The Devil's Point

A French Murder Mystery

Tom Becket

Copyright Page

This is a work of fiction. Names, characters, places, and incidents either are the product of the author's imagination or are used fictitiously. Any resemblance to actual persons living or dead, events, or locales is entirely coincidental.

Copyright © 2023 by Tom Becket

The right of Tom Becket to be identified as the author of this work has been asserted by him in accordance with the Copyright, Designs and Patents Act 1988

All rights reserved. No part of this book may be reproduced or used in any manner without written permission of the copyright owner except for the use of quotations in a book review. For more information, address: tombecketauthor@gmail.com

First paperback edition August 2023

Book design by GetCovers
Publisher: Colton Press

ISBN 978-1-7395117-0-8 (paperback)

ISBN 978-1-7395117-1-5 (ebook)

www.tombecketauthor.com

Preface

In the ancient French game of Trictrac, the eighth point on the board is known as the Case de Diable, the Devil's Point, because it is the second most difficult point to make, but reaching it does not mean that the game is won.

Prologue:

On a hot August day in 1943, in the cloisters of a medieval abbey in South West France, a young boy was sketching. Sitting on a low wall, drawing pad on his knees, he was copying a picture carved in stone at the head of a pillar; it was a biblical scene of David and the musicians, and all around the quadrangle there were pillars like this one, each with a different picture sculpted nine hundred years before.

A noise made him look up as two pigeons rose from the pantile roof and flew in a wide circle before landing on the great cypress tree that rose from the centre of the square. The sky behind them was a pure cerulean blue, an artist's light, he thought. He was dazzled when he looked back, but he could see a man standing in the gloom by the wall, watching him. Just then, an old, dishevelled priest emerged from the shadows, looked towards the boy and reached up to whisper in the man's ear. The man nodded, then walked quickly over to the boy and smiled.

'Look, Papa, I've finished number nine. Is it good?' said the boy.

The man leant over and looked at the drawing. 'It's good, very good. I think this is your favourite, no?'

'Yes, but can I draw another one, forty-seven or fifty? I like forty-seven.'

The man shook his head gently. 'No, David, I'm sorry, you can't draw any more, not today.' He reached out and took hold of the boy's hand. 'It's time to go now, it's time to go.'

Chapter One

The Present Day

Only a few minutes left.

Emmanuel Malraux stepped backwards into the dark alley. He lowered his head but kept his eyes fixed warily on the long, gaunt face of the man framed in the doorway. The man's eyes were hard and sad, he was tall and young, but weary, as if already drained by disappointments. And when he spoke, his face barely moved, a twitch and sneer of the lips, a slight rise and fall of an eyebrow. Malraux watched him intently, and it seemed to him that the sound of his voice came from deep inside the head through the bones and drawn flesh of his face.

'Thirty-three Impasse de l'Ange. That will pay him,' the man said.

'It's expensive.'

The man raised his arm then took hold of the door. 'Goodnight, monsieur, I see you have plenty of money.' The man shuffled back and slammed the door closed.

Malraux heard the metallic slotting home of numerous bolts. He dropped the small foil packet into his trouser pocket, stepped back and sniffed the air like an animal commencing the night's hunt. The alley was dimly lit, but he could make out a strange metal sculpture protruding from the wall above the adjacent door. He moved closer and saw that it was the shape of a fish, wrought in iron. His head was wonderfully clear and the next second it was like liquid, running with connections and ideas. He heard a bolt slide open again behind the door, so he moved rapidly away, walking close to the wall towards the lights of a broader street.

He reached the end of the alley and stepped onto a pavement. He looked up to see a street name, Rue Falhière. The alley behind him was like a channel where the sounds reached him clear and separated; the scratching of a cat on a wooden frame and the light tap of a man's footsteps. He crossed the street and headed towards the abbey. He had reached shops now: small secondary shops, a tobacconist, a tattoo parlour and a florist. He stopped at the window of a hairdresser, Camille's, and looked at his reflection. He touched his cheek and ran fingers through his thick, dark, curly hair. He glanced back along the street and cocked his head slightly to one side like a listening animal. He thought he heard the clear resonant song of a nightingale piercing the air, but then again, perhaps that was just inside his head.

He walked on, looking for the Impasse de l'Ange, number 33, Cul de Sac of the Angel, he smiled. It was mid-September, but the night was already dark. The air was moist, and a breeze blew up from the river and ruffled the leaves of the plane trees in the square. There were footsteps, there was a car starting up, and he heard the raised voices of a man and woman calling to each other in a language he couldn't understand. Or perhaps he could, but not tonight. There were definitely footsteps, but he couldn't see from where they came. He walked around the square looking at the street names in the dull lights. Rue de la Chasse. He followed this narrower and darker street that he believed would lead to the church. The street lights were absorbed into the leaves and branches of the trees, filtered, leaving shifting shadows on the road. The footsteps were quicker. He stopped beside a plane tree on the edge of the pavement. He raised his head up and breathed deeply, he could smell the bark and the branches of the tree. The nearby church bells struck the first note of ten. By the tenth strike, he was dying quickly, blood flowing from his neck and ear into the dust between the cobbles and the edge of the road. A small paper wrapper blew along the gutter and stuck onto the congealing blood, and flapped over his silent lips.

Standing on the small stern deck of his canal barge, Jacques Lecoubarry heard the church bells chime ten times. The pale glow from a street lamp slid across the oily waters of the canal. He looked down and smelled the faint odour of used water and diesel; a familiar smell, a quiet town, moments of respite. He looked back through the window into the cabin where the woman sat so still, absorbed, striking and inscrutable. He watched her for a while, she didn't look up or move. He shrugged his broad shoulders. A stroll, a small glass of Armagnac would fill that small space in the day that felt incomplete.

Bushes lined the towpath on the side of the canal where the barge was moored. He stepped off the boat between two bushes and onto the path. Without warning, a man, running, careered into him knocking him sideways. He grabbed at the man's arm for balance and they swung around, almost falling. The running man was tall and lean, Jacques was tall but more solidly built and his bulk saved them both.

'Pardon, monsieur,' the man gasped, as he wrestled away from Jacques' grip and started to run away, stumbling in his haste.

'Hey, you should be more careful,' Jacques shouted. 'Be more careful when you run.'

But Jacques saw that he was not a runner, not a jogger or a sports runner. He was wearing black trousers and a black, hooded sweatshirt. He pulled the hood back over his head as he ran off along the towpath. Jacques watched him go, past the lock and then onto the small footbridge that crossed the canal. As he reached the centre of the bridge he briefly looked back the way he had come. Too far away to see the details of his face, Jacques was sure of one thing, the face was white. The man came down off the bridge onto the path that led to the river and was out of sight. Jacques continued to stand there, a little shaken and uneasy. He looked along the towpath, listening. There was silence for a few minutes, and then he heard the distinct firing of an engine, and seconds later the sound of a motorboat pulling away from the shore. He listened for several minutes more until the sound of the boat grew muffled and faint.

Puzzled and annoyed. Jacques liked to describe things to himself in two or three words, particularly moods or the demeanour of people, he felt it helped him clarify and remember details: the woman in the barge, striking, inscrutable; the running man, rude, scared. This surprised him, he hadn't been aware of fear until that moment. Rude certainly, but scared, and why was he running along the canal at ten o'clock at night? And was the boat waiting for him?

The desire for a small glass of Armagnac was becoming a need. He walked a little watchfully along the towpath towards the town where he had earlier spotted a small canal-side café. There were a couple of scruffy, plastic, smoker's tables outside on the pavement, and through the window the interior looked dingy and drab. Perfect, he thought, as he pushed open the door. Leaning against the bar was a scrawny, little man speaking rapidly in a strong accent and making extravagant gestures with his arms and hands. Jacques thought he heard him say something like;

'It's an invasion, we've been invaded, this town, not just this town, all over France, a bloody invasion.'

He stopped and looked around as Jacques entered. The other two customers in the café looked up too. It was not easy to ignore Jacques; apart from the height and breadth, it was the strong, leonine head with its swathes of grey-brown curls like a mane, the beard and moustache swirling around his thickish lips and nose, and the dark blue, unflinching eyes. He had a definite animal king of the jungle look, and people were often wary at first. Would he bite? Could you stroke him? Most people tried initially to stroke.

'Good evening, monsieur. How are things going for you? From the boats?' the barman asked.

'Well, thank you. Yes, from the boats.' Jacques replied. 'An Armagnac… if I have time,' he shrugged, 'if there has been an invasion?'

'Ah well, that's just Michel. He is a… he is concerned about the number of Bulgarians who now live in the town,' said the barman, shaking his head loosely.

'Bulgarians?'

'Yes, fruit pickers, farm workers, you know.'

'Pick-pockets,' interposed Michel, building steam for another outburst.

'Now, Michel, enough. This gentleman doesn't want to hear your rantings'

'Tell me, friend,' said Jacques, turning to look directly at the scrawny man's eyes. 'That's a very serious accusation. Do you have any evidence of pick-pocketing or of any other crimes committed by these… Bulgarians?'

'Yes, everyone knows. The Maire has taken on thirty new police to deal with this wave of crime,' said Michel, and looked away.

'Michel, its twenty new police,' said the barman, 'and the crimes are not just Bulgarians. There are drugs and... your cognac, monsieur.'

'Thank you,' said Jacques. 'And how many Bulgarians are in this invasion force?'

'Nobody knows for sure,' said Michel. 'Too many.'

Jacques shrugged and sat down at a table in the corner. Michel walked out of the café and the barman raised his hands and mouthed an apology in Jacques' direction. There were so many issues to think about, so many uncertainties, so much baggage, so much personal cargo being carried along in the sturdy hull of his boat, the *Incognito*. He didn't think he needed to spend too much time worrying about the Bulgarian invasion.

Chapter Two

Madeleine le Courtier was eighty-two years old. She had lived in the Rue de la Chasse for nearly sixty years. First, as wife to a pale and generous man, whose generosity had not run to giving her children, and who had left her stranded there alone for another thirty years. A man who had died quietly in the armchair in the small sitting room where she had found him one evening after her class. Just sitting at peace, accepting, no sign that he had struggled to hang on to his life. Just a letting go, a heart pumping, then stilled. She was neither shocked nor distraught. It had seemed inevitable.

The second corpse she discovered in the Rue de la Chasse was very different. Each night, at half past ten, she lifted her little Pekinese dog, Flute, from her lap. The dog yapped as she clipped him to his leash and took him down the stairs to the street. She followed the same route every night, across the street along to the end, clockwise around the small square and then back along the tree-lined side of the street to her home. She saw the dark, twisted shape, like a large sack blown by the wind. She saw it from six metres away, and the dog stopped pulling, ran to her leg and sat down, growling softly. She looked without comprehension at first, her left hand raised to her mouth. She didn't scream. She saw the head twisted, the face looking up, something covering the lips. Dark liquid pooled along the cobbles. A young man, but no longer a man, an empty cask. Gone, violently, unready. She didn't recognise him. His clothes seemed inappropriate.

'Oh my God, oh my God,' she whispered to herself.

She knew that she needed to get help, an ambulance, the police, but she didn't like to leave him there. The way she had sat next to her dead husband for two hours before calling for help. It felt like a dereliction to leave them, raw and vulnerable. Nobody came for ten minutes, she simply stood and watched over the dead man. Then suddenly a light came on in the downstairs window of a house along the street. She rapped on the window, a face looked out and then came to the door. A middle-aged woman dressed for sleep. It was she who telephoned the police, while Madeleine continued to stand near the body, with her dog, caring for the dead.

When Jacques left the café there was movement on the main road through the town. He heard the siren and turned his head towards it, feeling the prick of unease in his stomach. Not for you, not in this little town, nobody knows you here, not for you now. He stopped outside a small corner shop, he had walked past it before but now it drew his attention. The sign said French and Bulgarian Goods. It surprised him, a Bulgarian shop here, in a small town in South West France. He imagined they sold food and clothes for the Bulgarian community; items that were missed by a displaced people, things that reminded them of home, food they had eaten all their lives. The canteen for the invasion perhaps. He must pay a visit, it would be interesting.

He walked back along the towpath, and as he neared where the barge was moored, he thought again of the man who had collided with him. There was something that he couldn't quite pin down. He wanted two or three words to clarify his thoughts. Scared and rude, yes, but more than that. But it wouldn't come, it had happened so quickly, and he was tired and 'mildly in his cups' as Armand would say. Poor dead Armand. He stepped aboard the barge. The lights were out, so he moved quietly through the cabin to the bedroom with its narrow wooden bed. He undressed and slipped in beside the woman. Her slim, strong body was turned away from him. He gently buried his face in her hair, but she didn't stir. She seemed a little frail and vulnerable like this and he felt the urge to wrap his large frame around her and protect her. But he was honest enough to accept that he was as much in need of protection as she was.

Chapter Three

When Jacques awoke the following morning the woman Celestine was gone. Her perfume lingered on the pillow and the sheets. He wondered for a moment and then he saw, through the narrow window, her slim, brown legs walking along the side of the boat. He met her in the galley.

'Coffee?' she asked.

'Coffee, yes,' he replied. 'But first I demand a kiss on both cheeks and on the mouth.'

'I think you're in no position to make demands, but you can have coffee to start,' she said, but she pecked him on both cheeks.

'I missed you last night. I went to bed alone. Where did you go?' she asked. Her voice was a little sharp and husky.

'Just to a little bar around the corner. For a nightcap. To check the spoor in the town,' Jacques replied. He shook his head as though to clear it of some dust. 'Funny, in the café there was a man talking about an invasion of the Bulgarians'

'A what?'

'An invasion of the Bulgarians,' he said. 'Swarming all over the French countryside, picking fruit and pockets.'

'In that order?'

'I think, according to the season.'

'Who was saying this?' asked Celestine.

'A man, a very serious but scrawny, ill-educated man. But, vehement and very pissed-off.'

Celestine seemed to ponder this for a moment as she sipped her coffee.

'It's true, there are quite a number of Bulgarians in this area. They come to pick fruit and do other agricultural jobs. We had a few in Bordeaux. They were not much trouble.'

'Surprising, there are certainly more pockets than fruit trees in Bordeaux,' said Jacques. 'But apparently, there are a lot of Bulgarians living in Lissac-sur-Tarn, and some of the locals aren't best pleased.'

They sat around a small rickety table on the bow deck to take their coffee. The sky was a perfect azure blue, cloudless, and the air was crystal clear. The canal was a dingy khaki colour, but the boats moored along its banks were gaily painted in reds and purples and greens. Plane trees lined the towpath on one side and the sun shone through the leaf canopies dappling the water with shade. The *Incognito* was what Jacques called a traditional barge and Celestine called seedy. At least a hundred years old, and in need now of several coats of paint, at twelve metres it was not as long as some barges. The hull was as sound as a bell, and the unpainted woodwork, the door and window frames, the seats and the tables were of fine hardwood, smooth and varnished.

'It's a sweet scene, don't you think?' said Jacques. He looked sideways at Celestine; her thick black hair was cut short, just reaching her shoulders, and she was running her fingers absently through it, twisting the ends around them in a way that made Jacques draw an extra breath. She was staring at the water in the canal.

'Don't you think?' he asked again.

She looked up. 'Yes, it is, it's very picturesque,' she said. 'And this canal goes on for how many kilometres more?'

'It's five hundred and twenty-five from Bordeaux to the Med.'

'And we've done how many?'

'Nearly two hundred, maybe.'

'Two hundred!' Celestine shook her head.

Jacques stood up. 'Breakfast. Let's go into the town and start the day properly. It's a nice town, you must see the cloisters and the church.'

They chose a café in a small square opposite the great church doors. They sat at a table outside, under a canopy of red and white barber stripes. A screen of trellis, and flower boxes, bursting with geraniums and begonias, separated them from the street. There were few patrons at this time and the waiter was at their table almost immediately.

'Oeufs Brouillés au Parme, for two,' Jacques ordered, 'and coffee and a petit pain for madame and a pastis for me.'

'Pastis?' Celestine raised her eyebrows. 'Pastis with scrambled eggs and ham. You've picked up some strange habits. Basque?'

'No. The coffee will accompany the eggs of course. The pastis is a small celebration that we have reached dry land again safely, and for a few days can enjoy the pleasures of an urban berth.' Celestine laughed at his absurdity, which she often did.

'You do live in a fantasy world, Jacques. We haven't just rounded the Cape of Good Hope, we've travelled at five kilometres an hour along the Canal de Garonne for ten days, no more than three metres from land at any point.'

'Sometimes, Celestine you are so prosaic,' he replied.

Jacques ate his breakfast with gusto, and then toasted Celestine with his small glass of pastis.

'Tell me about Lissac-sur-Tarn,' said Celestine. 'You've been here before?'

Jacques nodded. 'Yes, several times on business.'

'Dare I ask?'

Jacques shrugged. 'There was an antique dealer here, a Monsieur Pelissier. Claude Pelissier. He had a client who wanted a Louis XVI Trictrac table.'

'A Trictrac table?'

'Yes, Trictrac. It's an ancient game, a little like backgammon, same board, more or less, but the game's more complex, more subtle I would say. It was very popular among the aristocracy, not a game for the hoi polloi. That's why, after the revolution, a lot of Trictrac tables were destroyed, they were seen as a symbol of the ancient regime.'

'And were you able to locate one for Monsieur Pelissier?'

'Fortunately, I was. And I believe the client was extremely pleased with his purchase. A big-time wine grower in the region, I think he was.'

'And how much of the Louis XVI table was the genuine article?' asked Celestine sternly.

Jacques looked into her dark brown eyes, so fierce below the heavy lids. He looked down.

'Do you know how rare an original Louis XVI Trictrac table with fluted legs and ormolu castors is nowadays? The best examples are in museums or in the United States.' He paused and raised one finger. 'Fortunately, I was able to blend, and with great skill and attention to the most authentic details, a number of high-quality components into a superbly made example of this rare and much-envied piece.' He looked up at Celestine, sheepishly. 'The rich client was happy, Monsieur Pelissier was happy, and I, a humble carpenter, happy to have brought about such joy.' Celestine stared at him, unsmiling.

'And Monsieur Pelissier, is he still operating in Lissac?'

'No, sadly he died. Not long after our last arrangement.'

'Died?'

'Yes,' Jacques said. 'He drank heavily, smoked constantly and lived in a shop of dusty old furniture, breathing in the dead skin cells of previous owners. He was a great old fellow, doomed for sure.'

Celestine looked thoughtful. 'That's sad.'

'Sad. We've both seen death, Celestine, all too recently. Sad doesn't come near it. But there's death and death. Death after a long and fruitful life, there's nothing more natural. That's the one I have chosen for myself.'

'Oh, have you?'

'Yes, but death at the hands of another, before your time, that's a different beast altogether.' He suddenly looked dark and fierce, like a goaded animal, thought Celestine. She took a small guidebook out of her bag.

'The cloisters, it says here, are truly remarkable - Romanesque, one of the oldest in France, its original foundation date was 1100. A quadrangle of pillars, 118 of them, carved with different stories from the bible. And the door, just opposite, that great arched stone portal, is one of the greatest masterpieces of Romanesque art in France.'

Celestine looked up from her book. Across the cobbled street a group of schoolchildren, early teenagers, were swilling around the foot of the great church door, standing and sitting on the steps. Wearing a uniform of dark blue sweatshirts, skirts and trousers, with a gold crest or badge, they seemed to be waiting for something to begin. Then suddenly, like the host of a TV talk show, a nun appeared at the top of the steps. Arms outstretched, she walked down two steps and greeted the children in a strong and lively voice.

She waved the children to be seated, which they did surprisingly quickly.

'This will be interesting,' said Jacques. 'How long do you think the old girl will keep those kids' attention?'

'Ten minutes, no more,'

They listened for a few minutes.

'Is she talking about the door or the church itself?' asked Jacques.

'I think she's talking about the history of the Abbey.'

From across the square, depending on the noise in the street, they could hear snatches and then longer passages of what the nun was saying. She was very animated, pointing and continually waving her hands towards the children and then towards the carvings around the door. She was very short and slim, with square, wire-framed glasses. She was wearing a white calf-length habit and a white coif.

'She's tiny, but very enthusiastic,' said Celestine. 'She has an accent. I can't make out all that she's saying. I caught the Horseman of the Apocalypse.'

'No wonder the children are listening,' said Jacques.

'They really are.'

'They probably think this is the start of a horror film. "Mad nuns and the pale riders of the Apocalypse".'

'No, she's explaining the meaning and the symbolism of the carvings.'

'No one's asking any questions.'

'I think she's very thorough. The children do seem interested though. She's rather sweet. So enthusiastic. Enthusiasm is very attractive in a person, don't you think?' She looked across at Jacques.

The nun was asking questions and encouraging individual children to stand up and point to the carved figures on the frieze above, and when they did she clapped her hands and called out in a shrill and excited voice, 'excellent'. They noticed she was slightly stooped and her arms came away from her side when she spoke.

'She has an accent, she's not French, I don't think,' said Celestine.

'She speaks it very well, and with a good variety of adjectives from what I can hear,' said Jacques.

'Yes, she's rather splendid, a little bundle of enthusiasm, and she has captivated that group of schoolchildren and that's no mean task.'

'Amen,' said Jacques and polished off his pastis. The waiter came to clear the table.

'That lady, that nun, is she a regular at the Abbey gates?' Jacques asked him.

The waiter looked across. 'Yes, monsieur, she is a guide there. A few times a month you will see her with a group of children. Sister Agnes, Agnieszka. She is from the Convent.' The waiter pointed vaguely towards the hill rising behind the Abbey.

'Sister Agnieszka,' Jacques mused. 'So, not a French name'.

The nun finished her talk, and waving her arms like the sails of a windmill, whisked the children into the church.

'We should visit the church now. We can hear some of her explanations,' said Celestine. They paid the bill and wandered over to the great portal of the church. They stood looking up at the stone carvings. 'The elders of the apocalypse,' said Celestine, pointing to the figures. 'That's what the sister was saying.'

'The carvings are remarkable, eight hundred years old. I would like to have met some of those craftsmen, to have worked with them,' said Jacques.

'You are definitely out of your time,' said Celestine, smiling. She took him by the arm.

They walked through the portal and into the church, letting their eyes adjust to the gloom after the glare of the sun in the street. Celestine sniffed at the musty air, a smell so redolent of churches, of old stone, incense and dust. She pointed.

'There she is'.

The little nun was standing in an alcove surrounded by the children, who were still, more or less, paying attention. Jacques and Celestine moved nearer to listen. She was waving her hands towards a group of painted wooden figures that were standing watching, while two other figures lowered a half-naked body into a coffin.

'The entombment of Christ,' whispered Celestine. 'She's explaining who the various figures are.' Jacques nodded, he could hear her more clearly here, and her accent was more pronounced.

She was drawing the children's attention to one figure after another, using her hands like the conductor of an orchestra, engaging the children with her lively voice and her movement. Just then a plump, be-suited, official-looking man edged his way through the children to the side of the nun. He bent close to her and started whispering in her ear. The impact was remarkable; the nun almost collapsed like a punctured ball. All the life and energy seemed to drain visibly from her limbs. She staggered slightly, so the man took her arm and eased her towards a seat, where she sat down and dropped her head into her hands. The official turned to the children and began to usher them quietly away and out of the church. A number of the children looked back and you could see the concern and distress in their faces. The official turned to Jacques and Celestine.

'Monsieur. Madame, if you please. We would like to empty the church for a little while. So sorry.'

'Why, what's happened?' asked Jacques. The official just raised his hands.

'Please, if you wouldn't mind.'

Celestine looked over to the nun who was still sitting, head down, crossing herself slowly.

'Sister,' she called out as Jacques tried to draw her away. 'Sister.'

The nun raised her head once, sharply, and looked directly into Celestine's eyes. Celestine said later that the look was not unknown to her - it was sorrow, pain and fear, most certainly fear. They left the church and walked out into the sunshine. Celestine breathed deeply, glad to be out in the open air.

'That was bizarre,' said Jacques, 'That was some bad news she received.'

'The worst I think, I don't think I've ever seen someone change so much, so suddenly.'

The children were still standing around in groups, talking quietly. One of the girls, who had looked back towards the nun as she was leaving, spoke to Celestine.

'Excuse me, madame, do you know what happened to Sister Agnieszka?'

Celestine turned to her and smiled. 'No, I'm sorry, I don't know. I know no more than you.'

'Somebody's died,' said a boy nearby. 'Somebody died.'

'Who?' demanded Jacques.

'I don't know, I just heard.' He looked away self-consciously. Jacques turned to Celestine.

'Come on, let's go and look at the cloisters. It's none of our business.'

They walked around the side of the church to the entrance to the cloisters, but the entrance door was locked and a sign on the door said it was closed.

'That's strange', said Celestine. 'You can see the timetable on the door. It should be open at this time.'

'There must be a connection to what's just happened. Some kind of emergency.'

'Fairly serious, very serious,' said Celestine. 'That nun was shocked, but more than that, she was afraid. I saw that when she lifted up her face. I have seen enough of that to know it when it calls.'

'Fear,' Jacques mused. 'That's the second person in the last twenty-four hours, less, to have that look. Not exactly what I expected in this sleepy little town.' He took Celestine by the arm.

'Come on, I want to visit that Bulgarian shop to buy some cherries.'

'In September?'

'Well, cherry brandy then, and other Bulgarian delicacies for a festive table.'

Keen to shift Celestine's focus from the experience in the church, Jacques led her gently through the streets. 'The joy of wandering footloose, anonymous, through a strange town, known by no one, knowing no one, is not to be lightly dismissed,' he said. Celestine smiled, but in her mind, she could still see the anguished face of the little Carmelite nun.

The Bulgarian shop was also closed. Jacques peered through the window, but it was dark and there was little to see. Exasperated, Jacques waved his hand in a circle.

'Is everything closed in this town today? Is it Sunday? Saint Spoilsport's day?'

'Perhaps they have an earlier lunchtime,' said Celestine, 'When you work in the fields you tend to start early, it gets too hot later in the day.'

They turned to walk away when a young boy of about twelve rushed around the corner and almost bumped into Celestine.

'Izvinete,' he said. He stopped at the closed door, threw his arms out and uttered what was certainly a curse, although not in French.

'Do you know why it is closed?' asked Celestine gently.

'No,' he shrugged. He was dark-skinned, short, with lively brown eyes. 'No, maybe,' he shrugged again.

'So, it isn't normally closed at this time,' said Celestine to Jacques.

'No. The whole town is closing down. Slowly closing its doors and letting the apocalypse rage in the streets.'

'Hmm,' said Celestine. 'I think there may be a simpler explanation than that.'

Chapter Four

In the bright, new, concrete edifice of the Poste of the Police Municipale in Lissac-sur-Tarn, Commandant Jean-Philippe Grimard of the Police Judiciaire had commandeered two offices, and was now reading through the statements gathered so far. Having been instructed by the Prosecutor at two o'clock in the morning, he had travelled up from Montauban, where he was based, and had visited the scene of the crime at around dawn. The body of the young man was no longer there, but the dried blood remained and had left a macabre outline of the head and neck on the cobbled street. He'd looked around. A quiet street, residential, and with few street lights. Poor houses but not the poorest, a street in decline from respectable to more rundown and seedier. He would meet the old lady who had found the body later, after he had visited the morgue. Such violence in the streets of a small town was, in his experience, brought on by drugs, petty theft, often both together, or an argument or dispute that had escalated, perhaps the fission from the breakdown of a relationship. Which one was responsible for this particular crime, he wondered? And why, if this was the case, had the Prosecutor insisted on calling on him to lead the investigation? There were local police. He shrugged, perhaps the Prosecutor had seen something when he had viewed the body, perhaps because the victim was from outside the community, from Paris, perhaps.

Reading through the statements it was becoming clearer already. The man's wallet was missing, the wristwatch wrenched from his arm, and in his pocket was a small packet of cocaine. So, let us eliminate. He had drugs, but they were not taken. He had money for drugs and presumably more in his wallet, so theft. He ticked this one. Passion: apparently the deceased was a homosexual, and although there was no question that jealousy could arise in such relationships, it did not often, in his experience, lead to the violent and bloody, and let us remember, efficient, slaughter of the spurned lover. This remained unticked. An argument or dispute; this we would need to look into. Interview people where he worked, friends, family and others in his social life. No mobile phone, presumably also stolen. Grimard sighed. Such people often had very complicated private lives. But he believed it was usually simple to find the culprit in cases like this. It was either simple or else unsolvable. The scene was there. There would be traces. It was almost impossible now to avoid leaving traces that could be detected. He called through to his assistant in the room next door.

'Jerome, get me that young agent, Desmarais. The one first on the scene.'

'He's gone home, chief. He was on duty all night, so he went home to sleep.'

'Damn. No one sleeps in a murder inquiry, do they, Jerome?'

'No. Chief.'

'When's he due back in?'

'This evening at seven, sir.'

'Well inform him, sleeping or not, that I want to see him at six, understood!'

'Understood. Rabault has just come in with a witness who says he saw the deceased yesterday, arguing with a man in the town'

'Ok, that's more like it. Send Rabault up with the witness now.'

Grimard looked out of the window at the quiet backstreet. Yes, he said to himself, these small towns, it's always pretty simple.

Jacques and Celestine spent a leisurely afternoon on the barge. Jacques sketched the other craft on the canal while Celestine sat in a canvas chair with her feet up on the edge of the boat. Alongside her was a small table on which she had a notebook and pen. She kept scribbling quick notes as she worked her way through an adult puzzle book. It was, in fact, an extremely challenging puzzle book, issued by a section of Mensa France, of which Celestine was a member. It was not a society you could join by paying a subscription. There were tests to be completed, timed puzzles, and aptitude evaluations. The membership was exclusive, by ability only - the ability to solve complex, multi-layered and many-faceted puzzles. Without this intellectual stimulation, Celestine would feel a build-up of tension and frustration in herself that could lead her to strike out. Jacques was very aware of this need, and this zone of her being that was closed to him. It was intense and personal, and he encouraged her to take the time she needed.

He sketched, not well, but enthusiastically. He enjoyed the quiet rhythm of stroking pencil marks on paper. It was a quiet, contemplative activity and it often led him deeply into his own thoughts. His powers of observation were heightened by drawing a scene or a figure. He realised that he noticed more details and greater subtleties when attempting to transfer an image onto a sheet of paper. He was drawing the reflection of the plane trees on the surface of the canal, conscious of how the intricacy of the branches and leaves was slightly blurred by the thickness of the water. Looking from tree to tree he noticed the loss of clarity of detail. Then suddenly, the picture came to him again of the man in black who had nearly knocked him over on the towpath the night before.

'I'm going for a walk along the towpath,' he called out. Celestine, eyes closed, was making little counting movements with her right hand. She waved it briefly in his direction but said nothing.

He stepped over the side of the barge, emerging through the bushes carefully, and onto the towpath. He turned away from the town in the direction that the man had run. He walked past three other barges moored along the quayside. One of them looked lived in, although there was no sign of anyone moving around. The next one, a dingy, white cruiser, was locked up, with a small card in the window, for sale, and a telephone number. It was in poor condition, with a grey stain that seemed to spread from the water across the paintwork, around the windows and onto the flat roof of the cabin. *Just Left* it was called, although the leaving, Jacques thought, had been some years before. The third boat was awash with plants and gadgets; potted clematis, bicycles, solar panels, sky dishes and easels. It was painted a rich burgundy with gold letters on the side and stern. *Kaleidoscope.* Narbonne. It was a glorious, blue sky afternoon in the south of France, but as Jacques glanced in through the window he saw the grey light of a television screen and the back of two heads aimed in its direction. He passed the lock and reached the footbridge. On the other side of the bridge was a towpath along a wide cut in the canal that ran at right angles to it. At the end of this cut was another formidable-looking lock that gave access to the River Tarn. The river was lower, so to join the canal, boats had to enter the lock, close the two huge wooden doors and wait as waters leaked and then gushed in from the other end to gradually fill up the box, lifting the boat steadily to the new height. It could be quite claustrophobic the first few times, but you learned to trust the integrity of the structure. Just as well, you couldn't travel far down a canal being afraid of locks, thought Jacques.

The river spread wide before him, at least two hundred metres across to the far, tree-lined bank. He looked around. He had expected to see a jetty of some kind or at least a slipway where small boats could moor, possibly a boathouse or fisherman's hut, but there was nothing, just bushes and a small tree with its roots exposed. The water was quite shallow at the edge and you could see the bottom for about two metres until the depth and the murkiness made it impossible. Twenty metres upriver there was a sloping grassy bank, no more than a few metres wide, between the bushes and trees. The ground was hard at this time of the year after the long dry summer months so there were no marks on the grass, but Jacques noticed there was a tree, no more than a few centimetres thick, where the bark had been rubbed off. It was about half a metre off the ground and looked like the mark made by a rope, chaffing, or something similar. The current was not swift at this point but was strong enough to keep drawing a boat downstream if it wasn't tied securely. He looked upstream and down. About a hundred metres downstream he saw there was a short concrete jetty where a number of small boats were moored. They looked like the small GRP boats used by fishermen. Puzzled, Jacques looked again at the marks on the tree. The wounds were still raw, not darkened or sealed as they would be in time. These marks were made in the last few days, he thought. Why would you tie a boat up here when there is a perfectly good mooring place just a hundred metres away?

Jacques walked along the path toward the jetty. There were half a dozen boats, all in reasonably good condition. Four were clearly fishing boats, well used, scraped and scratched in places. The other two had small cabins and were more like pleasure boats for cruising on the river. They were clean and well painted and had both been used recently as there was none of the scum and detritus that builds up around boats left unused for a while on the water. He continued down the river and then turned back towards the town to cross one of the bridges over the canal and return to the *Incognito*. As he prepared to cross the road he was assailed by a voice from behind him. He looked around. It was the scrawny little man, Michel, from the café the night before. He walked up to Jacques, clearly excited.

'So, you see, monsieur, I was right,' he almost shouted. 'It has started. The bastards.'

His face, with the sunken cheeks and wandering eyes, was flushed and animated. He was wearing grey jogging trousers and a black T-shirt, and Jacques could smell the cigarette smoke on his clothes as he came closer.

'Monsieur, you remember me. In the bar last night. I explained. The Bulgarians.' Jacques looked at him hard.

'I am not sure explained is the word I would use. I remember you ranting something about Bulgarians,' Jacques said and started to turn away, but the man grabbed him by the arm and then dropped his hand quickly. He was a good fifteen centimetres shorter than Jacques, but he twisted his face to look up at him.

'But it has started, don't you see, the murder.'

'What murder?' asked Jacques.

'You don't know. Mon Dieu! The murder last night in our town. The murder of a Frenchman, a scholar, a professor.' He pronounced each description of the victim in an increasingly loud voice and with a roll of his eyes, his accent thickening and blurring the words. 'Murdered by a Bulgarian savage.'

'Hold on,' said Jacques. 'You say there has been a murder in Lissac. When?'

'Why, last night, in the Rue de la Chasse. Horrible murder. Throat cut from here to here.' Michel gestured with a finger across his own throat, his mouth open and his bad teeth stuck in a rictus of imagined horror.

'When last night?' demanded Jacques.

'Last night. Who knows? An old woman found him, walking her dog.'

'This morning or last night?'

'No, no. I said, last night.'

'And what has this to do with Bulgarians?'

'Why of course, they have got the killer. They have arrested a Bulgarian, one of the hordes.'

'So, they've arrested a Bulgarian for the murder of a French professor,' said Jacques slowly.

'Yes, yes. That's what I'm saying. I told you, monsieur. They must be expelled. Our town must remain our town.'

'Do you know anything else?'

'What more is there to know?'

'Then let me tell you, my friend. It would be wise for you to keep a lid on your trap. You can only cause trouble. You are a simpleton, and simple answers are rarely correct in these cases. Keep your trap shut!' he said fiercely.

'Pah.' Michel looked at Jacques with surprise and a little disgust. 'I will say what I see, is what I say.'

Jacques watched the little man walk away with his jerky, shuffling gait towards the town. He continued on his way back to the barge, seeing nothing, just deep in thought. When he stepped back onto the boat he found Celestine standing right on the edge of the stern deck staring down into the water.

'Don't jump, Chérie,' he said. 'The water is not, you know, very clean.'

Celestine started and for a second nearly over-balanced. Jacques grabbed her arm.

'What are you doing? Be careful, you really don't want to go swimming in there.' He looked at her, concerned. 'Were you calculating the depth by the width by five hundred and seventy-five kilometres, and how many bottles of wine it would take to fill it? Quite an easy puzzle for you,' he said. She stepped back and shook off his hand.

'No, I was just,' she paused and looked up at him. 'It's all so murky, and uncertain. I've never had such uncertainty in my life. I've always had a clear path, but it's gone. It's all so vague now. Drifting. Drifting down a canal.'

'We talked about this, C,' said Jacques calmly. 'It's just a period of transition. Time to let the dust settle. That was then and this is now. We agreed. Go with the flow, literally, and when the time is right, make decisions and set a new course.' He put his arm around her shoulder. 'I know this is hard for you, harder than for me, for sure. You had a career, you were someone. I've always been more flexible in my approach to life. But listen, you need to come and sit down, I have something to tell you and I need your professional advice.'

'I'm not a professional anymore,' she said.

'You'll always have that. You just don't have the uniform now. Which, you know, is rather a pity I think,' he added.

Jacques told her about the murder in the town the night before, about the arrest of the Bulgarian, and then about the man he had collided with, the look on his face, and the boat.

'Why would you run hell for leather through the streets of the town, get into a boat that was hidden from view and make your getaway?' Jacques asked, 'Or am I just blowing wind?'

'Well, we don't know that he was running through the town, only along the towpath.' Celestine reasoned. 'We don't know he wasn't running late to meet someone, to take him home in his boat. A lot of people live along the river. You said yourself, the boat would have been moored very conveniently for the end of the path. You'll have to show me the place.'

'Of course, let's do that now and you can judge.'

'Ok, but describe this man again,' said Celestine.

'I didn't get a good look at him, but I did grab hold of his arm to stop us from falling.'

'And how did that feel; strong, flabby, muscular?'

'Strong, strong-ish. Not feeble, you know, but not superman. Firm'

'Ok. Age?'

'Not very young, not a kid, more than thirty maybe. He was fit enough. He was running but not panting, not out of breath.'

'Ok. Height?'

'Tall, quite tall, one eighty-five, a little taller than me.'

'Build; fat, thin, broad?'

'Lean, not thin, but definitely not fat.'

'It's surprising what you remember when you go there in your mind,' said Celestine.

'I only saw his face briefly. He was wearing a black hat or hood low over his forehead. It was more an impression than a clear look. I was a bit disorientated. I don't think I'd recognise him. No, I wouldn't.'

'Clean shaven, beard, moustache?'

'Clean shaven, although I couldn't see the bottom of his face well.'

'And you don't think he was Bulgarian?'

'No, he wasn't. He was French. When he bumped into me, he said pardon. You know, it's involuntary, isn't it? You don't think, you respond. I said pardon to the galley door this morning when I bumped into it.'

'He could have lived in France a long time,' suggested Celestine.

'No. Remember when that boy nearly bumped into you outside the shop today? Remember what he said: Izvinete. That's pardon in Bulgarian. I looked it up. It's involuntary. If I lived in a foreign country for thirty years I would still say pardon,' said Jacques firmly.

'If you bumped into a galley door?' Celestine smiled.

'Or any number of doors or other inanimate or animate objects. It's involuntary, learned at your mother's knee.'

'You're probably right. Ok, let's look at the river bank.'

Jacques showed Celestine the marks on the tree trunk. He looked more closely and Celestine studied them and the angle to the water.

'It couldn't have been very big, there isn't the depth of water. And besides, the rope must have been quite thin, not a thick cord to hold a large boat,' suggested Celestine. 'And if it was tied up here, it would drift down a little with the current, but it would rest there in the bushes. It couldn't be seen from further down the river.' Celestine stood silently for a few minutes, absorbing the scene. For the second time in less than an hour, she found herself staring into the water. Finally, she said. 'You have to report it. You have to.'

'Anonymously, by telephone?' said Jacques, looking rather alarmed.

'No, you have to go in person. You must speak to the officer in charge of the case.'

'They'll want my name.'

'Yes, but that doesn't matter. You are not wanted.'

'No, but I was enjoying the anonymity. Nobody knows who I am, nobody knows where I am. There's some comfort in that.'

'Come on, Jacques, you're not a celebrity, you're not on the most wanted list. Nobody is that interested in you, if you're honest. Except me of course.'

'Thank you. Thank you for the afterthought. I have enemies,' said Jacques stubbornly.

'Only outraged customers you've sold dodgy antique furniture to,' said Celestine harshly. 'But you must go tonight. Before things get too solidified. Investigations start fluidly but can very quickly become rigid once a definite course has been set. If they have a strong suspect, then much of the work now will be directed at firming up the case they have. It's not supposed to be like that. They may be right, but until the evidence gathered is incontrovertible against the suspect, there must be room for questions or other alternatives,' she paused. 'And you must find out what they know. In fact, find out everything about the case. Who was killed, when, how, who are the suspects.'

'Whoa, whoa, Capitaine. Why would the police tell me all this? They would be more likely to tell you. You were one of them.'

'Yes, but you're the witness, and you could charm the angels off the altar,' said Celestine. 'For Christ's sake, you charmed me.'

'Ok, Ok, but...,' he stopped. 'Ok, I'll go now.'

Chapter Five

In the poste of the police municipale, Agent Paul Desmarais had had less challenging days. Twenty-four hours earlier he had been slowly typing up his report on the disturbance at the rugby club's new season dance. Then he'd received a phone call from a lady at the emergency services switchboard asking for the senior officer on duty. He had had to admit that he was not only the senior officer but the only officer on duty at that time. And then came the bombshell. A call had been received reporting that there was a body lying in Rue de la Chasse. It looked like he, it was male, had been unlawfully killed. Agent Desmarais had asked her to repeat the details. 'In Lissac-sur-Tarn, in Rue de la Chasse?'

'Yes, Agent, in Lissac-sur-Tarn. The caller is waiting at the scene. Hurry.'

Desmarais had put down the phone and drawn a deep breath. First time for everything he thought.

When he arrived at Rue de la Chasse there was already a small group of people standing around in a protective semi-circle a little away from the body. The process, that's what's important, he thought. Stage one, secure the scene. No, confirm the state of the victim. Gloves on. Dead obviously, but he placed his fingers gingerly on the man's throat, conscious of the blood caked on the side of the victim's head and neck. Now secure the scene.

'Stand back, please. Has anyone touched anything?' He called out. He had already called for assistance and he could hear a siren approaching through the streets. He would need them to cordon off the area, to control the scene. Nothing must be touched. Witnesses must be sought.

'Who found this man?' he shouted. He couldn't say the word body, it was too terrible.

'It was that old lady. She's in the house, sitting down. She's had a shock you know.' The woman said it as though it was his fault.

'Of course, of course, and you are?'

'I called the police. She saw it first and knocked on my window. It's terrible. She's an old lady.'

Just then two cars from the Gendarmerie pulled up and four officers jumped out. Desmarais stepped forward with his arms in the air and stood between them and the body.

'We have a murder. We need a cordon thirty metres around the victim. Call for a doctor, although he is dead and then…,' he couldn't remember who else to call, 'the other relevant authorities,' he finally said.

He turned back to the body, lying so exposed, so public, yet so alone. He felt a great wave of horror and revulsion and pity looking down at the dead man. Horrible, horrible, he thought. No one deserves that.

That was nearly twenty-four hours ago. He had waited by the body until five in the morning when it had been taken away by the Coroner's ambulance. The corpse had been photographed a hundred times, and studied by the local pathologist, who had arrived wearing a white operating gown over his pyjamas. A forensic team had spent two hours on hands and knees searching every square inch of the street for anything that might be relevant. It seemed like a sudden, well-oiled machine had been let out of its box, slick, efficient and impersonal. But it didn't feel impersonal to Desmarais. He felt that there was a desolation hovering a few feet above all this activity. And the feel of the dead man's throat and the darkening pool of blood had stayed with him, would stay with him, for a long time, he knew. He was a young man in his early twenties, with a full, generous, boyish face, and a shock of unruly brown hair crawling over his head. He had stayed until the Prosecutor had arrived. Had watched him, with his brisk efficiency, moving around the murder scene. But he'd seen also the horror and disgust on that man's lined, experienced face. He had answered all the questions thrown at him; where, when, who, and answered them like a machine. And then Commandant Grimard had arrived from Montauban, and the responsibility had been handed over to him and his team. Completely drained, Desmarais could barely walk to his car. As he sat down in the seat he realised that he had seen the deceased on two or maybe three occasions. He was not an easily forgettable figure. But where had he seen him? But exhaustion had left him unable to think clearly. He had driven slowly away from the scene.

After very little rest he had been called back into the poste to report to Commandant Grimard. That had not been comfortable. Desmarais had the impression that Grimard had criticised every single action he had taken, from the receipt of the call to the way he had driven his car away. He should have done this, it was necessary to do that. But clearly, what could be expected of a small-town flic dealing with matters far above their competence and their intellect. Very well, thought Desmarais, but now they have a suspect already, and perhaps Commandant Grimard could soon return to his golden temple on the hill in Montauban and leave him in peace. But, despite the condescension, Desmarais was also a little excited, this was an opportunity, this was serious policing. He must learn from the experience. Now, he had another visitor, a member of the public with information that might be relevant to the murder inquiry. The whole town and most of Occitanie now knew there had been a murder in Lissac-sur-Tarn. This would lie on the town's file for years. Desmarais looked through the glass partition into the reception area. Although there were seats available against the wall, the man was standing, feet apart, arms folded, and staring at the door through which Desmarais was about to enter the room. The man was a stranger to him, but quite striking, with his broad shoulders, thick legs in rough denim shorts, and a great shaggy head of greying brown hair and a full beard and moustache of the same hue. There was something about the way he stood, something forceful and confident. He turned to the other officer, sitting behind the desk.

'Who is that man, do you know him?' he asked.

'No. A Monsieur Lecoubarry. Wants to speak to the officer in charge of the investigation into last night's murder. Has information that might be relevant. Never seen him before. I'd remember, that's for sure.'

'I'll see him in room two. Can you bring him through?'

Desmarais switched on the lights of the small, musty interview room. He shuffled the items on the table and pulled out two chairs. He wasn't quite sure what to expect. This guy could be some nutter wanting to seem important, but that wasn't the impression Desmarais had gained, even from a cursory glance at the man, he looked serious and substantial.

'Come in, Monsieur Lecoubarry,' Desmarais said. 'Have a seat.'

Jacques remained standing. He extended his hand and Desmarais shook it. It was strong.

'Monsieur, l'agent…?' Jacques inquired.

'Sorry. Desmarais, Paul Desmarais. Please sit down.'

'But you are not in charge of this investigation?' said Jacques.

'No. No, that is Commandant Grimard. Unfortunately, he is not here at this time.' He saw the questioning look on Jacques' face and for some reason felt obliged to offer some further clarification. 'Commandant Grimard is in a meeting with the Maire and some of our local officials. This is a very serious occurrence to happen in this town you understand. It is not normal. I myself have never known such an event, a crime of this magnitude, no never in this town.'

Desmarais realised that he was becoming garrulous while the stranger stood rock still, looking at him. He fought off the sense he had that he was still a boy in a man's uniform.

'I am the agent, greatly involved in this case. Indeed, I was the first officer on the scene.'

'You saw the body?' asked Jacques quietly.

'Yes. I was first there. I ascertained the true state of the victim and I preserved the scene.'

'That must have been terrible for you. To see a human life cut short so horribly, with his throat cut, no?' Desmarais nodded. 'Was he robbed?'

'Yes, his wallet and a watch. Yes, it was horrible. But, it is part of my job,' he said uncertainly.

'Not a normal part as you've said. But tell me, was he a young man, a local, did you perhaps know him personally? Oh my God, that would be terrible.'

'No, I didn't know him personally, although I have seen him around, in the town. Youngish, but not local. From Paris, I think.'

'He was a professor, I believe. Studying here in Lissac?' asked Jacques.

'Yes. I think doing some research on our beautiful Abbey and cloisters. But, monsieur, I am sorry, you came here with some information that you think might be relevant.'

'Yes, I think perhaps it is,' said Jacques. 'But you have arrested a Bulgarian man, have you not?'

'We have, but this cannot be discussed. Are you a journalist?' asked Desmarais, suddenly wary.

'No, nothing like that. I'm a carpenter. I am here on holiday. We have a boat on the canal. We arrived yesterday.'

'A carpenter,' said Desmarais a little abashed. 'And what information do you have for us, monsieur?'

'Well really, I should perhaps speak to your Grimard. I think, if you don't know all the details of the case, you will not appreciate the relevance of my information,' said Jacques.

'Monsieur, I can assure you that I know enough about the case to be able to assess the relevance of what you have to tell me. And if appropriate, I will pass it on to Commandant Grimard.'

'So why have you arrested a Bulgarian, are you racist perhaps?' Jacques asked and looked Desmarais in the eye.

'No, monsieur, certainly not. He was arrested because the man was known to have argued with the victim that afternoon and threatened him. Also, there has been some evidence found at the scene, not much but some.'

Jacques sat down and smiled at Desmarais, waving for him to sit down also. It's as though he was interviewing me, thought Desmarais.

'Agent Desmarais,' Jacques began. 'I am content. You have clearly been through quite an ordeal. I will tell you my story, but you must pass it on, and also you must tell me if the information you now have renders my information invalid. I don't want to waste my time.'

Jacques told him everything about the running man, the look back, the fear, the boat moored in an unusual place.

'So, tell me, Desmarais,' said Jacques. 'Is your Bulgarian one-eighty-five? It seems to me they are, by and large, a shorter, stockier tribe.'

'No, he is as you say, short, very broad, very strong.'

'Does he speak French?'

'Some. He has lived in Lissac for a few years.'

'Then this was not a Bulgarian, the running man, he was as French as you or I. You are French, Desmarais? From which part?'

'From the Landes, near Saint-Paul-les Dax'

'Ah, we are almost neighbours. I am from Saint Palais, a Basque, although I was brought up in Bordeaux from the age of eight.'

'I did my training in Bordeaux in....'

'You understand that I have had little to do with the police in my simple life as a carpenter. But tell me, do you see the relevance of what I have told you? It's strange no? A man running, dressed in black, fearful. A motorboat waiting for a getaway. And at the right time of the night. Just after ten. And at what time did the old lady find the body? Oh my God, what a terrible shock for her to see that at her age. The poor Madame ...?'

'Le Courtier. Yes, she was very shaken. I interviewed her. Shaken, but firm, you know. Like the old people can be.'

'And the time?' asked Jacques.

'At 10.30. She walked her dog at this time every day.'

'But she saw nothing?'

'No, nothing. This town is very quiet, you know, at that time.' He shook his head.

'But you must keep an open mind, Desmarais. This could be an exciting moment for you, yes. An opportunity.'

Desmarais sat back. He felt quite drained again. He knew that he had been manipulated and twisted but in the most gentle and innocuous way possible, and that information had been shaken from him like pepper from a mill. But for some reason he didn't feel aggrieved. Rather, a small screen was opening in his mind, a different scene to the one he was used to running there, a more ambitious one, one where he could see himself gaining something, although he wasn't sure quite what.

'One last thing, Agent Desmarais,' said Jacques. 'It seems there are some hotheads in Lissac-sur-Tarn who think the Bulgarian visitors are a threat to the community. I met a fellow last night who called it an invasion. Although he was a stupid fellow.'

'Look,' said Desmarais, leaning forwards. 'There is some bad feeling in the town towards the Bulgarians. Not by all. They first came to Lissac for the fruit picking and grape harvest. They're needed. This area is prized for its fruit and wine. And they bring their families. Perhaps, at first, some of them behaved in a way that was not familiar, and quite uncomfortable for the French residents. For example; they stay out on the streets until late, in little groups, talking, it can be intimidating, but it's just their way. The French, as you know, are typically at home by nine o'clock and the streets are deserted. But it's not bad, just different. There was some fly-tipping, minor crimes, washing hanging out in the street at all hours.' Desmarais shrugged. 'But there has been a great effort to educate both sides, I would say. To understand, to explain what kind of behaviour is acceptable in a French town.'

'Then it would be a shame if things turned ugly in this nice little town,' said Jacques.

'You're right. But, monsieur, thank you for coming here this evening. I will be sure to pass this information on to my superiors.'

'Good. One more thing. If I should remember something else, some other detail, I would like to be able to tell you quickly. Do you have a number where I could call you directly? I would not want to trouble Commandant Grimard.'

Desmarais found himself handing a number to Jacques. He saw him to the door where they shook hands, then he turned back to the officer behind the desk who looked up and raised his eyebrows. Desmarais shook his head.

'I don't know, don't ask. An interesting man.' Very interesting, he thought.

Jacques walked slowly back through the streets of the town. There were few people around. It was a clean, quiet place, yet now the setting for the horrific murder of a young man. So, something was out of joint. Beneath the tranquil exterior of this sunny little town, something had happened, something had stirred, had caused a violent eruption so extreme that a life had been taken. Where would the anger, the passion, or the fear come from to drive one of its souls to slaughter? He stood below the great church portal and looked up again at the wise men of the apocalypse. What was the young man studying here? Did it have any link to his death? Or was it simply the result of anger, desperation, an argument, or an altercation that went too far? What sort of a man was he? Did he make enemies quickly? He wasn't from the town so it couldn't be a long-standing feud. To steal you don't cut a throat, you threaten, you slash or hit maybe. But to kill intentionally, for what, a wallet or a watch? Desmarais had provided him with so much more information than he could have hoped for. He stood looking at the church and thought of the little nun, waving her arms around like a windmill, entertaining those kids. What news did she hear? Now it seemed likely that it related to the death of the young man. She must have talked to him, perhaps shared her knowledge of the history of the church. She would take that sort of news hard, no doubt about it. But her reaction was also interesting. Celestine had said that there was fear in her eyes. And fear runs through murder like a sauce through a cassoulet. He sat down in the café opposite the church and ordered a beer. Celestine would be waiting to hear about his visit to the police, but it was that same visit that had given him the most tremendous thirst. He had never voluntarily visited a police station in his life before, and the first beer slid down without touching the sides as the second was on its way.

In the office of the Maire of Lissac-sur-Tarn, three men were seated around a low table. The men were Commandant Grimard; the Maire, Monsieur De Fournas - a quite recent incumbent, elected under the banner of the National Rally Party, and Monsieur Palomer - a councillor and owner of one of the largest and most prestigious vineyards in the area. There was an uncomfortable silence as Grimard shuffled his notes, preparing to leave. He had just provided the officials of the town with an update on the progress of the investigation into the murder of Monsieur Malraux. The Maire was a thin man in his thirties, with black hair severely combed back into a kind of reverse crest, and a sharp beak of a nose. This, and his penchant for wearing salmon pink shirts, had quickly given him the nickname of *the Hoopoe* among the wags of the town. He broke the silence.

'Monsieur Commandant. I was elected,' he began, in a high and querulous voice, 'to restore law and order in this town and to deal with the issue which concerns all of our citizens - the number of immigrants in the town, and their unacceptable behaviour.' He looked straight at Grimard. 'Now we have a murder,' he continued. 'The murder of a Frenchman, a scholar, an esteemed visitor here to study our heritage, our French heritage. Slaughtered in our streets by an immigrant, a Bulgarian.' His voice rose so high that the final words squeaked out. Grimard looked at him with some distaste.

'As I said, Monsieur le Maire, we do not yet know whether this man did commit the crime.'

'You don't know,' shrieked the Maire. 'You don't know. He was killed with a knife. These people carry knives. He was seen arguing violently with the deceased the afternoon before. You have physical evidence. A paper, a Bulgarian paper attached to the corpse.'

'Not attached,' said Grimard calmly, 'it was stuck to his face with blood.'

'A food wrapper. Bulgarian food wrapper.'

'Yes, but....'

'Did no one see anything, see him around the time of the murder?' asked Monsieur Palomer. 'Surely, in a small town.'

'It was late,' replied Grimard. 'I imagine these streets are quiet and quite dark at that time. We are of course making further inquiries and interviewing people living in the vicinity. We have appealed for any witnesses to come forward, but so far no one seems to have seen the actual killing take place.'

'So, no one saw anything?' pressed Palomer.

'At this point, it seems to be the case,' said Grimard.

'Then you must try harder, and find someone who saw that Bulgarian at the scene. Are there no traces, no DNA?'

'We are still waiting for the results and, of course, that could provide us with some more positive evidence.'

'You must keep us informed,' insisted Palomer.

'Gentlemen. I have an investigation to conduct, and how I do it is police business. I will of course show you the courtesy of informing you when there are further developments.' He stood up to leave.

'Of course, thank you, Commandant. Let us speak soon,' said the Maire. Grimard closed the door behind him and Monsieur De Fournas sat down again. He looked across at Palomer who was pulling absentmindedly on his left thumb. Of medium height, Palomer looked as though he had eaten and drunk far too well for fifty years. His belly sagged over the waistband of his trousers and his face was misshapen and jowly with fat.

'If not the Bulgarians, then who, Monsieur le Maire?'

'Who. Who. Of course it's the fucking Bulgarians. Nobody else kills in this town. Why would they? A professor from Paris.'

'A homosexual,' said Palomer.

'So! Look, this is just a distraction. It won't affect anything.'

'It had better not,' said Palomer vehemently. 'You keep right on top of this investigation. You let me know the instant you hear anything.' He hauled himself to his feet and walked out of the room without another word.

'Au revoir, Monsieur Palomer,' said the Maire, calling after him quietly. 'It's always an unmitigated joy to see you.'

Chapter Six

Earlier that morning, in a small bastide town some twenty kilometres east of Lissac-sur-Tarn, Bram Visser and his wife Lena were stringing the laces on their new walking boots and filling their rucksacks. They paid Madame Carpentier, the owner of the small Gite d'Etape which catered for pilgrims on the Compostela Way. Madame Carpentier smiled at them.

'You will enjoy the walk today,' she said. 'The countryside is gentle, you must take your time, you have to acclimatise you know.'

'Yes, we know. We are used to walking many kilometres every day,' said the man abruptly. His wife Lena said nothing and hurried out of the door. Madame Carpentier watched them walk away along the narrow, cobbled street, shuffling their shoulders and hitching their rucksacks higher. Quite a nice-looking couple, she thought, but not pilgrims.

A little further along the road, Lena stopped and pulled off her rucksack to adjust the straps. She tightened them and then hauled it back onto her shoulders. She looked at her husband's rucksack which was hanging too low on his hips, the straps were far too long. She took a hold of it to try and adjust it for him, but he shook her off. He was staring at the ancient walls of the buildings. The road was narrow, like a canyon, and the buildings were three stories high and pressed right up to the pavement. The walls were built from blocks of dressed white stone, but between there were also patches of thin red bricks and pieces of ancient timber.

'They're very old, the buildings,' she said. He didn't seem to hear her, so she moved to his side and noticed the look of bewilderment on his face. 'They're very old,' she repeated.

'How old?' he asked, not shifting his gaze.

'I don't know. Seven hundred years.'

'The fuck.'

'They're rather beautiful,' she said. 'That one with the fancy windows and shutters, the stone is….'

'They're not,' he said, and shaking his head he turned on his heels and continued walking. Lena followed him but she kept glancing at the buildings as they passed. There was definitely something beautiful about them, she thought.

Their route took them down through the old town and then the more modern suburbs and out into the countryside. They were following the red and white striped markers, and the walking was easy for an hour or so. They didn't talk much. The man walked some way ahead, looking in a narrow vector in front of him. But each time he spotted one of the way markers he would stop and point and shout back at her.

'There.' And it seemed to make him content and relieved that they were on the right path.

Lena liked to look at the fields, especially the fields of bright yellow sunflowers. But she didn't like the ones where the flowers had died and the heads were brown and drooping; they looked like a defeated army. She liked the trees, especially the poplars with their speckled trunks that lined some of the roads, although most of their way took them on tracks and along the edges of fields. When they walked through a patch of woodland Bram let her catch up a little, and he looked around and up in the trees as though they may contain dangers of some kind. By late morning, the day was warm and the air was fresh and filled with the scents of vegetation and dried earth. Lena felt this air filling her lungs more deeply, and the warmth on her bare legs made them feel somehow suppler. Her boots nipped a little, but she had always worn badly fitting shoes so that niggle was a minor thing. Bram had slowed down, and was complaining about his legs and the heat and the rucksack which was cutting into his shoulders. The land was starting to rise quite steeply, and she caught up to Bram and even tried to walk past him.

'What the fuck you doing?' he said. 'You have to find the markers, the red and white lines. That's how we know where we're going.'

She wanted to say that she was just as capable of this as he was, but she just didn't feel like arguing. So, the pace slowed as Bram shuffled up the hill slowly, breathing heavily and cursing. But she felt the air going deeper into her lungs, and her limbs were moving strongly, although she was not used to climbing hills - there weren't many hills in Amsterdam. They reached a top where the land fell away in front of them and the trees were set back and they could see far ahead into the distance. They could see down into a valley and then there was a great plain stretching beyond until it faded into the haze. Lena stood delighted, she could never remember ever seeing so far.

'That is amazing,' she said, turning to Bram.

'Yeah. It's a fucking long way. How far is that?' He shook off his rucksack, and although he was still breathing heavily from the climb, lit a cigarette from the pack in his pocket.

'I don't know. It feels like forever. It's like you could walk there forever,' said Lena.

'Not me. I'm not walking any more than we have to, for appearances. To seem like we're real pilgrims.' He sat down on the hard, dried grass and drew deeply on his cigarette. Lena sat beside him and took a water bottle and some food from her own rucksack. She handed him the map.

'Where are we?' she asked. Bram took the map and traced a line with his finger.

'On top of here,' he said, pointing. 'We've been walking for more than two hours, but we're not even halfway there yet. Jesus, it's going take another three hours, maybe more.'

'That's all right. It's nice being out in the countryside. I like it. Like nobody's watching you.'

'Just the fucking loonies and the bears and wolves and shit,' he said, and he made claw-like movements towards her. She laughed.

'There're no bears. It's nice.' She started eating, and they sat there in silence for a while. Then Bram reached into his rucksack and pulled out a long sheath knife, drew out the blade and stuck it in the ground. It quivered because the ground was so hard.

'When we get there, that fucking nun, I'm going to smack her one for every time. How many times?' said Bram, his hand resting on the hilt of the knife.

'Oh, I don't know.'

'How many? Twenty, a hundred. I'll give her a hundred slaps. Then I'll hold this under her nose and I'll nick it so the blood starts dripping and she'll think she's fucking dying then.' He leaned back and looked up at the sky.

'She'll think she's dying and she'll be all like, Jesus save me, all religious. Jesus save me, and I'll be like, no, you fucking nun, Jesus won't save you. I'm here with Lena, and we're like the, what do you call it, the antichrist. We are the antichrist, and Lena is going to make you pay for all the times that you were a fucking nun bitch. All the times and then some.' He laughed and started coughing and bits of sandwich spluttered out of his mouth. Lena listened and looked away. She was excited, but that, what Bram was talking about, was almost in another programme. She didn't want to think about it now. She wanted to walk and look at the countryside and feel the distance and the warm air.

'Yeah, we'll do that,' she said.

The walking was harder and then easier in the afternoon. Bram carried the knife in his hand and remained absorbed in finding the markers. Each time he called out 'there,' and then he didn't, and he just walked in silence. Lena was starting to feel tired but she kept looking around her, and it seemed to her at times that she had never lived on this planet before. Her legs were starting to ache a little and her feet were sore, but as they started to descend into the valley and passed the first houses she felt a little sad, she felt that she was leaving something behind. Bram put the knife away and let her walk closer to him. The markers were on street lamp posts now and he didn't shout out, just pointed. They passed the sign for the town of Lissac-sur-Tarn, which said it welcomed them, in two languages. That was strange she thought, and she looked over the road as they were passing the cemetery with its jumble of stone mausoleums and ornate graves and crosses. Welcome. She had never really been welcome anywhere, and she didn't think she would be here, if they knew.

They walked through the tatty outskirts, where the garages and the cheap restaurants were, and into the centre of the town. Bram had booked a small Gite, somewhere in a back street, and it took a while to find it. He was tired and bad-tempered, and she was tired so they didn't look around the town. They went to a café and drank beer and ate some thick, greasy food. Then they drank some more, especially Bram. He complained about his legs and his shoulders, so they went to bed in their dingy room, although it was still light outside. Lena lay there for a while, thinking. Thinking that she was lying again in a cheap bed in a dingy room and yet all day she had been untouchable, unrestrained, free, as she had moved through the countryside. It was a new feeling, and she lay there nudging it and wondering about it until she slept.

Chapter Seven

Celestine awoke early and angry. She eased out of bed past a gently snoring Jacques, and slipped on her running shorts and vest top. On deck, the morning was cool with a fresh breeze blowing along the canal from the west. She stepped over the side and began to run. The towpaths along the side of the canal are naturally flat and a runner's dream if you don't want to be faced with an unexpected hill to climb. Her intention had been to run five kilometres along the path, and then either return the same way or on the other side if there was a suitable bridge. But she found herself turning onto the footbridge and then jogging along the path towards the river. She stopped for a moment at the spot where they thought a boat had been moored. There was a path, less developed than the towpath, running along the side of the river away from the jetty and the town. The path was dry and clearly wide enough for cyclists to use; she could see the tracks of mountain bike tyres hardened in the softer clay at the sides.

There were no more than a hundred metres between the canal and the river at this point, and a few houses had been built there, but as the river began to curve away, woods and fields appeared on her left. The river bank was heavily wooded with only a few gaps where the water could be reached. Celestine was normally highly observant, she had been trained and had trained herself to notice fine details and to remember them. But when she ran she became virtually oblivious to her surroundings. To run was to push her body through its limits, to leave no space for thoughts or for self-doubt to emerge. She ran to exhaust herself and to cleanse her mind of the detritus, to leave a hard, sharp intellect ready to see the patterns forming in whatever was her focus at that time. It had used to be work; clear, uncompromising, worthwhile. But that was gone.

Where to focus? Where were the patterns? Who was Jacques, really? What was the pattern of their thrown-together life? She stopped running after twenty minutes and leant her hands on her knees. Was there a new pattern emerging? She could almost sense it. There were strands, seemingly unconnected, straying into her mind. Why had she chosen to run this way?

As she stood up, she heard the ringing of an old-fashioned bicycle bell. Coming along the track towards her was an old man on an ancient bicycle. He was wearing a large and torn straw hat tied under his chin with a ribbon, thick corduroy trousers and a stained, canary-yellow shirt. He stopped uncertainly in front of her, touched his hat politely, and said:

'Bonjour, madame, I hope I didn't startle you.'

'On the contrary, that bell gives you fair warning,' replied Celestine. The old man smiled. His face was deeply lined, and covered with several days' growth of pure white beard.

'You were a surprise. I don't often see people on the path at this time of the morning.'

'No, I suppose not,' said Celestine. 'I couldn't sleep.' The old man looked her up and down.

'No. Sleep is not always easy, is it? But you look very healthy, madame,' he said. Celestine was suddenly conscious that she was wearing very few clothes, and the shape of her breasts and long legs were very obvious. She wondered for a moment if he was being creepy and leering at her, but the look on his face was innocent and genuine.

'Do you use this path often, monsieur?' she asked.

'Oh yes. I live here you see, sometimes, along the path. I have a residence, a small boathouse. Nobody uses it, not for many years, so I stay there when I am in the area.' He spoke quietly and slowly with a warm, cultured, southern accent. Celestine noticed more about the bicycle. There were panniers strapped to either side behind the seat, which were bulging and misshapen and held together by old pieces of string. In front of the handlebars was a wire basket in which a large shopping bag had been placed. Again, it seemed full, although Celestine could only make out an old grey woollen jumper and a newspaper tucked in the side.

'You travel a lot, monsieur?'

'Yes, from here to there. I like it here at this time.'

'How long have you been here?' Celestine asked. His eyes were suddenly wary. 'I only ask because I was wondering if you had seen something I was interested in when you were riding along the path,' she added.

'What are you interested in?' he asked, the wariness still in his eyes.

'A boat. My friend and I thought we heard a boat on this side of the river the other night. Late. And we saw the marks of a rope on a tree, as though a boat had been tied up there. I just wondered.'

The old man pondered this for a few moments.

'I am Monsieur Lefebvre, Henri. I am not stupid, but I don't always remember everything.' He paused. 'Perhaps I saw a boat, but you must show me where.'

'Very well. You cycle and I will run. The place is just before you get to the lock on the canal.'

'Perfect, I am going that way to town,' said the old man, and he suddenly grinned. 'Enchanté, Madame …?' He held out his hand.

'Celestine. Celestine Courbet.' His hand was rough and dry, but Celestine held it and looked into his weather-beaten face. She was taken with his eyes, which smiled as broadly as he did and seemed to belong to a man at least twenty years younger.

They set off with the old man in front, but he rode so slowly that Celestine overtook him and raced on past. She reached the place where they thought the boat had been moored. Behind her, the old man trundled along, slightly erratically, on his sturdy-framed bicycle with its bulging panniers and overflowing basket. I wonder how old he is, thought Celestine. Are they all his worldly goods attached to that bike? How reliable a witness would he be? The old man came to a halt and leaned his bicycle against a tree at the side of the path. Breathing rather heavily, he said:

'You run quickly, madame.'

'I'm sorry, I didn't mean to rush you. I would happily have waited another five minutes for you. And please call me Celestine.'

'Certainly, Celestine.' He nodded. Celestine showed him the rope marks on the tree.

'You see, we think a boat was tied up here the other night. My partner saw a man running to this place and then heard the engine of a boat. We are curious. We wondered why someone would moor a boat here when there is a perfectly safe jetty just a hundred metres away.'

Monsieur Lefebvre was silent, clearly chewing over what Celestine had said. 'Why is this of interest to you madame, Celestine?' he asked in a surprisingly firm voice.

'Well, there was a crime committed in the town at about the time Jacques, my partner, saw the man. It seemed strange, perhaps nothing, but we want to be sure,' Celestine said. 'Do you remember seeing anyone here?' He didn't answer but again looked at her warily.

'What is your work, Celestine?' he asked. 'Do you work in Lissac?'

'No. I came here on a barge. We are on a long holiday.'

'But your work, when you are not on holiday,' the old man pressed.

Celestine looked into his face. The eyes were kind but there was also a determination there. This was not idle curiosity and this old man was nobody's fool. He smiled at her encouragingly.

'I was a police officer, in Bordeaux, for twenty years.'

'Ah,' the old man nodded. 'But not now?'

'No. I resigned.' Celestine heard the bitterness in her own voice. 'I was disappointed.'

'I see.' And he really gave the impression to Celestine that he did see. Perhaps something similar had happened to him. Now, an itinerant living on a bicycle, perhaps he had also had to change his life within a matter of weeks. 'Thank you, Celestine, let me think.' He cast his head back slightly and half-closed his eyes. He stayed like that for a minute or so. Finally, he straightened his head and opened his eyes wide. 'I have seen a man in a boat, not at night you understand, I don't like to ride my bike in the dark, I have no lights, the battery is dead.' Celestine noticed the old-fashioned lantern on the handlebars of the bicycle. 'But I have seen a man in a dark boat,' he added, 'a thin, sharp boat, passing along here twice in the last few days.'

'Did you see his face perhaps; would you recognise him?'

'I've never seen the boat here, but I did hear it start up one day, just before I got to this place. I saw the boat through the trees, going upstream. I saw the same boat once more, much nearer to my habitation, on this side of the river.'

'Did you see who was in the boat?'

'I did, a man, sitting of course, but I think, not short, dark hair.'

'Just one man? Did you see his face?'

'Well yes, I think I did.'

'Would you recognise him again?'

'Perhaps, in the same place, you understand, the same location, context.'

'I understand,' said Celestine. Monsieur Lefebvre looked again at Celestine with his kind, but firm eyes.

'Do you think this is important, Celestine?' he asked.

'I honestly don't know, Monsieur Lefebvre. It might be a wild goose chase.'

'Perhaps you haven't quite given up your previous job yet.'

Celestine smiled ruefully. 'That's not easy. It was a shock, an unexpected change in my life. Perhaps you've had something similar, monsieur?'

'Perhaps,' he said and looked away.

'You've been most helpful, Monsieur Lefebvre. I hope I haven't put you to any trouble.'

'On the contrary, it's a pleasure to talk to someone so young and beautiful, if I may say, and who doesn't treat me as just a useless old man.'

'Certainly not that. But tell me, how long will you be staying in this area?'

'Oh, another week or more yet, and then I will head further south as the weather changes. I'm like a bird you see.' He flapped his arms gently and grinned.

'I see,' said Celestine, and then surprised herself by asking: 'Well, perhaps you would come and have dinner with us, this evening, on our boat. I am sure Jacques would like to meet you, and he's a very good cook.'

'A dinner invitation,' replied the old man, and seemed to swirl the idea around his mouth to see whether it suited his palate.

'Of course, I would be delighted,' he said finally.

'Nothing formal of course,' said Celestine.

'Good, good. May struggle to locate my dinner jacket, you see.' Celestine laughed.

'Please come as you are, Monsieur Lefebvre. We'll be delighted to see you. Say seven o'clock. Our barge is on the town side of the canal. A rather murky green and burgundy colour, with the name, *Incognito.*'

'*Incognito,*' he smiled, 'an interesting choice of name. I don't live by the clock now, I have no watch, but I'll listen for the church bells.'

They parted, and Celestine jogged back to the boat, wondering why, oh why, did I just invite a homeless wanderer, a tramp, for dinner. But she knew. He was clearly an educated man who had lost something, fallen or jumped into hard times, and she worried that, although not close at this stage to his level of destitution, she was on that same spectrum. She shivered, despite the rising heat of the day. The sun was already quite high in the cloudless sky, and the boats on the canal were splashes of colour and gaiety in the tranquil and picturesque scene.

'Let the light drive out the darkness,' she said to herself, knowing that the only light that mattered to her was the truth.

Chapter Eight

Lena lay uneasily in the gloom. Light filtered vaguely through the old curtains that hung listlessly down the window. The sun rose so early at this time, it wasn't yet seven. She lay there thinking about the kilometres she had walked the day before. She was tracing the path in her mind; the surprises, the smell of the warm vegetation, the distances she could see from the hilltops.

She was waiting to be poked – the poking ritual. There had always been spaces in her life that people had suborned, taken for their own purposes, as though those spaces didn't belong to her. She had always known that she had no right to those spaces. Even yesterday, she had at times felt guilty, even illicit in the countryside; walking, seeing, with no right to be there. She listened to the breathing noises of the man. She slipped quietly from the bed and tip-toed into the tiny bathroom, lifting her clothes from the chair where she had folded them. She washed and dressed, her face pale and drawn, dark shadows around her eyes. She knew she was pretty, but she looked haggard in the stark fluorescent light. She listened again in the room. Then, taking her bag, she eased gently out of the door into the dingy corridor, down the stairs and into the street.

The streets were so quiet, not at all like Amsterdam. The air was fresh, not hazy or fumy. It was already warm, pleasantly warm; she almost felt bathed in it. She wandered through the narrow streets, crossing each time to the sunny side. She walked over a bridge and looked down at the small canal below. It was all on a different scale, different to Amsterdam. She felt she could walk from one end of the town to the other, she could do that, in a day, no an hour. She could never have imagined walking through Amsterdam like that. Here she could walk in all the spaces, all her spaces. She felt a little light-headed. She crossed back over the canal and sat down at a small plastic table outside a café that had opened its door. She ordered coffee, and it came, strong and dark. Another woman sat down near her, dressed for the night before, and lit a cigarette, spluttering at the first draw. Lena looked away from her and stared at the building opposite, shutting things out.

Leaving the café, she walked and found herself at the bottom of a steep lane leading to a convent and a viewpoint called Calvary. Now she realised why she was here, why she had chosen to come out alone this morning. This was her past only. This was the past that she had come here to diffuse, to bleed, to cauterise. Yes, to cauterise. The path was steep, but she soon reached the high iron railings that were an entrance to the Convent chapel and the guest house. The gate was open and she climbed up the steps and stood by the cross and looked at the church. She didn't feel awkward. She knew this place, these places, she knew their atmosphere, their rules. She could blend into the very air of the place. She was twelve years old, she was thirty-two years old. The door of the guesthouse opened and a workman came out. He smiled at her and politely held open the door. She walked in. The room was both entrance hall and refectory, and she saw people in hiking clothes sitting at the long benches. There was light over the tables, but she stood by a pillar in the gloom. She knew every scent. She saw nuns, two, sitting in their pure white robes, looking down at their food, silent.

Then she saw that nun. Unmistakeably that nun; very short, slim; that walk, a little stiff, self-aware, self-controlled. She was carrying a tray of food which she placed in front of the guests. She smiled at them, that insincere, lip-deep smile. She raised her arms to the side, in that gesture. Lena stepped away from the pillar and into the light, and the nun looked towards her, sensing another person there. She peered through her wire-framed spectacles, her head turned a little to the side, puzzling. Lena saw the actual moment when the nun recognised her, and she watched all the emotions of an era flicker and then spread across her face. The nun literally started and stepped back, her eyes blinking as if to clear themselves of what she had seen. And then her face collapsed. Lena saw the deep lines etched into her cheeks, the crow's feet around her eyes behind the wire-framed spectacles. The nun turned and stumbled, catching her foot on the legs of a chair. Lena saw the stiffness in her walk, so much stiffer now, saw the slight bending of her spine, the early stoop. She was so much smaller than Lena remembered; tiny, stiff, pathetic even. When the nun glanced furtively over her shoulder she saw only the back of a ghost as it walked out through the door. Lena gulped in the fresh air and felt a coldness coming over her, like a dark hood covering her skull, tightly. She stumbled down the steps and took the path into the town. She could feel the newly stretched muscles in her legs, so she walked across the small town, right to the other end.

Chapter Nine

Jacques and Celestine sat in the café in the square, opposite the Abbey portal. The street was quiet and the pigeons were hopping undisturbed near the café tables, pecking at crumbs. Celestine finished her coffee and took out her notebook.

'We need to find out exactly what Malraux was doing here, what he was studying, who he had contact with, who he met, how he spent his free time and where he came from. There will be connections, there always are. We have to know the man, the victim. We'll start here at the Abbey where he was working. Did he discover anything? Did he make friends? Confide in people? Are you listening?' Jacques mopped his mouth with a napkin and sat back.

'I have heard and understood every word, Celestine. But I have one question.'

'Only one?'

'I think it's a big question, and that is, why? Why are we doing this? Why are you getting yourself involved in a criminal investigation? This is a police matter. I'm sure that when you were a police officer you didn't exactly welcome the assistance of the "amateur".'

'I'm not an amateur, Jacques, and you know fine well that the police have their limitations.'

'Happily so,' said Jacques ruefully.

'And you started it with your running man and mysterious boat, and now I'm hooked. So, even if it's just as an intellectual exercise, I need this. But it's more, and I thought you were with me on this. It's abhorrent, the killing of another human being. And if we can help to catch whoever was responsible, then we should do it. Even if we just find out some information that the police can use. That would be useful, wouldn't it? I need to be useful.' Celestine's eyes flashed and she clenched her fists and glared angrily at Jacques.

'Ok, Ok. I just don't want this dragging up any of the pain from what happened in Bordeaux. We're supposed to be in the process of healing now.'

'Healing. I think this just might be part of the healing, you know.' She reached over and wrapped her hand around Jacques' fist.

'This is me. I need this, Jacques. Maybe it's a kind of warming down. But let's do this properly and see where it leads.'

Jacques nodded in acquiescence. He stood up and put some money on the table. They walked across the street and climbed the stone steps through the portal of the church. Jacques looked up again at the dominant figure of Christ and the seated wise men of the apocalypse, their heads turned towards the Messiah.

'I'd like the wisdom, but without the apocalypse, if you don't mind,' he whispered to himself, and followed Celestine into the church.

The nun wasn't there, but they saw the same official, arranging candles on a small table by an alcove. Celestine walked over to the wooden tableau that Sister Agnieszka had been describing when she'd been interrupted. Jacques approached the church official. 'Excuse me, monsieur. Could you tell me a little more about the wooden figures standing around the body of our lord, on the tableau over there?' He pointed.

'Of course, monsieur,' and he drew himself up to his medium height. 'I am the Deacon of this church. Let me explain them to you.' They walked over to the tableau and the Deacon nodded to Celestine.

'The Entombment of Christ, Fifteenth Century, a little primitive perhaps, but beautiful work, the colours….'
'Well preserved,' said Celestine.

'Repainted in the 18th century. And the figures, such sympathy, such sorrow.'

'Do we know who the figures represent?'

'Well, clearly the Virgin Mary, the holy mother, and next to her Saint John. This figure here is Mary Magdalene with, it is believed, a vase of perfume.'

'Ah, Mary Magdalene,' said Jacques. Celestine interrupted him quickly.

'Monsieur. We were here yesterday. We saw a nun with a group of schoolchildren. She was so enthusiastic. We saw her on the steps too. What a wonderful manner, so inspiring.'

'Sister Agnieszka.'

'But you said something to her and she seemed to change, so suddenly, as though a light had gone out,' said Celestine. The Deacon looked at them quickly.

'We were here. Actually, we were listening to her. She was irresistible. You asked us to leave the church.'

'Yes, yes, of course, I remember. I am sorry, but I had just learned some tragic news and she took it rather badly.'

'Was it the news about the murder?' Celestine asked pointedly.

'Yes, it was,' he said in a flat voice that suggested there was nothing more to be said.

'He worked here, I think, the victim?' persisted Celestine.

'Worked no. He was studying here.'

'Here in the church?'

'Some, but more in the cloisters, I believe. He was a professor, from a university in Paris.' The Deacon was moving slowly away from them.

'I see, and was Sister Agnieszka close to him?' asked Celestine.

'I really couldn't say. I can't think so. He was a very flamboyant character. But who knows, perhaps they talked. Now I must leave you to look around the rest of the church.'

'Just one more thing, monsieur,' said Jacques. 'Is there any great mystery in the cloisters? Anything that hasn't been studied before? Perhaps some new information that has come to light, to cast doubt on...?'

'I don't think so. The cloisters are a heritage site. They have been studied by great scholars for many centuries. I can't think there's a new angle,' he snorted to himself. 'But look for yourself. They are a wonderful example of 12th and 13th century ecclesiastical architecture, sacred art I should say. You must see them for yourselves.' He nodded and walked away.

'Yes, we must,' said Jacques.

This time the entrance to the cloisters was open. In the glass foyer there were stands where books on the Abbey and related topics were displayed. Celestine looked quickly around. There were two women seated behind a long desk - a girl and an older woman of about Celestine's age. The girl was taking the entrance fees and handing out tickets from a machine. Celestine whispered to Jacques.

'We'll go in separately. We're not together. We'll meet inside, but don't approach me.' Jacques nodded. He walked up to the counter and smiled at the girl. She printed out his ticket, handed him a leaflet, and he walked through the glass door into the cool of the Abbey courtyard. Celestine approached the older woman who was typing on the keyboard of her computer. She looked up and scowled.

'Excuse me,' said Celestine, smiling. 'I wonder if you could help me. I am looking for a more detailed guide to this period of church history. I see some of the books but they look a little thin.'

'Medieval Religious Architecture, Laurence Proux,' spat out the woman and looked down at her keyboard again.

'Could you perhaps show me that? You see I am studying a very esoteric aspect of medieval carving.'

'You are an academic, madame?'

'An amateur, but also a wood carver myself. An unusual field for a woman, I know, even now. But it's my metier.' The woman smiled for the first time, a wan and uncomfortable smile, but she came around from the counter and led Celestine to one of the stands farthest away from her desk.

Chapter Ten

Urbain Lamy's house in the little alley of Sainte Marta was raided at midday by eight police officers in full protective clothing. It took some minutes to break through the heavily bolted front door; enough time for Lamy to throw a small number of packets into the toilet bowl and flush them away. The girl lying on the threadbare sofa had grabbed three packets and thrust them inside her pants. The door burst open and police flowed into each of the rooms. The bathroom door was also bolted, so the officers hammered on it and screamed for it to be opened. Slowly, Lamy unbolted the door and let himself be dragged out of the house and into the street. As they marched him to the open doors of the van he saw the dogs jump out of the back of another van and, straining hard on the leash, bound into the house. His girlfriend was being bundled into the back of a police car, and he knew there was not a centimetre of his house that would not be meticulously searched.

An hour later, Grimard himself sat down opposite Lamy in the small, airless interview room. He stared for a minute at the gaunt, twitching figure. Then he slapped his hand loudly on the top of the table.

'Eh bien, Lamy. You are a dealer of drugs. A pathetic and disgusting occupation and one that deserves the maximum punishment allowed. We have discovered evidence enough to prosecute you now, and you will of course be incarcerated. For some time. We have found packages of cocaine, just like this one.' He held up a small foil packet. 'We found them in your house, and in the underwear of your girlfriend, Marie Carre.'

'I don't spend any time there,' said Lamy, stupidly. Grimard ignored him.

'She's a young girl. She'll tell us everything we want to know. We will have more than enough.' He shrugged and paused for a minute or so. Then he held up a small package in his right hand.

'This is one of yours I think, at least, I know.' He held it close to Lamy's face. 'It was bought from you on Tuesday night, at around ten o'clock perhaps.'

'Don't know what you're talking about.'

'It was bought from you by a Monsieur Malraux. A man who, shortly after he bought this packet, was mercilessly cut down in the street only a few hundred metres from your house.'

'I heard. Nothing to do with me.' Lamy sat back and folded his arms. 'Why would I do that?'

'Money. You would have seen the money he had in his wallet, which was stolen along with his watch. Do you have a watch, Lamy?'

'No. I didn't see anything. I don't need to steal for money.'

'No, you make, made, a living, let's not say good, from your filthy trade. At an end now. What we have to decide is how serious is the trouble you are in.' There was a long silence, broken only by the nervous tapping of Lamy's foot on the floor. Finally, he spoke.

'I saw something that night. I stepped out for a minute, maybe around ten o'clock.'

'What did you see?'

'A couple, man and woman, along the street, end of the alley. Arguing, shouting at each other.'

'Could you hear what they were saying?'

'I could hear it, but I couldn't understand it. They were speaking in a foreign language. Bulgarian maybe.'

'Bulgarian. You're sure?'

'Not sure, but it wasn't French or English.'

'Would you recognise them again?'

'It was dark, maybe, don't know.'

Grimard stood up abruptly. 'So, you admit selling drugs to the deceased, Monsieur Malraux?'

'I didn't sell him anything. It was a gift. He was going to meet a boy. I wanted to help him, that's all.'

'Name and address.'

'Marc. I don't know. He's just a poor kid. I'm sorry for him.'

'We're not finished yet,' said Grimard. 'You need time to think about the details of your story. Believe me, you had better give us the full picture. That's the only thing that will help you.' Grimard strode out of the room and Lamy slumped back in the chair.

Jacques walked slowly through the cloisters. Although a deep sceptic, he could still appreciate this as a beautiful place, a place of harmony and tranquillity. The cloisters were arranged as a quadrangle around a lush green lawn, the rooves of the arcades were supported by stone pillars with wonderfully carved capitals, each one was of a different theme; there were stories from the bible interspersed with intricate patterns of leaves, birds and mythical creatures. Despite himself, Jacques was soon absorbed, checking the guide pamphlet to try to decipher the details of the carvings. Twelve was the Devil Unchained, thirty-five was the Wedding at Cana.

A group of schoolchildren were spread out along two sides of the quadrangle. Most were sitting on the low wall with their backs against the pillars, they were sketching the carvings. He stopped by one of the pillars and looked over at the sketch that a young girl was making. She looked up warily, but he beamed at her and she smiled, despite herself. He nodded at her drawing. 'That's very good,' he said. And it was, and it surprised him that in this modern, secular world, children should be here sketching these old motifs. He hardly noticed Celestine sidle past him. She stopped by one of the pillars and appeared to be studying it carefully.

'I'll see you later this afternoon, at the boat,' she whispered, as Jacques walked past. Very well he thought, then I shall buy some Bulgarian delicacies for my own lunch.

Chapter Eleven

Jean-Luc Ducrozet slipped out of the side door of his house and onto a narrow back street. Wearing shorts and a dark T-shirt, and carrying a small black rucksack, he looked around quickly before quietly closing the door. It was Thursday and he should have been at work. His wife was at the hospital and his two children were at school. His place was at the Abbey Museum where he was Chief Curator. Instead, he was shuffling, head down, through the narrow streets leading to the canal. In his stomach were sharp biting creatures tearing at him. He had felt that fear so many times. The fear of a catastrophe about to engulf him. The terror and the loss. He crossed the canal on a narrow road bridge and looked down at the water, and at the colourful barges leaning against the quay. People were talking, laughing and reading, a man was standing on the roof adjusting an aerial of some kind. People were oblivious, content, not a hundred metres away, and of course, they didn't know the agony he was in.

    He followed the road slightly downhill until he reached a broad green park area beside the river. The path ran diagonally through the park, cool under the trees, until it reached a short, concrete jetty where five small boats were moored. He climbed aboard the third boat, a white motor cruiser with a covered area and a canvas hood. He opened a hatch and leaned down to check the levels of fuel in the tank. The engine started on the second attempt, and he leaned out to untie the painter from the small capstan set in the concrete. Then he eased the boat away from the shore and headed for the centre of the river. The current was quite strong, and he upped the throttle and pointed the bow upstream. He saw only one other boat on the river; a small fishing boat near the far shore, and the fisherman looked up but didn't wave.

Looking straight ahead, Ducrozet continued up the river until it curved and the town behind was out of sight. It was heavily wooded to the water's edge, and he slowed the boat right down and looked carefully at the banks on either side. He was looking for movement of any kind. Satisfied, he took hold of the rucksack and drew something out of the front pocket. It was wrapped in cloth, and he uncovered it and looked at it wistfully. It was a knife with a blade about fifteen centimetres long, the handle was of whalebone with scrimshaw markings of a fantastic wild animal and a young native boy naked under a palm tree. He lifted the knife to his lips and kissed it. Then, taking one last look around he dropped it into the water. He felt the tears stinging his eyes so he took off his T-shirt to wipe them dry. Then, as the fear and anxiety continued to nibble away at his bowels, he had the desperate urge to literally strip himself of everything. He took off his shorts and underpants, and naked, pushed the throttle on the boat to the maximum and headed directly upriver.

Celestine returned to the *Incognito* at around three o'clock. Jacques was sitting, sketching on the bow deck. Next to him was a small table on which there were the multi-coloured remnants of his lunch. Celestine bent down and kissed him on the cheek.

'You seem to have lunched well,' she said. 'Not much left.'
'No. What you see are the skid marks of my Bulgarian lunch.'
'Bulgarian?'
'Yes, Bulgarian. And I have some information for you.'
'As have I for you.'
'Have you lunched?' Jacques asked.
'Yes,' said Celestine,' 'but not as well as you I think. I need a coffee and I'll tell you what I found out.'
Coffee cup in hand, Celestine leaned on the side of the boat and put her foot on the edge of Jacques' chair. 'Catherine Tallandier is the assistant curator at the Abbey, and a very disgruntled woman, for many reasons, but principally with her position as assistant curator. She gave me a long and rather one-sided discourse on the finer points of Romanesque ecclesiastical art. I told her a little of my deep interest in medieval carving, and the upshot was that she invited me for lunch.'
'This interest seems to have gone deep very quickly.'

'I know, but I had to think on the hoof. Anyway, I spent some time looking through the cloisters, and at twelve-thirty precisely, when the Abbey doors were closed, I found myself accompanying this disgruntled woman to a small restaurant in the main square. We sat at a table outside where I had tried to direct her as far away as possible from other people, so she wouldn't feel inhibited to talk. I needn't have bothered. She hardly stopped.'

'Did you eat well?'

'Not even that,' replied Celestine. 'I waited to see what she would order, so as to order something similar.'

'Like a kindred spirit.'

'Exactly. But a pale vegetable soup and a limp goat's cheese salad was....'

'Just what you deserved.'

'Probably,' said Celestine, and nudged his thigh with her foot. 'But nevertheless, it was an interesting lunch for many reasons. For example; the Head Curator, Catherine's boss, is a Monsieur Ducrozet, and he hasn't been at work since the night of the murder. More than that, Catherine assures me that Malraux and Ducrozet were having a passionate relationship. Almost from the day Malraux arrived. Now, Ducrozet is a married man with two children. Catherine described the relationship several times as Rimbaud and Verlaine.'

Jacques pulled gently at his beard. 'I know something of that,' he said.

'Yes, I thought you might. Rimbaud was a rather wild, enfant terrible of the literary scene in the 1870s. He had a relationship with Verlaine, another poet, who was quite a lot older than him. The relationship was passionate and also violent. At one time Verlaine shot Rimbaud through the wrist, he also slashed at him with a knife. Apparently, they attacked each other, even in public, and caused injury to both. Now Catherine was adamant in referring several times to her boss's relationship as Rimbaud and Verlaine.'

'And Ducrozet hasn't been to work since the murder?'

'No. But she thought the affair was over several days, even a week before. Her boss had been storming around like a bear with a sore head, shouting at staff, and criticising the work of Monsieur Malraux.'

'What about the work Malraux was doing?'

'Well, it seems that initially he was more interested in the archives, both here, and at the Convent, and also, and I didn't know this existed, at the Museum of the Jewish Scout Movement which is here in Lissac. Latterly though, he had been spending more time at the cloisters and the church, much it seems to the annoyance of all the staff.' Celestine paused and sipped at her coffee.

'He was a very extravagant person, it would seem, this Malraux. Given to wild exuberance and grumbling self-pity. Very overtly gay, and often, Catherine suggested, he was out of his head. Drink or drugs, although she said he didn't smell of alcohol and was in fact very fastidious about his appearance.'

'What of the nun, Sister Agnieszka? Was he close to her? Seems unlikely doesn't it?'

'She didn't think so, but they definitely spoke here and at the Convent, where he said, she had been most kind and helpful.'

'Ok, so this Ducrozet, did she say if he had been in touch at all since the murder?'

'Only to tell them to close the Abbey, and that he was sick.'

'But did he come in on the morning of the murder? As we saw, the news only reached the church in the mid-morning.'

'Apparently, he didn't come in. He just telephoned and told them to close the Abbey. Catherine was really scathing about that.'

'I bet she does a good line in scathing, from what you've said. They, the police, must have interviewed him by now. He'd be one of the first, wouldn't he?'

'I don't know. Catherine said they hadn't interviewed all the staff there yet.' Celestine stood up in disgust.

'They think they've got their man. The minds are closing, like you said,' suggested Jacques.

'It's bloody basic. Family, friends and work colleagues; draw a picture of the man early, his relationships and his movements. Basic, basic stuff.' Celestine walked once around the boat, holding onto the handrail on the roof, and then sat back down again next to Jacques.

'Did you really eat all the food you bought?' she demanded.

'In the spirit of investigation, I felt it necessary,' replied Jacques.

'In the spirit of your belly more like.'

'Ok. The man they've arrested is called Krastyo Dacheva, I think that's how it's pronounced. He's a kind of family head to a few other groups of relatives. A cousin to the woman I met in the shop. The shopkeeper.' Celestine raised her eyebrows.

'They're very family-focused, and there's a lot of distress and anger at his arrest. They claim he's not a violent man, just hardworking and decent. He leads a team of men and women who work on the farms around here, picking fruit, weeding, etc.'

'Ok, but what about the argument?'

'There was an argument in the afternoon. Apparently, Malraux met a young Bulgarian man, a youth really, in the street, or maybe before. The boy was a nephew of Dacheva. He heard the boy shout out some Bulgarian slang and came out to see what was happening. The boy was swearing. They said it was true that the uncle threatened Malraux and pushed him along the pavement, away from the boy. They're strong little fellows these Bulgarian workers, good in a fight, low centre of gravity. Anyway, that was the end of it. And the men I spoke to in the shop swore that Dacheva wouldn't do any such a thing as kill somebody. I think they're a bit old-fashioned in their views, especially in relation to sexuality. They didn't say as much, but I think maybe Malraux propositioned the boy.'

'You spoke to some men inside the shop. Were they antagonistic, suspicious, what?'

'Suspicious at first. They were standing outside while I was trying to order the food. It was funny, we were laughing in the shop. I guess they thought we were having too good a time. Anyway, I spoke to them, in a concerned way, about the arrest and they relaxed a bit. It was all in broken French. But they were keen to give as much information as possible.'

'Did they have an opinion on who could have committed the murder, if not their compatriot?'

'I asked that, but they basically shrugged. He was a homosexual, like it was bound to happen sooner or later.'

'What about an alibi? Couldn't any of them confirm where the guy was at the time of the murder?'

'They'd asked around, but he was out of the house, perhaps with a woman. His wife died apparently and he… takes comfort.'

'How old is he?'

'They said around fifty.'

Celestine opened her notebook and drew out a pen. She spent a few minutes writing, occasionally looking up into the distance and then writing some more.

'Suspects,' she said finally.

'Yes,' said Jacques, 'suspects.'

'One: The Bulgarian; argued with the victim, can't trust family loyalty. Strong, capable of violence, and protective. Police have some evidence. You need to speak to your friend Desmarais.'

'Friend?'

'We'll need his insight. The forensics should be back by now. There are details we'll never know without him,' Celestine said forcefully.

'Ok,' said Jacques.

'Two: Your running man; a definite sighting of the boat. Wait till you listen to Monsieur Lefebvre this evening. He gives quite a clear picture. But who is he? Why was he running? What's his link with Malraux? We don't know this yet. If any.

Three: Ducrozet the curator; unrequited passion, a violent relationship, fear of exposure.'

'To his wife?'

'Yes. Perhaps to the wider community. He has quite a prestigious position in a small town.'

'Yes, but your lunch mate knew, so he wasn't particularly careful. And from what you suggested, she wouldn't be one to keep it to herself. Perhaps there was a professional disagreement. Maybe Malraux discovered something that discredited Ducrozet's position,' suggested Jacques.

'He did write the guidebook to the cloisters.'

'Ducrozet?'

'Yes. It's very detailed, and in Catherine's view, very dull.'

'We need to find out more about Ducrozet. I think that must be one of the next things we do.'

'Four.'

'Four?'

'Four: An unconnected party; a thief, junkie, drug dealer, take your pick. Plenty of those, even in a small town like Lissac.'

'Ok. His wallet and watch were taken. But do you kill for a few euros and a Rolex?'

'Was it a Rolex?'

'I have no idea,' said Jacques. 'But you know what I mean. A Patek Philippe.'

'I got the impression he wasn't short of money.'

'Did he have a car?'

'Catherine didn't say. But he came down from Paris by train.'

'Then everything he needed to study must have been within quite a narrow area. Where did he stay by the way?'

'There's a small apartment for visiting academics in the Abbey complex. He was staying there.'

'The police will have already searched that, won't they?'

'Undoubtedly.

Five: Religion; we have a scared and upset nun. A man studying and perhaps expressing opinions on religious matters. Could someone want to silence him? Stop the blasphemy.'

'Why blasphemy?'

'He could have been expressing anti-Christian views. In the eyes of some extreme religious figures his whole lifestyle, his orientation, is blasphemy.'

'This is France,' said Jacques, 'not Alabama.'

'No, but we need to keep the religious angle open,' said Celestine firmly.

'Six.'

'Six. Oh my God.'

'Six: Someone with a relationship that is not apparent at this time and who had a compelling reason to kill him.'

'Is that it?' said Jacques, rolling his eyes. 'Please don't go as high as eight or I can feel myself being dragged into this list of suspects.'

'I can't give you an alibi, I was sleeping,' said Celestine, and grabbed his wrist like a handcuff.

'Not even in jest. But what do we do next?'

'We need to know why the victim came to Lissac. And we need to know more about the other suspects, particularly the Curator. And we need to find out who your running man is,' said Celestine.

Chapter Twelve

Monsieur Lefebvre rode slowly along the canal towpath a few minutes after the church bells had chimed for seven o'clock. Wobbling slightly, he peered at each of the barges in turn. Celestine leaned out and waved as he came nearer, and relieved, he walked his bicycle between the bushes and up to the barge.

'Bonsoir, bonsoir, *Incognito*, bonsoir, Celestine,' he called.

'Bonsoir, Monsieur Lefebvre, you are very prompt for a man without a watch,' said Celestine. Monsieur Lefebvre beamed, reached into one of the panniers on his bicycle and pulled out a slightly bedraggled, but very colourful, bunch of flowers. He handed them formally to Celestine who took them and lifted them to her nose.

'Thank you so much, Monsieur Lefebvre, they're beautiful,' she said. She was fairly sure that the gardens of the houses she had passed along the bank of the river could spare a few blooms for a man in Monsieur Lefebvre's situation.

'Jacques, Monsieur Lefebvre is here, help him with his bicycle.' Jacques emerged from the galley wearing a scarlet apron and a scarlet face.

'Bonsoir, monsieur, welcome,' he said and lifted the bicycle over the side of the boat.

'Wow, this is a very substantial bike, not carbon fibre I think.'

'No. Valerie was built in the age of steel,' replied Monsieur Lefebvre. He looked around quizzically. He was wearing a pair of grey, flannel trousers, plimsolls, and a white formal shirt which was worn, a little stained in places and two sizes too large. He had trimmed his beard, although it was still uneven and tufty. He'd replaced the old straw hat with a faded blue cap, almost nautical looking, but with a plastic spoke sticking out of a hole in one corner. Jacques liked the look of him immediately.

'Welcome to the world of *Incognito*,' said Jacques, grabbing Monsieur Lefebvre's hand and pumping it for half a minute. 'Let me show you around. I'm cooking, but I think everything is under control.' Jacques took him by the arm and led him down into the cabins below. In the galley, two pots were bubbling on the stove. 'A Blanquette de Veau, a veal stew, served with rice. I hope you'll like it.' Monsieur Lefebvre just nodded and smiled gently. Jacques then took him onto the deck again and around to the stern, where a small table had been laid with three places.

'Sit down there and I'll send the waitress to take your drinks order. A small aperitif before dinner perhaps. I have to see to the cooking.' Monsieur Lefebvre nodded and sat down carefully on one of the chairs. Jacques spoke to Celestine who had been arranging the flowers in a vase in the salon. 'Get the old fellow a drink. Poor man looks a bit dazed.'

'I don't suppose he's met many people like you recently,' said Celestine. 'With your great scarlet apron, you look like a demented bullfighter with his cape wrapped around him.'

Jacques grinned, and Celestine poured two glasses of chilled white wine and went to join Monsieur Lefebvre on the deck.

'So, Celestine,' began Monsieur Lefebvre slowly. 'You live on this boat. For how long?'

'About three months now. It was moored near Bordeaux. It's Jacques' boat.'

'And Bordeaux, that's where you were a policeman?'

'Police capitaine, yes. A detective.'

'And Jacques?'

Celestine paused. 'Jacques is, well, a carpenter, but a specialist in the restoration of antique furniture.'

'A carpenter.' Monsieur Lefebvre again gave the impression of swilling the words around his mouth to taste their meaning. 'Not a policeman then, although he's a strong-looking fellow.'

Celestine laughed. 'Yes, he's strong. But no, he was never a policeman.' Monsieur Lefebvre looked at her in his quiet, determined way.

'And now you live together on a boat. And is it your intention to continue…?' He waved his hand vaguely.

'Yes. I don't really know. This is a kind of experiment for us.'

'Of course, I see. I'm sorry, I don't mean to pry. I'm afraid I have few of the social graces now, if I ever had them.'

'I understand,' said Celestine and looked him fully in the eyes. 'You can say anything at all to me, I won't take offence. But tell me, Monsieur Lefebvre, again if you don't mind me asking, how long have you lived in your way?'

'The honest truth is, I don't know. Is it five years or six? It's hard to keep count. Years mean only changing seasons to me. I'm not destitute you understand. I have my pension, and when I need it I can draw on this, but,' he stopped and his eyes clouded. Celestine immediately put her hand on top of his.

'You don't need to say another word. It's not our business. Let's talk of other things.' With that, Jacques emerged carrying steaming bowls and set them on the table.

'Bon appétit, Monsieur Lefebvre. I am so glad you could join us for our meal today,' said Jacques forcefully.

They ate in silence for a while as Monsieur Lefebvre picked slowly and carefully at his food, nodding occasionally at the plate and at Jacques.

'Tell me, what do you eat normally, day by day?' asked Jacques. Monsieur Lefebvre sat back and pondered for a moment.

'I eat a lot of fish; tins of fish, mackerel, tuna, sardines. And fruit. Fruit, always in season,' and he gave a low chuckle. Jacques roared.

'You're a forager. Is that why you come to this area at this time of the year, for the fruit? It's a great area for plums and apples and grapes of course.'

'Partly,' replied Monsieur Lefebvre. 'Partly I come for the fruit, but also because it's next to the canal. The canal you see is perfect for cycling. It's flat, there's a good path all the way, there are no cars and it runs through good farmland, but also through the cities. In the winter the cities are a better place.'

'And where do you come from, originally?'

'From Toulouse. I was an engineer, in the space industry.'

'An engineer,' said Jacques. 'But....'

Celestine nudged him. 'Jacques, that's none of our business.'

'I'm sorry, of course, I was just curious.'

'That's ok, Jacques, and you must call me Henri now, after such a fine meal.' He smiled and looked thoughtful for a moment, and he stared into the waters of the canal. Then he turned to them and said in a matter-of-fact voice. 'There are thunderbolts, you know, they come out of a clear sky. Then nothing is the same, nothing can be the same again.'

'How true,' said Celestine hurriedly. 'Tell Jacques about the man in the boat, tell him what you saw.'

'Yes, I will. I have thought a little more about what I saw.' The old man described again hearing the boat taking off from the bank, and on another occasion hearing it further up the river. 'But now I remember better. I saw your man, wearing a black shirt as you described him. I did see his face, he had dark hair and a plump face, yes plump, so the features were a little vague from a distance. But also, I remember now, he was facing in my direction. He was speaking on a mobile telephone.'

'Could you hear anything?' asked Jacques.

'He was shouting of course, because of the noise of the motor and the rushing water, but more than that, I think he was shouting because he was angry.' He stopped and looked drained, as though unaccustomed to speaking for so long.

'But he was French?' demanded Jacques.

'Oh, certainly French. Southern French perhaps.' He sat back in his chair.

'Tell me, Henri. What is upriver from where you stay, are there other houses?'

'Yes, there are some farmhouses and a chateau, although I think it's just an overgrown Vintner's house. It's an area of vineyards, for the Chasselas grapes, you know. Large vineyards.'

'And are these houses near the river? Do they have boat houses?'

'Yes, quite a few. There are quite a few boathouses. Mine is the first one you come to. It's not in a good state, and it hasn't been used for many years, I would say. But it's dry and shady under the trees.'

'No boat?'

'No boat, some old oars and ropes, but no boat.' Jacques was suddenly deep in thought.

'Jacques was thinking of taking a trip up the river, to see if we can spot the black boat,' said Celestine.

'And you must come with us, Henri. What do you think? You might recognise the boat or the man.'

'Jacques, that's too much to ask,' said Celestine. There was silence for a few moments.

'No. Jacques is right. And I would like to take a trip on a boat. Yes, I would enjoy that,' piped up Monsieur Lefebvre, his eyes smiling again.

'Settled. Can we pick you up from your boathouse?'

'Yes, I think so. There's a small wooden pier.'

'Tomorrow afternoon then, after lunch,' confirmed Jacques. Monsieur Lefebvre smiled widely, and his creased and weather-beaten face became smoother and more relaxed, suddenly at ease.

'But I almost forgot,' he said. 'Today, this afternoon, I saw another strange thing upon the river. I saw a boat coming fast, a white boat, Jacques, not a black one, coming fast upriver, and in it was a man, standing, not sitting, and he was erm… naked, absolutely without clothes.' He chuckled again. 'Stark naked, imagine.' Jacques and Celestine looked at each other. Celestine smiled.

'I think you lead a very interesting life on the waterways of France, Henri.'

'Perhaps, but no, most of the time it's not very interesting. I'm surviving as best I know how.' His face creased again and he seemed to draw in on himself. Shortly after, he rose, shook both their hands, and thanked them for the invitation and their kindness.

'First, we have a gift for you, Henri,' said Celestine. Jacques produced a new bicycle lamp.

'I didn't know what size of battery your lamp uses, but this one should help until you get a replacement.' Monsieur Lefebvre smiled broadly, a smile that changed his face so completely from a lost and withdrawn old man into a member of human society again.

'You are too kind. I won't forget your kindness,' he said. Jacques lifted his bicycle back onto the path. 'You take care now; don't you go falling in the river.'

The light was fading and he would have need of the lamp. Jacques watched him until he had disappeared over the road bridge heading for the river. He stood there long after the old man was out of his view, feeling a sadness, unexpected but tangible. He realised that he needed the arms of a good woman and he stepped back onto the barge.

Chapter Thirteen

Sister Agnieszka put aside her reading. It was nine o'clock, and normally at this time she would have been preparing to retire to her plain and simple room in the Convent, to pray and to sleep. But this night was different. Inside she was in turmoil such as she hadn't felt since her novitiate, some thirty years before in Poland. She was deeply troubled. The events of the last two days had shaken her world, her faith was being stirred and tested and she was racked with uncertainty. And this day something had appeared from her past; a ghost, a faint memory and a niggling, sharp, hard feeling of guilt. She slipped on her thin cotton cloak. The nights were still warm, but she felt a little chilled. Raised in a cold, northern climate, she was still amazed at how mild the evenings could be. But she was also aware that the cloak was more than a covering, it was almost a disguise. She became almost unrecognisable in the cloak; a small, harmless, religious figure. She stepped quietly out of the main door. There was a little movement at the far end of the building where the kitchens were, but the rest was in silence. She walked in shadows across the courtyard and opened the small street door set in the high wall that surrounded the Convent. The door opened a little noisily, she glanced back towards the building. There was no movement, so she closed the door as quietly as she could and stepped out into the narrow street - the street which led downhill to the town and uphill to the viewpoint of Calvary.

Earlier that evening, she had received a note, addressed to her and brought to her by Sister Josephine, who was as large as Sister Agnieszka was small.

'I found it in the offertory box just now, it's addressed to you. And there was a fifty euro note.'

The offertory box was kept on the wall just inside the gate, and people could post offerings through a slot on the outside. Often these were small denomination coins or notes, deposited there by pilgrims on the Compostela Way. Rarely anything larger than ten euros.

'It's not the correct place for correspondence,' said Sister Josephine. 'You must tell them to communicate with you through the normal channels. Who's writing to you anyway?' Sister Agnieszka looked at the envelope and then tucked it into her sleeve.

'I don't know. Probably from the Abbey. I don't know when I'll start work there again.'

Sister Josephine sniffed and waddled away down the corridor. Sister Agnieszka walked to her room, closed the door behind her and sat down on the bed. She drew the envelope from her sleeve and gently opened it. It contained a single piece of paper. There was no address and no greeting. It was printed, as all letters were now. She read it twice and then bowed her head in prayer. She sat like that for ten minutes or more before raising her head again. The envelope had fallen to the floor but she tucked the letter into her sleeve. There was no question about her next course of action

That had been two hours earlier, and now she stood listening in the quiet lane. She could hear the sound of a few cars in the streets below and then the surge of noise as a train hurtled along the railway line which ran by the edge of the town. After the train had gone the silence seemed more complete. She tucked her cloak around her and headed up the hill, her thick, rubber-soled shoes making little sound on the concrete path. She left the last house behind, and now there were only bushes and trees at the side of the path and a dark field beyond. The trees waved gently in the wind, covering and uncovering the few street lights. Shadows danced across the pavement as the bushes swayed. Head down, she walked slowly, mouthing words and snatches of prayers in French, but then also in Polish; something she did very rarely these days.

She reached the top of the hill, a little out of breath, so she stood by the metal railings looking down into the town of Lissac-sur-Tarn, where the roads were ribbons of light and the great Abbey was illuminated to display its grandeur and dominance. She could see the bridge over the great, wide River Tarn. She moved over to where the large white statue of the Virgin Mary was surrounded by a metal fence. She looked up and crossed herself. The right hand of the figure was raised in a blessing, the left one touching the cross. For a moment her own arms raised, and she held the same pose as the statue. She wondered if she was too late and called out quietly. For a moment there was no reply, so she called out again, a little more loudly, although her voice sounded strangled and tremulous. Then she heard a noise from the darkness of the trees. A figure was moving slowly towards her.

'Bonsoir, I am Sister Agnieszka, you sent me a note.'

'Oh, I know who you are, Sister Agnieszka.'

The figure came closer, walked right up and stood in front of her. She looked up, puzzled. Then she gasped as she felt a sharp pain in her chest. She looked down, the knife was tangled in her clothes. But then it was violently pulled out and upwards. She started to speak, but her breath was cut off and she choked and clasped her throat. She felt the warm blood flowing over her fingers. There were no more breaths. Her head was suddenly light and she felt herself falling backwards, panic, the terrible panic of having no air in the lungs, and the pain, the terrible agony, and then the darkness as her blood seeped out onto the stones at the foot of the statue of the Virgin Mary.

Chapter Fourteen

Bram and Lena Visser were ready to leave their lodging before seven o'clock, but unfortunately, they were not the first. A young French couple and a middle-aged man were fastening themselves into their rucksacks by the door.

'Good morning, join us,' said the young Frenchman and smiled encouragingly.

Bram raised his hand in acknowledgement. Lena bit her lip and bent down to tie her laces again. They left the building together and strolled into streets which were slowly coming to life with the early workers. They walked past the entrance to the church and the middle-aged man stopped to look up at the great carving above the door. He took a quick photograph on his mobile phone and crossed himself ostentatiously. Bram sneered. He and Lena walked slowly, Lena with her head down - they didn't want to be part of a group. By the time they reached the narrow road leading to the Convent, the French couple were already fifty metres ahead and the middle-aged man a few paces behind them. They turned at the sign pointing to the Santiago de Compostela Way and started to climb the hill. When they reached the Convent, Lena hesitated, then stopped, and looked at the austere walls. Feeling bleak and emptied, she muttered again the phrase from her childhood. Then she hurried forwards to catch up to Bram. They left the last house behind, Lena breathing heavily now as the path got steeper. They had just paused to catch their breaths when they heard the scream, a screech of absolute horror. Despite themselves, they hurried to the top of the hill. The French girl was staring, hands in front of her face, keening uncontrollably, breathlessly, as she stood before the bloody and mutilated body of the nun. The young French man grabbed her by the shoulders and forced her away, towards the railings that look over the town. She kept screaming, gulping for air, just to scream some more. The middle-aged man was cowering a few metres from the scene. He kept shaking his head and looking away before looking back again.

'Oh my God, oh my God,' he kept repeating.

Bram and Lena walked slowly up to the corpse, ignoring the reactions of the others. Lena gasped, and then stood, woodenly, staring at the distorted face of the nun. She seemed uncertain for a moment and then nodded slowly. She looked up at the statue of the Virgin and crossed herself. Bram glanced down once, and then holding Lena by the elbow forced her to walk away. They stood near the French couple, looking over the town that was peacefully stretching itself on the plain below. The French girl was now sobbing in great gulps, still gasping for air, her partner stunned, kept his arm around her shoulders. The middle-aged man walked a little distance from the body and shook off his rucksack. He took a mobile phone from one of the pouches and dialled 112.

'I have to call the police, an ambulance,' he said, looking wildly towards the others. He spoke rapidly, breathlessly on the phone.

'We are not to touch anything,' he said out loud. 'We must stay and protect, er... make sure no one else, you know.' And he suddenly looked around, occurring to him for the first time that perhaps the killer was still nearby.

'Stay together, keep together, don't move anything,' he almost shouted, as though the others were children to be warned. He placed his rucksack in the middle of the path at the top of the hill, and stared resolutely towards the town below. The French girl was now sobbing less uncontrollably, and her partner was enclosing her in a huddle, shutting out the world. Bram slipped out his mobile phone and shuffled over to the corpse. He took three quick pictures, then walked back to Lena. He took her by the arm and led her away, down and along the path that led to Santiago de Compostela.

Commandant Grimard was not a religious man, but there was something 'unholy' about this crime. A sister of Christ, murdered beneath a statue of the Virgin Mary. Her throat sliced through, her heart pierced and her clothes slashed and torn. He shuddered. Years of police service couldn't immure you to this kind of scene. He looked around again and then waved for the pathology and forensic teams to start their work. There was a small group of civilians standing beside the ambulance, one of them, a young woman, was sitting on the steps, a paramedic was talking to her and she had an oxygen mask in her hand. His subordinate, Bedeau, came up. Grimard nodded toward the group.

'I'll speak to them myself presently. Did they see anyone around?'

'No. They came up from the town this morning, pilgrims. They found her lying there. It's been quite a few hours since.... The woman's hysterical and the other young one is her boyfriend. The man is a Monsieur Toussaint. He made the call. They didn't see anything else. They're deeply shocked.'

'That's hardly surprising. I'm shocked myself. What is it with this town?'

'The girl's in a bad way; the medics want to take her to the hospital, she's hyperventilating, she might need sedating,' continued Bedeau.

'OK. I'll speak to them briefly. Be sure they know they mustn't leave town today, we may want to speak to them again. After they've got over their shock they may remember something.'

'Oh, there's one other thing,' said Bedeau. 'There was another couple with them, Dutch they think, pilgrims as well. They left, just walked away.'

'Walked away?'

'Yeah, just walked away down the trail there.'

'Ok, get someone to pick them up. If they're on the Way they won't be difficult to find. It's a long shot but they may have seen something the others didn't. Walked away.' He shook his head vigorously. He was doing a lot of that lately.

Chapter Fifteen

At ten o'clock, Jacques was sitting on the bow deck of the barge surrounded by small pieces of lacquered wood of different shapes and sizes. He was placing them into groups according to some pattern which, from the outside, was hard to decipher. He heard a car door slam nearby, and he looked up quickly. The sight of a police officer striding along the towpath towards the barge caused a sharp contraction of his stomach. The officer stepped through the bushes and up to the barge.

'Monsieur Lecoubarry. Bonjour. It is I, Desmarais.'

'Bonjour, Agent Desmarais, come aboard,' said Jacques. There was an intensity in Desmarais' face that subdued Jacques' natural ebullience. He stood up slowly and pulled another chair up to the table. 'Come, sit down, a pleasure,' he said.

Desmarais looked around him uncertainly and then uncomprehendingly at the wooden pieces on the floor. He waved his hand vaguely towards them.

'It's a Japanese personal secret box, a puzzle box. Early nineteenth century. Must have fifty-four steps. I'm repairing it. It's bloody complex, I can tell you. Please sit down. Coffee?'

'No, thank you. I shouldn't be here. But there is something.'

'What, go on, you look a bit shaken.'

'Shaken, yes. You see, there has been another murder. This morning or last night. She was found this morning.'

'She?' Jacques raised his eyebrows.

'Yes, she. A nun from the Convent. Murdered, stabbed, by the statue of the Virgin on Calvary Hill.'

Jacques felt a cold tremor creeping up his back and shoulders to his scalp.

'A nun,' he said slowly. 'A nun, Sister Agnieszka?' Desmarais looked at him astonished and then with suspicion.

'Yes, Sister Agnieszka. How could you know?' he demanded.

'I didn't know,' said Jacques,' but I feared. I should have done something. I didn't think they'd harm a nun.'

'They, who?' asked Desmarais. His eyes wide, he looked more than ever like a young rabbit astonished by the presence of a man with a gun. 'Monsieur Lecoubarry. Who is doing these things?'

'I don't know,' said Jacques, turning his face away. He could feel the anger rising like a reflux in his chest. 'Why did you come here, Agent Desmarais?'

'I came, I don't know why I came. I thought perhaps you knew more, or that I could talk to you about this.' He hesitated. Jacques said nothing. 'I need help. We cannot have these horrors in our town.'

'Isn't Commandant Grimard investigating these horrors? At least he can't blame this on the Bulgarian. I presume he's still in custody.'

'Actually, no. He was released last night, subject to restrictions. He couldn't be held any longer.' Desmarais looked so downhearted and anxious and young that Jacques softened towards him. He thought quickly and came to a decision.

'Look, Desmarais, Paul. It's good you've come here. I appreciate that it's difficult for you. But yes, we have made some progress, not much, but I'll share it with you and we can form a plan together. But first, I'm going to make some coffee, and I want you to meet my partner Celestine. Sit down.'

Desmarais sat down and visibly sighed, the excitement and the horror of the morning gradually subsiding as he took in the tranquil scene of the boats on the canal. Jacques returned shortly with a pot of coffee, and Celestine followed.

'Paul, I want you to meet my partner Celestine. Celestine this is Agent Paul Desmarais.'

Celestine smiled and Desmarais stood up and shook her hand.

'Enchanté, madame,' he said and looked at her shyly. A gradual sign of recognition spread over his face. 'Why, madame, I know you. We have met I think, although not introduced.' Desmarais kept looking at Celestine.

'Yes, Agent Desmarais,' said Celestine, raising her eyebrows.

'But yes, madame. You are Capitaine Courbet. I was trained in Bordeaux. I saw you several times at the academy and at the Headquarters. I had no idea.' He looked at Jacques. 'Now I understand.'

'You understand nothing, Agent Desmarais,' she snapped. 'No longer capitaine and I would appreciate it if you didn't mention seeing me to anyone. Anyone on the force.' She corrected herself. The sternness of her look and the firmness of her words made Desmarais pull back. Confused he said.

'You are in trouble, madame?'

'In trouble, Agent Desmarais,' she said. 'No, I'm not in trouble. I am simply following a different course in my life right now. A course that is taking me down this canal, on a barge, with my lover. Will that suffice?'

'Yes of course, madame,' stuttered Desmarais. 'I'm sorry, I don't imply anything.' He looked at Jacques helplessly. Jacques snorted.

'Take a seat, Celestine. We have a lot to discuss with Agent Desmarais.'

The next hour they spent going over the actions they had taken, the things they had seen and the ideas they had. As much as he could, Desmarais brought them up to speed with the information that had been gathered through the police investigation. Celestine was distraught when Desmarais described the scene at the hill of Calvary that morning. She had to walk away, and took some time to compose herself. When she came back there was a new hardness and anger in her eyes and in her voice.

'Who would kill a Sister of Christ? That little nun who had the children eating out of her hand.' She shook her head and growled. 'This man, I think it must be a man, has to be caught soon. There's some terrible secret here. This guy is cold, a risk-taker.'

'You think then this is the same person, the same killer?' asked Desmarais.

'Don't you, Desmarais?' she almost shouted. 'Same method, stabbing, throat cut, at night. You have no murders in this town for how many years?'

'Twenty-three.'

'And then you have two in two days. The same person for the same reason.' She walked along the side of the boat and then returned. 'There has to be a connection to the work Malraux was doing here. What was he really studying? We need to speak to that curator of the museum. He may know more, and he is not out of the picture by any means. And I need to speak to the sisters at the Convent. That won't be easy; you'll have to help me there, Desmarais.'

'Unfortunately, the curator, Monsieur Ducrozet, has gone missing. His wife called yesterday to say that he had not returned to the house and that he was very depressed by the murder of a colleague. Oh, and his boat is missing.'

'He has a boat?' said Jacques. 'That brings him straight into the spotlight, don't you think?'

'Yes. Apparently, a motorboat. We had intended to start looking this morning, but with the....' he shrugged his shoulders.

'Indeed, how is it that you're here at this time? Were you not required at the murder scene?' Celestine sounded like a superior officer uprating a junior.

'I was there, but I have been on duty all night. I was allowed to go home. Grimard has his own team working with him.'

'Then, if you have been up all night, I suggest you go home and get some sleep,' said Celestine. 'We have a lot of digging to do and a boat trip up the river this afternoon. Do you have full access to the Cranien computer system?'

'Almost all.'

'Good. I may need you to access some information for me, but not yet.'

'Of course.' Desmarais almost said Capitaine.

'That's a good idea, my friend,' said Jacques. 'Go home and get some rest. You did right to come here. We must keep communicating. We'll call you later today. Don't worry, we won't say a thing about your visit, to anyone.' Jacques ushered him off the barge. When he looked back, Celestine was rhythmically kicking the wooden side of the boat and staring into the waters of the canal.

For the next two hours, Celestine sat alone in the cabin with her laptop and notebook. She sent Jacques off to the town with various instructions.

'I want you to walk the route taken by Malraux, from the drug dealer's house to the murder scene. I made a note of the number from Desmarais. Just look and observe. How close is the route to, for example, the Abbey, the Bulgarian shop and the curator's house? Look at the way from the Abbey to the Convent. And then I want you to walk back the quickest route possible from the murder scene to the canal here. You may have to try a couple of routes. And again, notice anything that might reasonably be of interest. Just look.' She stopped and thought for a minute. 'But don't walk up to the Convent or Calvary. We must do that this evening, together.'

'And I'm looking for what?' asked Jacques.

'I don't know, maybe nothing. But just look. There may be something that strikes you as relevant. Keep your eyes and mind open. You have a mind that sees pictures. Look through the obvious, see the pictures, use your intuition.'

'Ok,' said Jacques.

'Oh, Jacques. I think we can expect another visit from the police today. Not Desmarais, you understand.' Jacques looked at her questioningly. 'The police will now be going over all the evidence again. They will look at your statement and I would expect them to want to talk to you. I would rather be out of sight when that happens.'

'I understand.'

'But also, if I were in their shoes, I would want to speak to everyone staying on these boats. A murder happens, two murders, the first time in twenty years. People come to town and then leave again in a few days, they're disruptors. They're not the normal citizens of the town. They represent new factors in the equation,'

'You mean we're suspects?'

'No. But we could be of interest, just could be, you understand.'

There were no longer any signs in the Rue de la Chasse that anything unpleasant had happened there. Perhaps a small area of the pavement and the road that looked a little cleaner where the blood had been scrubbed off. There were no tapes, no signs, nothing to say a man had died there. There were no notices asking for any witnesses to come forward. Jacques stood for a few minutes, looking at the cleaned ground, trying to imagine the scene. The victim, a flamboyant, drugged maybe, stranger to the town. Standing beside the tree. Did he know his assailant? Did he quietly greet him, smile? Or did he feel fear and terror? Did he recognise the danger he was in? The blows must have come fast, unexpected. Of course, no one expects to be attacked like that. Jacques looked around; it was a quiet residential street, not well-lit like the centre of the town. A street of small, undemonstrative lives, good, bad, kind, unkind, the usual balance in any chosen street like this. Not people like the professor, who seemed to have been loud, articulate and even outrageous to some. No, this is not where he would have expected to breathe his last.

So, to walk or run to the canal, I should take which road? he asked himself. He set off walking along the main route which seemed to be going towards the canal, but the street changed direction part of the way down and took him away from the canal towards the wide road that circumvented the town. He retraced his steps to the Rue de la Chasse. Instead of heading directly towards the canal, he continued walking along a road that seemed to run parallel to the canal, assuming that an alternative route would appear which would allow him to turn in the direction he wanted to follow. But the road continued to run parallel, and he found himself back on the edge of the market square. If the running man came this way he would have run right through the centre of the town, and he would surely have been seen by someone. And it's a long way around to get to where I saw him that night. There must be a shorter, quicker way, he reasoned.

He returned once again to the Rue de la Chasse. There was a choice of only two streets. He started down the first street again, and then he saw, only thirty metres or so from the corner, an alleyway between two tall houses. He turned into it. It ran narrowly at right angles to the road. It was roofed over, so he thought it was probably a connection to the gardens at the rear. It was gloomy in the middle of the day but would have been jet black at night. Jacques followed it, expecting at any stage to find himself facing a dead end, but the path went past the houses and edged between two high, brick, garden walls. At the end, there was a broken wooden gate, and the cut continued behind a row of dark and shady gardens. Jacques kept walking. The path, now paved, led him between two old houses and then it ended, and Jacques emerged into bright sunlight on a road he recognised that ran down to the canal by the lock keeper's cabin. It had taken very little time from leaving the Rue de la Chasse, and he hadn't hurried. Admittedly it was daylight, but a man who knew the route, with a small torch, would comfortably run the distance in a matter of minutes. There would also be little likelihood of being seen or a least recognised by anyone on that path.

'Our running man knows Lissac well,' he told Celestine later. 'You wouldn't find that route if you were a stranger to the town.'

Chapter Sixteen

After a hasty lunch, Jacques and Celestine headed for the river and a rendezvous with Gilbert, the man from the boat hire company. Jacques was thoughtful. He turned to Celestine.

'You know you talked about investigations, when they find a course, they tend to run on it.'

'They take the path of least resistance, yes,' replied Celestine. 'Confirmation bias is a big danger; looking for things to confirm your theory and ignoring, wilfully or not, other evidence. There's a lot of training done on that now.'

'Then do you think that maybe I've taken one of those routes? Focused on the running man, decided straight away that he was involved in this crime, crimes, and yet we have no real evidence that he had anything to do with it at all?'

'That's true,' said Celestine. 'But I've been working on other possibilities and they may turn out to have more merit than your running man. However, you thought immediately that there was something at odds there, and you have good instincts. There's the coincidence of it occurring just minutes after the murder. Think of it as a process of elimination. If we find there is no link, then it closes down one route and we can concentrate on others.'

They reached the river and began to walk toward the jetty. 'But you know,' began Celestine, 'the second murder normally narrows down the range of suspects, rather than widens it. If there is a connection between the two deaths, and it seems inconceivable that there isn't, the people who felt the need to kill two such divergent types cannot be many. Only one person or group of people needed both Malraux and Sister Agnieszka dead, and I am convinced it had something to do with the work he was doing. I'm convinced of it.' She took Jacques by the arm. 'I did some research this morning into

Monsieur Malraux, social media, academic websites etc. I'll tell you about it later, this looks like it could be Gilbert.'

Gilbert was a young man of toothy bonhomie; dressed in a white shirt bearing the rental company crest, and shoes so pointed you could extract mussels with them, he was so delighted to be renting out a boat to such as they. He practically drooled over Celestine's shoulder as he stood too close behind her while she signed the paperwork. Exquisite seemed to be his favourite word; an adjective appropriate for the weather, the boat, the potential for sight-seeing on the river and any action taken by Celestine. Jacques smiled to himself. He had often seen the disturbance his partner made on the equilibrium of impressionable men. To Jacques, from behind, with her long, bare, brown legs, she certainly looked exquisite. But when she turned around and you looked at that face, with the blend of North African and white European, the dark fiery eyes, with their sleepy lids, the full lips, the high cheekbones, the long nose and firmness of the chin; that was exquisite, that's when your equilibrium was so disturbed you never thought you would stand on firm ground again. That was how it was for Jacques, in any case, and he recognised it. Gilbert escorted them to the jetty, and holding Celestine's hand a little too long, helped her to step down into the boat. He waved them off effusively, staring like a man slowly emerging from a reverie.

Jacques eased the boat confidently out into midstream. The current flowed more strongly there and they could see both banks clearly. Celestine sat looking over the side, a little tense, holding onto the seat. Jacques headed the boat upriver, and when they looked across they could see the little grass bank, between the trees, where the black boat had been tied. He brought them closer to the near shore, keeping about twenty metres from the bank. Long beds of reeds grew in the shallower water.

'Look out for anything unusual, anywhere a boat may have come ashore again,' he said.

For a few hundred metres the trees at the side of the river were dense and the path was hidden from view. Then the trees began to thin out again and there were spaces where the bank was visible. They had travelled for about twenty minutes when Celestine called out.

'There's Henri. There's the boathouse.' Monsieur Lefebvre was standing on a rickety wooden jetty, straw hat in hand, waving gently at them. Wearing his bright canary-yellow shirt and a pair of baggy, khaki shorts, he called out. 'There you are, over here, come alongside here.' Jacques expertly manoeuvred the boat in towards the shore and alongside the jetty.

'Bonjour, Henri, in you come,' he said. Celestine took hold of one of the wooden planks to hold the boat steady, and Jacques reached out and guided Monsieur Lefebvre into the boat.

'Splendid, splendid,' he kept repeating and sat down next to Celestine, smiling broadly as he looked all around. 'Up the river we go, splendid, splendid.'

Jacques kept the boat far enough from the shore to avoid any hazards like fallen trees or sand banks. He really is very competent at this, thought Celestine.

'Of course, the boat could easily have come from the other side of the river,' she said.

'I've thought of that,' replied Jacques. 'But Henri said he saw the boat almost alongside his boathouse on this side, so I'm working on that assumption at the moment. We can return along the other bank if we find nothing.'

Monsieur Lefebvre had gone quiet, he seemed almost in a trance as he waved his head slowly from side to side, trying to take everything in. It was a glorious, blue-sky afternoon, perfect for a leisure trip on the river. But this didn't feel like a jaunt to Celestine. She focused all her attention on the river margins. The long, tousled branches of oak trees hung out over the water, in some cases the roots were half-exposed, soil washed away in the winter floods. Where there were no trees there were straggling bushes, clumps of brambles and dying stands of stinging nettles. Then, easing around a gradual bend in the river there was suddenly grass, clearly mown and well-kept grass. Everyone tensed, and Monsieur Lefebvre stopped moving his head. There were about fifty metres of grass bank and then a small outcrop of land covered in low trees. Tucked in behind the trees was an inlet that led to a boathouse. Jacques turned in, throttled down the motor to idle, and they drifted slowly alongside. It was well-built and in good repair, with oak-framed walls and a clay-tiled roof. Inside they could see a low platform with several ropes and life jackets hanging on the walls. There was no boat.

'There are some handsome houses along this stretch of the river,' said Monsieur Lefebvre.

'Can you see them from the river bank?' asked Jacques.'

'You can see one or two of the houses, but sometimes there's just a path leading through the woods.'

'It's quite difficult to see the boathouses until you are right alongside them, isn't it,' said Celestine.

'I would think that you could walk right past that one, on the path, and not see it,' said Jacques. 'It looked in better shape than yours, Henri. Perhaps you should move up-market.'

Monsieur Lefebvre chuckled. 'That boathouse looks as though it's used regularly. I wouldn't feel safe there,' he said.

They continued a little further upriver and there was another boathouse. This one contained a wooden rowing boat and, hung up on the wall, a small flat-bottomed motorboat.

'Blue,' said Celestine.

'Oh no, not like that,' said Monsieur Lefebvre, and Celestine realised that he was concentrating intensely on the task of finding the black boat.

They passed another empty boathouse and then the landscape changed. There was a wide grassy margin by the side of the river with the occasional specimen tree. The land behind was clear and rose gently from the riverside. At first there were fields, well cultivated, and they could see two horses grazing, flicking their ears and tails against the flies. Behind the field, on ground that rose more steeply, they could see row upon row of vines. The whole of the gently sloping hillside was covered with the ranks of an army of vines. Nobody spoke. The river curved again slightly, and through the trees of a small orchard, they could see a house, a chateau.

'Nice spot,' said Celestine.

As they came closer they could see the house was a long, three-storied rectangle, with dormer windows in the roof. The first-floor windows had blue shutters and each had a small wrought iron balcony. The ground floor windows were wide, also with blue shutters; and at one end there was a tower with a pointed conical roof of grey tiles. There were stone steps leading from a circular, gravel turning place up to the main entrance. In front of the house were lawned gardens with flowerbeds. A white, wooden, swimming jetty protruded into the river and Jacques nudged the boat out a little to avoid it. Then, where the land extended further into the river, and a few trees were growing, they saw a boathouse. In fitting with the house, it was built on a grand scale, with a concrete slipway and another wooden jetty running alongside. Jacques eased the boat out a little more as the boathouse extended some twenty metres into the river. They came alongside it and Celestine and Monsieur Lefebvre peered into the gloom. There was a long cabin cruiser moored in the first point. Gleaming white and silver, and very expensive looking, the name in gold letters on the side was *Vencidor*. Then, as they passed the stern of the cruiser, they saw it; a long, low, sleek, black motorboat. Monsieur Lefebvre raised his hand and pointed, his mouth was open but no sounds came out.

'That one, Henri,' said Celestine. 'Is that the boat you saw?'

'Yes, yes, most certainly,' he said, nodding his head vigorously. 'Yes, it is just like it. Like a black swordfish or some species of boat shark.' Jacques cut the throttle and they drifted towards the boats.

'Go in closer, Jacques,' said Celestine. Jacques turned the motorboat delicately into the waters in the front of the boathouse and edged it forward until they were almost touching the black boat. It was, as Monsieur Lefebvre had described it, like a long, sleek, dark fish. It was low in the water, and even looked a little menacing, thought Celestine.

'It's a Skater. Very fast, more useful for racing than throwing out a fishing line,' said Jacques. Celestine leaned over to look into the bottom of the boat. There was one seat, wide enough for two, slim people. A curved Perspex shield and a sharp water-slicing bow all gave the impression of speed and power. On the bottom of the boat, there was only a small black cloth. 'You're sure this is the boat you saw, Henri?' asked Jacques.

'Yes, I do think so, yes. Quite a belligerent-looking boat, don't you think?'

'Can you see the name on the side, Celestine?'

'Yes, *Vencidor II.* Same name as the big cruiser.'

'It's Occitan,' said Monsieur Lefebvre quietly. '*Vencidor.* It means something like, to win, or to triumph.'

'Modest little title then,' said Jacques. 'So, *Vencidor II*, who hag rides you in the middle of the night, I wonder?'

'We should go now,' said Celestine. 'We don't want anyone to know we're interested in them.'

Jacques agreed, reversed the boat out of the boathouse and turned it upstream. They looked back at the house, and as they passed it they saw that the land on that side was similar, with a flattish field cultivated with rows of fruit trees and above, on the sloping hillside, row upon row of vines.

'Who are you? Who lives in this house?' Jacques turned to Monsieur Lefebvre. 'Do you know, Henri?' Monsieur Lefebvre, who had looked quietly satisfied and vindicated, shook his head.

'No, not part of my social circle, I must admit.'

Jacques chuckled. 'You have a dry sense of humour, for an engineer,' he said.

'Former engineer,' smiled Monsieur Lefebvre, and looked quickly at Celestine.

'Keep going, Jacques, let's see how the land lies further on,' said Celestine. They continued for another half a kilometre before the view changed; trees came closer to the river and the horizon was obscured by woodland.

'That's quite an estate,' said Jacques. 'We must find out who lives there. It shouldn't be too difficult, neighbours will know. We'll look it up on the map when we get back, then we'll ask a few questions. I'd like to see the actual driver in the boat, see him and talk to him,' said Jacques, a hard edge to his voice. Celestine stood up next to him as he steered the boat.

'I have an idea about that,' she said, 'but let me think it through first and then we'll discuss it, ok?' Jacques looked at her quizzically, but she looked away and sat down again. She rested her hand on Monsieur Lefebvre's arm.

'Well done, Henri, you've been a great help.' Monsieur Lefebvre grinned, but then suddenly became very serious.

'But you, my dear, and Jacques, you must be very, very careful now.' He nodded his head gravely, and Celestine saw there was a slight dampness in the corner of his eyes. They continued upriver for another kilometre or so. The terrain was changing gradually to flatter, more cultivated land; fruit trees, maize and fields of ripened, brown sunflowers.

'Ok, we've had more than half our time. Let's go over to the other side and work our way back,' said Jacques. 'And look out for your naked boatman, Henri.'

'Oh, I think he could be many kilometres away by now.'

'Where's the next large town on the Tarn?' asked Celestine.

'Montauban.'

'Montauban,' she mused.

They came back down on the other side of the river. As they passed the house and boathouse again they slowed down and peered across, but there was no sign of life. They could see the land on either side of the estate more clearly, and where the other boathouses were, they could see the roofs of houses nestling in the trees. Jacques steered the boat gradually across the river and they soon arrived at Monsieur Lefebvre's boathouse. Jacques brought the boat alongside, and Celestine jumped out and tied the painter to what was left of a wooden mooring post. They helped Monsieur Lefebvre onto the jetty where he shook their hands vigorously. Celestine put her arms around his shoulders and kissed him on both cheeks.

'Henri, it has been a pleasure having your company this afternoon, and thank you again for all your help. I have an idea, and I think I'll need your help some more, if you're willing.'

'Of course, anything.'

'I have to talk to Jacques first, and we'll need some equipment. But if you're agreeable, I'd like to call on you tomorrow, early. I'll take my run along the path to your boathouse.' Monsieur Lefebvre nodded.

'When you wish,' he said.

Celestine climbed back into the boat and Jacques pulled away from the jetty. She looked behind when they were underway and saw that Monsieur Lefebvre was still standing, looking after them, tattered straw hat in his hand. They returned the boat to the grinning Gilbert and walked into town. They came through the side streets to the café opposite the Abbey.

'You see how confusing and convoluted some of these little streets are,' said Jacques. 'You would need to know your way around this town well to choose the quickest and quietest route.' Celestine agreed. But she remained standing when Jacques chose a table and sat down.

'Order yourself a drink. I'm going to buy a detailed map of the area, but first I want to talk to Catherine, before the Abbey closes.'

'Do you want me to order something for you?'

'No. I'll have something when I get back.'

She crossed the street and around the corner to the Abbey. Jacques watched her, the firmness of her walk, the slight tip back of her head so that her short dark hair dusted the tops of her shoulders. So, incredibly, it comes down to this, he thought. I have become even more protective of her. I believe I would kill, in only these circumstances. But I would kill to keep her safe. The waiter took his order for a beer, then he took out his phone and called Desmarais, who answered almost immediately.

'Jacques, where are you? Two of Grimard's men called on you today, on the boat.'

'I was out on the river with Celestine.'

'Well they need to talk to you, they want me to bring you to the poste, the police station.'

'Well, you need to come and find me then. I'm in the café opposite the church. I need to talk to you, too. Are you on duty yet? I'll buy you a drink.'

'No. Not till seven. Ok. I'll be there in fifteen minutes.' Jacques sat back and sipped his beer.

Chapter Seventeen

Monsieur Ducrozet, fully clothed but unshaven, unwashed, and wearing a creased and stained shirt and shorts, sat at a rear table under the canopy of a large café in central Montauban. In sunglasses and a battered sailor's cap, pulled low over his eyes, he was aware that he was looking decidedly unsavoury. Although no one seemed to be remotely interested in him, he still felt conspicuous. He was paranoid, afraid, on edge and just a little bit angry. He had telephoned his wife the night before to say that he was safe, but needed a few days to clear his head. He hadn't answered any of his wife's questions, hadn't told her where he was, and had instructed her to tell the police, or indeed anyone else asking about him, that he had gone walking in the Causses for a few days. He had rung off quickly when he'd heard the first gulp, knowing that tears were coming. He had passed an uncomfortable night, cramped in the boat, moored in the shadow of a bridge. He hadn't been hungry, but he had bought a bottle of wine from a cheap bar near the river and drunk himself to sleep. Gagging with thirst the next morning, he had walked into the town and drunk litres of water and coffee. And now he was sitting, hiding, at the back of this café. He ordered a croque-monsieur and more coffee, but when the coffee came he realised that his hand was shaking so much that he could hardly lift it to his lips.

He tried to focus on the people passing by in the street. There was a smartly-dressed young woman carrying an attaché case who looked so clear and full of purpose. A middle-aged man on a skateboard drew his attention. He was at least forty, the same age as Ducrozet, dressed casually, but cleanly; he was carrying a small rucksack and skating at ease down the street, balancing effortlessly as he weaved around the other pedestrians. Ducrozet watched him until he was hidden by a group of college students coming the other way. He was gripped with envy of the easy-going, carefree manner of the man, and wondered why he could not be like that. He could no more imagine skateboarding down the centre of a public street than he could see himself dancing naked around a campfire. Although, the naked aspect had become more and more dominant in the last few weeks. He cringed when he recalled the hours he had spent nude on his boat. How many people must have seen him? Yet it had felt good, too. Kind of unshackling and sensuous. His mistrust of his own mind and body soared. What the hell would it draw him into next? It was as though he had no control over them. Urges, imperatives, would suddenly surface and he seemed powerless to resist them. It was pathetic.

He recognised when this modification had started; it had begun with his first encounter with Emmanuel Malraux. It was in Malraux's small apartment, Malraux carrying a bottle of wine and talking constantly, Ducrozet uncertain, but drawn, unable to resist. Malraux had placed the bottle of wine on the table, and then immediately removed all his clothes. Ducrozet had stared at the young, hairless, clearly aroused body. Malraux had made an impatient gesture for Ducrozet to follow suit, and then reached into a cupboard for two glasses and a corkscrew. Ducrozet had clumsily removed his clothes, struggling with his shoelaces. When he'd stood up, Malraux had come close to him, body to body, handed him a glass of wine, emptied half of his own glass and then kissed him. At the same time, he had run his fingers in a scratching motion down across his nipples, over his belly and wrapped them around his penis. Naked, always naked. Malraux washed, fucked, slept, cooked, read and fought naked. Ducrozet had learned to do the same; to be naked, to be just about bodies and their reaction to the actualities of another man's body. And to fight naked. At first, just play, slaps, hard squeezing of buttocks, face slaps, nipple twisting. But play became violent; disagreements, recriminations, deliberate provocations from Malraux until Ducrozet had wanted to tear him apart, pierce him, stick him. One night, he had watched in horror and fascination as the blood seeped out of a wound Malraux had given him on the thigh, with the end of a corkscrew.

Ducrozet shook. He drank down his coffee and ordered another, and water; his mouth was as dry as the desert sand. He could see that his madness, for clearly it was an episode of temporary insanity, had coincided with an increasingly frenetic state of mind in Malraux. When he arrived he was very excitable, but he seemed to exude erudition, with a fine academic mind and a disciplined approach to his field of study. But as he made progress, he seemed to lose all sense of the discipline needed to elucidate truths and reality from his studies. One day he would be sniffing around the cloisters like an animal trying to find a suitable nesting place. He found him once, lying on the floor, looking up at one of the friezes, one eye open the other closed. Then he would rush up to the Convent and spend hours searching through archives, only to return like a beaten dog. After one such visit, he had burst into Ducrozet's office, leaving the door wide open, looking wild and forlorn, he'd come right up to Ducrozet's desk, leaned over it, and mouthed a string of curses and sexual obscenities. Ducrozet was certain that his staff would have heard, and he quickly walked around and closed the door. That was the instigator of another of their increasingly bitter fights in which he had been slapped around his head and shoulders.

All that in what, three weeks, a little more. Towards the end, Malraux had cooled down, treating Ducrozet with professional courtesy and detachment. The fury had ended for him, he had moved elsewhere. It left Ducrozet with such anguish, breath-taking jealousy, emptiness, and a feeling of something truncated, raw, a limb cut off as the body continues somehow to function. There was also, it had to be said, in lucid moments, some relief. It was hard to deceive so many people; wife, children, colleagues; to make up lame excuses to explain the absent hours, the physical marks. Yes, a little bit of relief, and then there was also the intellectual curiosity. Malraux had made progress in his research. Ducrozet had discovered that this was not really an academic project, more a personal one. He had been looking for evidence, and he'd believed that he had found it. But that evidence had sent him again into a frenzy of searching and scouring the finest details in the Abbey and the cloisters. When Ducrozet had asked him directly what it was he had discovered, Malraux had replied: 'A message from the dead, my dead, a message too long concealed.' And when asked what the message had told him, he'd cast his eyes up to the ceiling and said:

'To keep searching, of course. I have a key now but I can't find the lock. I have to crack the code to find the lock.'

Ducrozet had smiled at this melodrama, and Malraux had kicked out at him, catching him on the knee and sending a searing pain up his leg.

'Perhaps, you can help me. You know the fucking cloisters better than anyone.' Then he had put his arm around Ducrozet's shoulders and leant closer to him. 'Tomorrow, you can help me, now, go home to your wife.' And they were done.

Malraux had come to him the next day as though there had been no physical relationship between them. He'd addressed him formally as a respected colleague and an equal. He had laid a small square of paper on the desk. There were seven numbers written on it in Malraux's purple ink: 67 53 47 69 54 25 75

'What's this?'

'That is the code.' Malraux had looked at him with blood-shot, but fierce, staring eyes. 'The code, the cloisters, the Abbey, what do the numbers mean?' Then he'd softened his look, and coming around the desk, he'd put his hand on Ducrozet's neck and moved his face close to his. Ducrozet could smell the acidity of old wine on his breath, but the intimacy of the gesture had released the intoxication he had come to feel close to this man. 'Help me with this, help me my friend, I must solve this.' With that, he had walked out of the office, leaving the paper behind on the desk, and Ducrozet in a state of confusion and arousal.

Now sitting in this café in Montauban, with all that had happened, he knew he had to think very, very clearly.

Chapter Eighteen

Agent Desmarais slipped into the seat opposite and shook hands with Jacques. He looked tired and worried.

'How are things with you? Beer?' asked Jacques.

'No, no. Coffee, please. I'm on duty in an hour.' He looked down and took out his notebook. 'Things are complicated,' he said.

'Complicated.'

'Yes. First, you must tell me what you have found out. Then I'll tell you what I can. And then,' he looked up at Jacques hopefully. 'Then you must accompany me to the poste to speak to Commandant Grimard or one of his men. Agreed?'

'Agreed,' said Jacques. 'There's an old Basque proverb that says, "The truth will out, but it saves time if you tell me what you know".'

'Is that a real proverb? I don't speak Basque.'

'Words to that effect.' Jacques told him about the trip upriver and finding the black boat. Desmarais raised an eyebrow when he mentioned Monsieur Lefebvre.

'An itinerant, an old tramp, that's not very credible is it?'

'Oh yes, without doubt. But you don't have to mention him. I wouldn't want him to get involved. He's a singular old man, but very clear standards of what is right and wrong. Keep him out of it.'

'Ok, go on.'

Jacques filled in the rest of the details and gave him some more information about the scene at the church - the nun and her reaction.

'You mentioned that. You must talk to Grimard about this. A second murder, you see, it's just well, incomprehensible.'

'It is until you see a connection to the first.' Jacques took a long drink of his beer. 'So, what progress? What has Commandant Grimard discovered so far?

Desmarais looked around a little guiltily. 'Well,' he hesitated. 'The Commandant is still of a mind to recommend pursuing the case against the Bulgarian, but he still needs a little more certainty in the evidence, another piece. They have a sighting of the victim, the first victim, in the street, and a positive identification of the Bulgarian, Krastyo Dacheva, walking in the same direction as Malraux.' He paused. 'We have the physical evidence, the paper stuck to the lips.'

'Which could have come from anywhere?'

'Yes, yes.'

'A murder weapon, DNA, traces of fibre?'

'The house of Dacheva was searched, with another search taking place today. I don't know if anything was found.'

'Why don't they search all the Bulgarian houses in Lissac and really stir things up?' said Jacques angrily.

'Jacques, please, let us focus.'

'Ok. What about the curator, Monsieur Ducrozet?'

'Monsieur Ducrozet left home yesterday afternoon, and as far as I am aware he hasn't returned. I spoke to someone in the station and they said his wife had been visited again, but she wasn't certain of his whereabouts. Walking in the Causses was suggested.'

'Doesn't Grimard find that extremely suspicious?' asked Jacques.

'I think he's keeping an open mind until Ducrozet is located, but he is a person of interest.'

'Especially since he was having a wild fling with Malraux. Rimbaud and Verlaine, as it was described.'

Desmarais opened his palms and shrugged. 'What does that mean?'

'Well, these two poets, Rimbaud and Verlaine, had a passionate and violent, extremely violent, affair. Well known and scandalous at the time.' Desmarais nodded and scribbled in his book. 'And Sister Agnieszka?' demanded Jacques, more aggressively than he had intended.

Desmarais' shoulders sank and he shook his head slowly. 'I can't begin to imagine, to understand,' he said. 'I only know what my colleague told me. They are waiting for the autopsy and the forensics, which will take twenty-four hours at least. They say she received a letter or note, last evening. She went out. Nobody knows why, perhaps the note. It wasn't found on her person. And there is a Dutch couple, pilgrims. They were among the group which found the body but they didn't stay, they walked away. The Gendarmes are trying to locate them, it shouldn't be difficult. They walk a well-signposted route. It may be nothing, but perhaps they might have seen something. Anyway, Grimard is very angry, you shouldn't leave a crime scene.'

Celestine appeared from the church and crossed the street to meet them. Desmarais stood up to formally shake her hand. 'Please join us, madame, but I'm afraid I will have to take your partner to the police poste shortly.'

'That's ok, Agent Desmarais, take him. Jacques, I'll see you back at the boat, I still have a few errands to run.'

Jacques stood up, kissed her on both cheeks and said, 'If I'm not back in two hours, call that hot-shot lawyer you know, and come and break me out.'

'I can assure you, Celestine, this will only take half an hour. Just a statement of what Jacques has told me,' said Desmarais quickly.

'He's joking, Paul. Bonne soirée.' Celestine walked off along the street, both men watching her in silence.

Two hours later, Jacques returned to the barge where Celestine was waiting.

'At last. We must go now. I thought they'd kept you in,' she said.

'No. I spent half the time waiting in an uncomfortable chair before being invited into a miserable little cupboard by a bored, uninterested junior, who could barely be bothered to take notes.'

'Is that it?'

'No. As I was leaving, he thanked me for fulfilling my civic duty. Surreally, he did ask me if anyone had bumped into me on the night that the nun was killed. Like murderers had some mad instinct to find and bump into me just after they've committed a murder. Maybe something they're taught in murder school. I couldn't tell if he was being serious.'

'Be useful if they did. A bit uncomfortable for you, but we'd clear up a lot of killings quickly. Anyway, come on we have to go,' said Celestine.

'You said that. Go where? And when do I get to eat dinner and other essential human activities?'

'Later. We're going to the Convent and the hill at Calvary.' Jacques grabbed a jacket and they walked out in the darkening streets.

The Bulgarian shop was closed and only the café gave out a dim light. The streets were very quiet.

'This town is in shock,' said Celestine. 'Two murders, violent killings. A nun struck down. People think if someone can kill a nun, they can kill anyone.'

'A serial killer. Is that what they're afraid of?'

'Why not. Would you take a chance?'

They stopped at the bottom of the hill leading up to the Convent. Celestine gripped Jacques' hand.

'I have a lot to tell you,' she said.' But it will take some time, and I want to see these places in the dark, at the same hour as the victim.'

'Sister Agnieszka received a note yesterday evening, Desmarais told me. Nobody knows who from, or what it said, but she left the Convent sometime after receiving it,' said Jacques.

'And they didn't find it on her body?'

'Apparently not. Her clothes had been searched. They may have been looking for the note, or something else.'

'How do they know she received a note?' asked Celestine.

'One of the other sisters gave it to her, found it in the offertory box.'

'So, a note, inviting her to a meeting at night. Why would she go if she was afraid? Did she think it was something to do with Malraux or something else?' They stood silently under a street lamp at the foot of the hill. Hardly a car drove along the roads, no one was walking, and no children were playing.

'We must follow her route, the walk from the Convent to the hill. Try to see what she saw, imagine how she felt, the sounds, the smells even. Keep your eyes and your mind open.'

They reached the high stone walls of the Convent, the great wooden gate was closed and braced against the night and the outside world.

'It's a refuge. Why would you leave its protection, at night? Knowing what had happened just two days before,' Jacques questioned. 'There must have been some urgency or some entreaty to her.'

'Or a threat.'

'Perhaps she felt she had a duty.'

'Religious duty?'

'Presumably. But if that was the case, why wouldn't the person have come to the Convent or the Church? And why specifically Sister Agnieszka?'

'That's what we need to find out,' said Celestine firmly.

As they walked alongside the high walls, they could hear, from the Convent, the low, melancholic sound of a repetitive chant being sung. It was an eerie and disturbing sound at that time and in that place.

'The sisters in mourning,' said Celestine and shivered. 'How do they approach a terrible incident like this? They live in such seclusion. Where do they find the resources to deal with it? God, I suppose.'

'And his mysterious ways. Where does this fit into the great plan? You callous bastard,' said Jacques vehemently and looked accusingly at the sky.

'So, sister A. left the Convent through this door at... nine, ten o'clock?'

'Desmarais said the sisters were interviewed, and someone, a helper, thought she heard a noise, possibly of a gate opening around nine.'

'Ok, so about this time,' said Celestine. 'And she would have left through this small side door, not the great big carriage door. Quite dark. She looks around. Downhill and uphill towards Calvary. She might have been expecting to see the person she was going to meet on the way to the rendezvous.'

'But was she early or late?'

'We don't know. But she started walking up the hill. It's quite steep and she wasn't young. She would have felt it.'

'Maybe, but she walked everywhere on those sturdy, black shoes,' said Jacques.

'Yes. Did you notice her no-nonsense shoes? Rubber-soled, quiet. There's no one living nearby.'

'No. The houses stop. It's unlikely anyone would have seen or heard her.'

'Or the murderer if he came this way,' said Celestine. They kept climbing as the old-fashioned street lamps thinned, and the trees and bushes grew over the narrowing path. 'Not many women would feel comfortable walking up here in the dark. There are shadows everywhere.'

'Yea, though I walk through the valley of the shadow of death, I will fear no evil,' said Jacques, surprising himself.

'Something like that,' said Celestine. 'It's difficult to get into the mind of someone whose life and beliefs are so alien to ours. But we need to understand what committed her to making this walk; I mean, given all the circumstances of the last few days.'

At the top of the hill, the path was partially blocked with blue tape, but a route had been made around the viewpoint so that walkers could pass alongside the railings and continue on the Way. The statue and the ground below were obscured by a canvas tent and a high screen. Only the head and shoulders of the Virgin were visible. Celestine stood at the scene for some minutes while Jacques leant on the railings and looked down into the town. Celestine then walked around the statue, keeping outside the tape, to where there was a small car park. Jacques came to stand next to her.

'So, our killer could easily have come here by car. And I'll bet there are no CCTV cameras along this country road.'

'There are a few houses set back, in the trees. Quite a salubrious area of Lissac-sur-Tarn I would think; with views over the town. One of them might have a camera,' suggested Jacques.

'Maybe, but we have to trust to Grimard to check that one out.'

'They could have just walked back down the hill, you can see how quiet it is,' said Jacques.

'They could have. It's an additional risk though. You never know who is going to be walking there, or even at the bottom of the hill by the main road.'

'Why here?' asked Jacques. 'Why meet here?'

'It's close to the Convent, it's religious, symbolic, the Virgin on Calvary. You imagine a nun might be more willing to meet someone there than say, Jacques' Take Away.'

'Jacques' Take Away. Now there's an idea.'

'Come on,' said Celestine. 'Is there anything else you feel or think about the place?' Jacques was silent for a moment.

'Yes. If I wanted to kill a nun and make a point, a religious point, this is exactly where I would choose,' said Jacques. 'But also, if I wanted, needed, to kill a nun and make it look as though there was a religious element, again this is where I would choose.'

'So, are we looking for two killers or one?' asked Celestine, more to herself, as she looked down at the town of Lissac-sur-Tarn spread out below.

Twenty minutes later, sitting in the cosy warmth of the boat's salon, Celestine poured Jacques another glass of wine. 'I'm just getting warm now,' she said. 'I've seen quite a few murder scenes, all of them horrible, but rarely anything so cold as this.'

Jacques leaned over and stroked her hair. 'Come on, Capitaine, tell me what you found out this afternoon.'

Celestine took a sip of wine, uncurled her legs from under her, and planted her feet firmly on the floor. 'Ok. Catherine told me some more about the work Malraux was doing in Lissac. According to her, this was a personal project he was engaged in. The academic side was just a cover for his own research. He came with a very good reputation, doctorate and professorship at the Sorbonne. A medievalist. Brilliant apparently. But when he came to Lissac, although he spent a little time looking at the church and the cloisters, he then went to the Convent and spent days looking through their archives. He said he was looking for links to the founding of the Abbey, but they were hundreds of years apart, and the church has its own archives. He also started walking around the countryside outside of Lissac, and visiting other museums in the town, although they don't really have a medieval bent. There's a museum of everyday life, eighteenth and nineteenth century. A museum of the Jewish school, but of course, he was Jewish, so that may just have been a personal interest. Oh, and there's a museum of the local wine.'

'I didn't know he was Jewish,' said Jacques.

'Yes. I found that out this morning, online. I spent some time looking at his profile and his social media. He was,' Celestine hesitated, 'very active, and with a wide range of partners I would guess. Some quite explicit stuff there. Monsieur Ducrozet gets a mention; a strange choice, very different from the other friends he's pictured with. He was a good-looking young man, but you could already see the dissolution in his face. He certainly took drugs regularly. Well, we know that already. Altogether a bit of a tornado to descend on a little country town like Lissac-sur-Tarn.'

'Would that be enough to get him killed?'

'It could be. He no doubt upset a lot of people.'

'Including Ducrozet, who has now disappeared, and no one seems to know where he is.'

'His wife does,' said Celestine, enjoying the look of surprise on Jacques' face.

'His wife. How do you know that?'

'Because I visited her this evening, before I came back here.'

'You did?'

'Yes. I visited her, said I was a friend of Catherine Tallandier, that we were worried about her and her husband, and did she want to talk about it. And she did. She's at her wit's end. She's worried for his safety. She says he's not stable.'

'Unstable enough to commit murder?' mused Jacques.

'Oh no, not that. She doesn't think for a minute that he killed Malraux, although she knew about the affair. It's not the first time he's had relations with a male.'

'But?'

'But she loves him. In a way, he's a good husband, his children adore him. She knows and understands his devils, she said.' Celestine took a deep swig of her wine. 'He came home with all kinds of physical marks for a few weeks, quite savage cuts, bruises and even a small stab wound to his thigh, which he tried to keep hidden. But to go back to what I learned from Catherine. Ducrozet was working quite closely with Malraux, particularly in the last week or so. Apparently, one day Malraux just came back to the Abbey, no more Convent, and threw himself into a study of the cloisters. He had a new intensity, is how she described it, and Ducrozet was dragged back in.'

'She's quite observant this new friend of yours, Catherine.'

'She is and quite vitriolic at times too.'

'Figures.'

'Anyway, it looks as though Malraux must have made a discovery in the archives which led him back to the cloisters to start studying them in greater detail.'

'Personal or academic. Do we know that?' asked Jacques.

'Personal. Catherine is convinced it was personal.' Celestine looked up at Jacques a little uncertainly. 'And talking about personal; tomorrow is Saturday and she has invited me to have lunch with her at her home.'

Jacques looked horrified. 'You're leading her on. Is that fair?'

'No. But we need information, and she is proving to be a very valuable source. It's not… She knows about you. She's just a little friendless. I feel a little sorry for her.'

Jacques looked unconvinced. 'We must find out what Malraux was searching for, and if he found it, and did it get him killed,' said Jacques.

'That's the conundrum. We could spend a lot of time looking for motives that are actually not relevant, when he might have been killed by an angry drug dealer, a spurned lover or a Bulgarian.' Celestine sipped thoughtfully at her wine. 'But you know, the second murder really does make it more likely that there was a link to the work. We know Sister Agnieszka was in regular contact with him, and may even have been helping him with his research at the Convent. She may well have known exactly what he had found there. No, the more I think about it, the more convinced I am that there's a link.'

'You said Madame Ducrozet knows where her husband is.'

'In Montauban. He let it slip. He phones her regularly to say he's all right.'

'He's all right, what about her,' said Jacques irritably.

'I'm sure he asked about her too, and the children. He's a good husband in a way.'

Jacques looked dubious. 'But, you know,' he said, 'from what you've told me; if he worked closely with Malraux, just like the nun, he could be in danger, too. Perhaps that's why he disappeared?'

'One of the reasons, I'm sure. He is unstable, as his wife said. It's not the first time he's gone up the river in the boat and stayed away for a few days.'

'She must have the patience of Jove.'

'Job. Yes, I think she has, but she is very, very worried now.' Celestine took a deep breath. 'That is why tomorrow, you are going to take her, in her car, to Montauban, to meet him and to convince him to trust you.'

Jacques sat back on the bench, stretched out his arms and flexed his fingers. He looked at her with narrowed eyes. 'You will need to conjure up some very high-quality coaxing for that to take place,' he said.

'Wait. Just think. If he knows enough about Malraux's research, we might be able to establish why, or if, he was killed for it, and just as importantly, who or what could be damaged by this research.'

Jacques stood up, his large frame filling the neat space in the salon. 'I need to sleep, Celestine, I'm exhausted by all this action,' he smiled. 'But you, you look more alive than I've seen you in weeks.'

Chapter Nineteen

Monsieur Palomer awoke early, with a gnawing feeling in his stomach. He tugged on his silk dressing gown, paddled along the corridor and down the wide ornate stairs to the hall. The sun was just starting to slide in through the high, east windows. He unbolted the door, walked out onto the terrace and looked around uneasily. He could not recall ever feeling such disquiet in his insides. He wouldn't show it. His facial features, long since bloated by the folds of fat and sagging skin, would remain bland whatever turmoil was bubbling inside him. He had taught himself to neutralise his face, even his eyes, on demand. He just let his face and his voice and his arms and hands slide into a kind of neutral; a flat voice, a dull eye, it made him impossible to read and that was how he liked it.

He paced around the terrace, occasionally glancing sideways at the rows of vines, spreading out like an army on parade. Stripped of their fruit, they were waiting now for the secateurs to cut them back down to size. This morning the sight gave him no pleasure. He sat down heavily on one of the cushioned wooden benches and put his feet up on the low table. It was too bad, too bad. So much at stake, far too much to lose. Too much had been done for years and years. You couldn't take that back, you couldn't take it away.

The sun was filtering through the trees along the edge of the river. He walked down the wide stone steps and onto the lawn which sloped to the water's edge. The grass was finely cut and the flowerbeds were properly cared for, no weeds pushed through, no dying flower heads. Everything was under control. He walked alongside the boathouse, onto the slipway, and stared at the slowly moving waters of the great river. Today, he must take the boat out, the best boat on the river for many kilometres. Take the boat up and down the river, and eat pâté de foie gras and drink champagne.

Moor in the town. Perhaps invite that narrow-minded Maire for drinks on the boat. Power. Remind him of the source of power in this little region. A light, cool breeze rippled the waters, chasing shadows across the surface, shivering the leaves on the oak trees beside him. Feeling a little calmer, he turned and padded slowly back to the house.

Chapter Twenty

Celestine, comfortable after a good night's rest, stepped over the side of the barge and began to run along the towpath. She breathed deeply, and marvelled at the clear blue sky, so absolutely cloudless. A gentle breeze teased back the wisps of hair on the side of her face. It felt like a fresh dawn, a beginning, not just to the day, but more. She felt strong, physically and mentally, and she ran quickly for the first two kilometres then settled into a steady, easy rhythm she could maintain forever. A group of waterfowl skittered across the water from the bank, as she startled them in their leisurely, morning paddle. There was something not quite autumn yet, but there was a subtle change in the air quality, in the luminescence of the sky; each sight was clearer and sharper, as though the haze of summer had been washed away. When she reached Monsieur Lefebvre's boathouse, he was sitting on an old wooden seat at the end of the jetty. He looked as though he was expecting her at exactly that hour, although Celestine suspected that he had been sitting there for some time.

'Bonjour, Henri. How are you this morning?'

'Bonjour, very well thank you, and you. You run like the wind. I shall call you wind-runner,' he smiled.

'Nice compliment, but not completely appropriate I think. I've slowed down a lot since I was a young woman.'

'Young woman.' Monsieur Lefebvre snorted gently. 'But come and sit next to me. I can't offer you coffee and croissants, I'm afraid.'

'Don't worry. I have water, and I didn't come for breakfast.'

'Oh well. It's changing, the season. This morning is different to yesterday morning. Summer is slipping away.'

'And you, Henri. Will you be slipping away soon?' Celestine asked kindly.

'Soon yes, not now, but in some days.' Celestine had a sad vision of Monsieur Lefebvre in the winter, not in the mildness and generosity of summer in the South of France.

'Are the winters very hard for you, Henri?' she asked.

'They can be. Yes, it can be more of a struggle. I don't like the cold and the days are short. I like to be outdoors. I think that's where we belong. I think I'm only once removed from a hunter-gatherer. A simple, outdoor life, like our ancestors.'

'I believe you are,' said Celestine. 'Perhaps we've all come too far from those ways.' They sat quietly for a minute or so, each following their own thoughts. 'But now I'm going to drag you rudely from the Stone Age to the twenty-first century in one leap.'

She opened her small backpack and took out a box. From the box, she extracted a mobile phone. Monsieur Lefebvre looked at it calmly, smiling gently at her.

'What exactly do you want me to do with that?' he inquired.

Celestine explained that she had charged the phone and prepared the speed dial with her and Jacques' mobile numbers. She showed him how to switch it on and how to find the numbers to call. 'So, if you see the black boat coming down the river towards Lissac, call us immediately, so that we can be there to identify the driver when he arrives. Nothing else, unless you want a quick chat,' she smiled. 'And I promise you that I'll take it away again as soon as this is completed. Promise. Hunter-gatherers didn't have mobile phones.' Monsieur Lefebvre listened carefully and nodded. 'Can we try it?' suggested Celestine. 'Just call me. There's a good signal here.'

Monsieur Lefebvre took the phone in his creased and dirt ingrained hands. 'Like this?' he said and quickly pressed the buttons. Celestine's phone began to trill almost immediately. She looked wryly at him.

'You are constantly a surprise. I'm sorry if I seemed to treat you as someone incapable.'

'It's nothing at all. But you know, I have had a mobile phone in the past. Not as pretty as this pink one. Pink is not a traditional colour for me.'

'I'm sorry, that's all I could find. I wanted a phone that was light and easy to use, and cheap. A phone for one purpose only.'

Monsieur Lefebvre looked away. 'I have enjoyed our brief....'

'Friendship,' said Celestine, as she felt he was stumbling over the word.

'Well, well then, friendship, yes. I will do exactly what you say and remain vigilant. That boat will not pass by here without my remarking it. No, definitely not.'

Celestine hugged Monsieur Lefebvre, left him a small bread flute and a haunch of cheese, and took her leave. He watched her go until the path curved away and she disappeared from sight. Then he sat down to eat the bread and cheese and to watch the river.

Chapter Twenty-One

Madame Ducrozet was a thin, uneasy woman. Her face was not unattractive, but it was dull, without animation. Her long, light brown hair was carelessly tied back in a kind of rope which hung halfway down her back. Her eyes, which were a fine dark hazel, flitted constantly, never looking directly at the person in front of her. It was difficult to get any sense of her character. Her hands moved ceaselessly, tugging at things, rubbing fingers against thumbs. Jacques decided she was like a fly fringe, shifting all the time to stop any human gaze from alighting on her. She was around the same age as Celestine, but her clothes were of a woman much older. She didn't smile when she invited Celestine and Jacques into her house, she seemed almost resentful. She led them into the gloomy living room and flapped her hand at the sofa.

'Sit down,' she said, but Jacques remained standing. He took a step towards her and tried to look her squarely in the eye. She moved her head to the side, picked up a cushion and began plumping it up. He stood in the middle of the room, looking at her.

'Madame Ducrozet,' he began, his deep, rich voice enunciating every word in a warm, southern accent that was not too broad, but with strong vowels, definitely not Parisian. 'We must face facts,' he said. 'Your husband is in a very vulnerable position. He is in danger of himself and of others. I know you don't know us, and this is difficult for you, but we do not mean any harm to you or your family. On the contrary, we want to set things right. To help you.' Madame Ducrozet let out a light moan. Her head was tilted to the side, but she had stopped moving and was listening carefully to the voice. He's almost hypnotic, thought Celestine. Maybe that's what he did to me. That's exactly what he did to me - permanent hypnosis. Jacques continued. 'We must go to find your husband. I'll go with you. You know that Celestine was a high-ranking officer in the police in Bordeaux. I worked with her on several occasions. You can trust us implicitly. We have to find your husband, and I must talk to him. Then we will find a way to bring him home safely. Home to you and the children.' Madame Ducrozet's eyes flicked to Jacques' face and for a moment rested there.

'You will protect him, save him?' she said, in a voice that was strained with emotion.

'I will. We will do what we can for him, but he will also have to trust us and be open with us. Do you think he'll do that? Trust us.' Jacques looked at her so earnestly that she almost stepped back.

'I don't know. I don't know his mind.'

'Yes, you do. You're his wife, whatever his inconsistencies. He is your husband. You know him. Do you think he'll trust us?'

'I think so, perhaps. He's not a firm man.'

'I understand,' said Jacques, nodding his leonine head.

'You must go to Montauban with Jacques,' said Celestine. 'Do you know where you can find him?'

'Yes, I think so, I think I know where he is.'

'Then I suggest you pack a bag with a change of clothes, some food and water, and a little money. He may have all of these things but….' Celestine looked up at Jacques. For a minute she thought he was going to mention the clothes, or the lack of them, but he restrained himself. Madame Ducrozet disappeared for a few minutes and returned with a big blue canvas bag.

'I have money,' she said.

'That's good. He may not need it but best be sure. It rather depends on what we decide to do next.'

As Jacques was about to climb into Madame Ducrozet's little car, Celestine whispered to him,

'Gentle, be gentle with him. He'll be very wary.'

'I know, don't worry. "Gentle words with strong actions tame the falcon in its gyre".'

'Basque proverb?' Celestine asked, raising her eyebrows.

'Words to that effect.' He kissed her on both cheeks and folded his large frame into the passenger seat of the small Renault Clio. As the car pulled jerkily away from the kerb, Jacques turned to Madame Ducrozet. 'Please call me Jacques and I shall call you?'

'Chantal,' said Madame Ducrozet shyly.
'Chantal. Ok. Allez.'

The drive to Montauban was uncomfortable and awkward. Jacques sat cramped into the narrow seat, and no one spoke for several kilometres until the rhythm of the drive and the period of proximity seemed to help the woman next to him to settle down. He started to talk slowly, gently coaxing out the facts of her life; her life with the children, the work she had done before the children, and the life with her husband.

At one point she took both hands off the steering wheel to explain to Jacques. 'He really is such a good man, a good man. Very clever, not brilliant you understand, but clever and conscientious. And caring. He has a lot of, well,' she hesitated, 'love in him.' She drove on a little further. 'But he is not strong. He can be turned easily, charmed. And he has this thing in him. This need.'

'Did you know about it before you were married?' asked Jacques quietly.

'No, and yes. I think I knew or suspected, but it was nothing. And he was so attentive and interested in me. And it does hurt, of course it does. But I know he is sometimes in need of ... male sex.' She almost gasped as she said it and gripped the steering wheel tightly.

'Chantal. This happens many times, we are all complex, multi-faceted creatures,' said Jacques.

'I'm not,' she said vehemently. 'What you see is what you get.'

'Yes, but you've described a man with many admirable qualities, rare qualities. A good father. There can be no higher praise for a man than that. My father died when I was eight. I barely knew him. Yet, he was a loss. A good father, even with his other foibles, is still a fine accolade for a man.' Chantal smiled for the first time in Jacques' presence.

'Thank you, yes, he is a good father.'

'Then we must bring him safely back to his children and to you,' he said.

The Canal Port was a short walk from the centre of the town. There, the canal had been widened into a broad rectangle where pleasure boats, barges and cruisers could moor quietly in the still waters, but also have access through a lock to the river. Chantal pulled the car into a parking place in the shade of a spreading oak tree. She sat back and took a deep breath. Jacques could sense her nervousness starting to rise again. He rested his hand lightly on her arm.

'Where do you expect him to be?' he asked.

'Somewhere near the boats. He'll have come through the lock and moored at the far side of the port. There's a café there. We used to go there with the children. There's a little playground you see.' Jacques looked across.

'Ok, Chantal. It's important that you go first, not with me. So he's not spooked. I'll follow and keep an eye on you. When you find him, talk to him, sit him down and explain about Celestine and me. When he's ready, put your hand up and I'll come over. I won't be far away. Just tell him it's ok, he can trust us.' Chantal nodded. 'Go on, off you go. Everything will be fine.'

Chantal set off along the path that led to where the boats were moored. She came to where the first boat was tied to a pontoon, and she seemed to hesitate. She was looking at the boats carefully, but these were large houseboats, exuberantly painted in garish yellows and greens; some had small wooden extensions, like garden sheds, tacked on the sides and decks till they had lost all the shape of a boat. Ducrozet's craft was a small motor cruiser, it wouldn't be moored there. Chantal walked on slowly, peering along each pontoon, head slightly on the side. Like a wading bird, scanning the shallow waters for food, thought Jacques. She came to the end of the boats on that side, straightened up, and looked towards where Jacques could see the roof of the café. She immediately quickened her pace and set off in that direction. Jacques stopped in the shade and watched as Chantal walked unsteadily towards the building. She walked so stiffly, so full of uncertainty; not for the first time, Jacques felt immensely sorry for her and for the position she found herself in. He saw her wave tentatively to someone inside, but he couldn't see who it was. She disappeared towards the back of the café and he lost sight of her, so he strolled away from the boats and entered the café from the other side. He soon spotted her, with her back towards him, her head bent as though listening carefully. Jacques took a seat at a table about five metres away, facing the bay. Eventually, the man sat back. From the corner of his eye, Jacques saw him almost rise and saw the restraining hand on his arm. He could make out the sound of Chantal's voice, thin and sharp, pleading with him. Jacques saw the man's face for the first time, his dark beard and black-framed spectacles. As he bent forwards he saw that he was balding on top where his dark hair was parted.

A waiter approached their table, but Ducrozet waved him away with a flick of his hand. He came over to where Jacques was sitting and Jacques ordered a coffee. He picked up the menu from a stand on the table and appeared to be studying it. He could see that the pair were in deep conversation. He couldn't hear what they were saying, but he picked up the sound of Chantal's voice, again and again. The man's voice was lower and quieter and he moved his head a lot, shaking it from side to side, then nodding slowly. Then he lifted up his head, sat back and started looking around. Chantal raised her hand, beckoning, although she didn't look to see where Jacques was. Just at that moment, the waiter arrived with his coffee.

'I'm sorry, could you take it to that table there? I've just spotted two friends of mine,' he said and smiled.

'Of course, monsieur.' The waiter walked over to their table, nodded to Chantal and her husband and placed the coffee in front of the empty chair. Ducrozet looked confused, the waiter smiled and Jacques walked around the table.

'Monsieur Ducrozet,' he said. 'My name is Jacques Lecoubarry. I am here to help. And that is my coffee, may I?' He held out a hand to Ducrozet, who looked sick and uncertain, unable to look Jacques in the face. Jacques took his hand and gripped it firmly. 'I'm very pleased to finally make your acquaintance. I have heard many good things about you from your charming wife.' He sat down still holding Ducrozet's hand. He turned and smiled at Chantal. 'You've explained my presence here?' She nodded. 'Then we have a lot to talk about, and we have some problems to solve. We'll do that together.' He let go of Ducrozet's hand who sat back and looked at it for a few seconds as though it had been enchanted.

'I didn't kill Emmanuel Malraux,' he said, and for the first time looked at Jacques. 'I would never do that. I was…, we were lovers. I'm sorry.' He looked towards his wife. 'This is so terrible, so terrible for Chantal, for me. How can we ever….' His voice trailed off and he looked like a man completely defeated. Jacques realised then how close he was to the edge.

'You must trust me, Monsieur Ducrozet, Jean-Luc. But I can't work miracles. You are going to have to work with me. To help me help you.' Jacques paused. 'I don't believe you killed Malraux, but I intend, we intend, to discover who did, and Sister Agnieszka.'

'Oh my God, Sister Agnieszka, I can't imagine who....'

'At the moment we're working on the assumption that the deaths are linked and that somehow it relates to the research he was doing. You're going to need to help me with that part. We need to understand everything. Do you see?'

Ducrozet nodded. 'I don't see why. I don't see why anyone would kill people. The research he was doing wasn't like that. It wasn't valuable or world-shattering. Nothing like that.' Jacques could see him stiffen, his voice a little firmer.

'Ok. Then you must explain to me exactly what the study was about, and what point he'd reached. Also, how Sister Agnieszka helped, and what she knew about the research. Who else knew about it? Did any of you speak to another person, however casually? And is there a way for the research to continue without Malraux, to see where that leads?' Jacques sat back. 'Are you ready to do that?'

'Yes, I think so. Perhaps you're right. I can't really think straight at the moment.'

'No, but this will help to calm you. Talking helps to clarify thoughts and you'll be doing something positive. That's very important.' Jacques pulled a small sketching pad from his inside pocket. 'I like to draw,' he said. 'I'll make some notes.'

For the next half an hour, Ducrozet described in detail the course of Malraux's investigation. As he talked, some light came back into his eyes, he straightened a little and occasionally, he was able to look directly at his wife and at Jacques. He described the early, fruitless and frustrating studies in the Abbey, which included, in his own words, a number of kindly interceptions on the part of Sister Agnieszka; how he had seen them one day deep in conversation in the church, beside the wooden figures lowering the body of Christ into the coffin. You've seen it. Of course, they didn't use coffins in the Middle East two thousand years ago. A sixteenth-century interpretation. Jacques quickly brought him back to the main subject. After the long talks with Sister Agnieszka, Malraux had started visiting the Convent, and spent days there, sometimes coming back to the Abbey inflamed with frustration, angry and reckless. And then one day he had rushed into Jean-Luc's office, waving papers, a letter, with some numbers on it, like a code.

'A letter from whom?' interrupted Jacques.

'He was Jewish, you know, and the letter was from his great-grandfather.'

'His great-grandfather? A letter here in Lissac?'

'Yes. There were a great many Jews here before and during the war. There was a school, a movement, the Scouts. A movement that helped to save Jewish children from the Nazis. There's a museum, just below the Napoleon Bridge.'

'Yes, I saw there was a museum. I didn't put the two things together. Where's the letter now? Do you have it?'

'No. I presume the police took it with his possessions from the apartment. Perhaps your partner could obtain it?'

'Perhaps,' said Jacques. 'But did you read the letter or did Malraux tell you any more?'

'Not much. It was a letter from his great-grandfather to his son, Malraux's grandfather. In it there was a set of numbers. Malraux seemed to think this was a code and that the answers lay in the cloisters of the Abbey. He'd started working there feverishly. He kept asking me to help him but I didn't really know what I was supposed to be looking for. A code. I am not mathematical.'

'No, but I know someone who is,' said Jacques. 'So, do you think he had reached a conclusion on the day he died? I'm sorry, but I have to ask. Did he say anything then? And did he share this with Sister Agnieszka or anyone else?'

'I don't know, I really don't. He talked a lot, he was very extroverted, you know. It's not impossible....'

Jacques placed his hand on Ducrozet's arm and looked at his face. 'You've done well, really well, but I need you to wrack your brains. Was there anyone else who knew about this? Let that idea swim around in your head a little and see if you come up with something, a name, an impression, anything.' Ducrozet looked calmer now but drained. Madame Ducrozet was drawn into herself. She had listened to all this, all the details about her husband's lover, and shrunk further and further into herself. But she looked up at Jacques and smiled wanly. Somehow, in all this mess, Jacques had given her the impression that everything would be all right, that life could go on, that boats could be righted.

It was a confidence that, at that moment, Jacques didn't really share.

Chapter Twenty-Two

Bram and Lena Visser were picked up by the gendarmes outside their small Gite d'Etape at eight o'clock that morning, just as they were setting off to walk back to their car. In small towns and rural areas, everyone has connections, and it didn't take the police long to find them. Bram remonstrated loudly and tried to walk away, but he was grabbed and bundled into the back of the vehicle. Lena was pushed in beside him. They didn't speak on the quick trip back to Lissac. But when they arrived at the police station Bram started up again about how they'd done nothing wrong, they were pilgrims, and how he trusted they would be taken back to where they could resume their walk to Santiago de Compostela. One of the gendarmes just grunted.

'Commandant Grimard is very angry with you. You left the scene of a serious crime. That's an offence. I wonder why you did that.' Bram continued to shout and complain as they were separated and taken into different rooms. Lena walked in quietly, head bowed. She hadn't uttered a word since the arrest.

Commandant Grimard was indeed angry, but this was caused by a whole range of issues. Another citizen had volunteered that they had seen Krastyo Dacheva in the vicinity of the murder site, but not actually at the scene. The scientific evidence was slightly more encouraging; some fibres had been found on Malraux's sleeve which matched the sweatshirt of the Bulgarian, but they could have come from the earlier confrontation. In addition, there were a dozen other fibres, some unaccounted for, and some which might be matched with furniture in the house of Urbain Lamy. It was not enough; and now he was being asked to tread carefully in his pursuit of the Bulgarian by the head of the town's Municipal Police. At the same time, the Maire and his local officials were telling him to accelerate his pursuit. All of which he would ignore, and would pursue the investigation at his own pace and with his own degree of intensity. He could not though find a link through to the murder of the nun. There were no sightings of the nun talking to Bulgarians; they were a different church weren't they, one Catholic, one Orthodox. He shook his head. No, that was a dark tunnel he didn't want to go down. He believed implicitly that the Bulgarian was the most likely culprit for the first murder - hot-blooded, easily insulted, homophobic, from a different culture. A culture where men still acted to protect their own; less restrained than the soft Western European, he imagined. He just needed more evidence. Someone knew something, and if he had to shake it out of the community he would. He had requested two more translators to work with his officers. He would send them door to door again, but this time with a little more aggression. Something would break, someone would talk.

There was a tap on the door and his assistant leaned his head into the room.

'We've got that Dutch couple in the interview rooms,' he said. 'Only something interesting. The woman, we've got their passports, she's not Dutch. Look at the name on the passport. She's Polish.'

'Polish?'

'Yes, sir. Polish, like Sister Agnieszka.'

Grimard grabbed the passports. 'Right, let's see where this leads us,' he said.

Chapter Twenty-Three

At eleven a.m. precisely, Monsieur Palomer reversed the cabin cruiser, *Vencidor*, cautiously out of the boathouse, and turned her head downstream. Sitting in the boat with him were his daughter-in-law, Jannine and his eldest son, Jean-Michel. The daughter-in-law looked bored before the boat had reached mid-stream. Her long dark hair was tied back in a scarlet, satin scarf. She adjusted her sunglasses, pulled her linen top around her with her folded arms and glared at the far bank. Jean-Michel dipped his head into the small cabin and put his hand into a large cool box lying on the floor. He took out a bottle of beer, flipped off the top and put it to his mouth. His father looked at him angrily.

'Can't you wait? There's champagne for later, for lunch.'

'I'm thirsty. Lunch is a long way off,' he replied and sat back, put his feet up on the seats and looked lazily over the side.

Palomer steered the boat carefully. He enjoyed the control he had over the boat - a classic, expensive boat, the best boat on the river. He liked the control and he liked the appreciation. It was always disappointing that there were so few people on the river at this point, although there would be more as they neared Lissac. The river was wide and flowed smoothly, and there was a clarity in the air that Palomer liked. He liked the sharp air. He liked the first frosts as they limed the branches of the fruit trees and the wires where the grapes would grow the following year. He liked clarity and sharpness. But it was a pity there weren't more people on the river to watch him pass by.

There was one person who was looking at the river at that time - an old man, sitting quietly on a ruined wooden jetty beside a decaying old boathouse. Jean-Michel caught the slight dissonance in the scene and for a second looked directly at the old man.

Monsieur Lefebvre started slightly, unsure at first. He watched the boat go past, saw the bow wave spread out behind it and lap softly on the shore near his feet. He hesitated for a moment then reached into the small bag, took out a mobile phone and dialled a number with ease.

Celestine's phone rang as she was leaving a fine goods shop in the centre of the town. 'Monsieur Lefebvre.' She listened. 'You are sure, Henri? Just this minute. Are there other people in the boat? Ok, yes, I see. Thank you yet again. See you soon.'

Celestine thought quickly. She walked swiftly through the side streets leading to the canal. On the *Incognito* she stored her purchases in the small fridge and cupboards in the galley, combed her hair and slipped a dark sweater over her bright red T-shirt. She thought of calling Jacques but decided that he didn't need to be disturbed, his mission was tricky enough. She put on her darkest sunglasses and locked up the boat again.

There were two possible landing places for the *Vencidor*. There was the quiet jetty which the fishermen used, or the port where many of the cruisers moored. She opted for the second as the most likely. She recalled that the boat was large and ostentatious for a river cruiser, all chrome and gold lettering. She crossed the canal on the narrow road bridge and walked across the park towards the river. Through the trees she could see two sailing dinghies skidding across the water, their bright red sails bulging in the stiff breeze. As she reached the edge of the little bay that was the port of Lissac-sur-Tarn, she saw it - a white cabin cruiser with gold lettering, sitting high in the water.

From behind one of the electric charging pillars, Celestine could see the head and upper body of a man in a Panama hat, and when he turned away she could see the rolls of fat on his neck. This was not the man Monsieur Lefebvre had described. Disappointed, she leant back against the pillar. Monsieur Lefebvre had definitely said that there were at least three people in the boat when it passed him. Then she heard raised voices, and peering around she saw a younger couple walking towards the cruiser. The man appeared to be trying to placate both her and the man in the boat. He was quite young, maybe early thirties, she thought, with very dark hair, tall, lean, not fat like the other man. He was wearing light-coloured chinos and a navy blue, short-sleeved shirt. His forearms, she noticed, were thick and hairy. Was this the man Jacques had collided with that night? The woman started shouting again, then turned and stomped off. Celestine could hear the sound of her heels clacking on the cobbled roadway for several minutes after she had left. The younger man watched her go for a few seconds and then turned back to the boat. The older one was speaking to him in a serious voice and he leant forward to catch the words. She could see him nodding, and then he turned away and started walking towards the town.

Celestine quickly headed back through the park on a parallel course. She waited by a cypress tree until he walked past, and then moved smoothly onto the pavement some fifty metres behind him. He crossed the bridge over the canal and seemed to be heading for the centre of the town, but then suddenly veered off to the right and entered one of the narrow side streets. Celestine followed cautiously at a distance. The lanes they were walking through were gloomy, like canyons between the high buildings; they were old warehouses, empty and shuttered. They came to the end of one of the lanes and onto a wider, residential street. At the end of a road, the man stopped and stepped over to the side of the pavement. Celestine ducked quickly into a gateway to watch him. He stood there for more than five minutes, his head moving occasionally from side to side, as though looking at different angles. At one point he reached into his back pocket for his mobile phone, and started photographing whatever he was looking at in the road ahead. Then, as suddenly as he had stopped, he started walking again, crossing the road and heading in a different direction. Celestine waited for a minute, then, keeping a close eye out in case he returned, walked slowly to the end of the road. She could see him moving quickly towards the centre of the town. She put herself in the same position he had taken, and looked down and across the street. A shiver ran from the top of her scalp to the base of her back. It was clear that what the man from the boat had been studying so carefully, was the house of Monsieur and Madame Ducrozet.

Badly shaken, something shifted in her and she felt the anger building. She set off in pursuit, determined to find out who this man was. At the end of the road, she entered the broad market square, where a small crowd of people were shuffling along the aisles between the stalls. She spotted him easily; he was tall and moved with purpose, while most of the other people in the square were strolling in a leisurely, Saturday fashion. She followed him across the square and along the pedestrianised street that led to the Abbey, almost jogging to keep up with him. He walked past the great church portal and around the side of the church, and she was just in time to see him enter the glass lobby of the cloisters. Celestine paused; this was exactly where she should have been heading at this time, to meet Catherine Tallandier. She was a little early for the meeting, but was determined to get close enough to the man from the boat; the man, she now felt certain was the one who had collided with Jacques on the towpath.

Catherine saw her immediately and came from behind the counter to greet her. She looked a little flustered, and kissed Celestine clumsily on both cheeks.

'I'm a little early,' said Celestine, catching her breath.

'Don't worry. Have you been running?'

'Just walking quickly. I got confused with the time,' she smiled. 'Do you think I could just spend a little time in there, in the cloisters, until you're ready?'

'Of course, go through. We'll close in fifteen minutes. I'll call you,' said Catherine.

Celestine stepped into the cool shade of the courtyard. She walked slowly, pretending to look at the pillars and their carvings. It was quiet, there were a couple of elderly, bewildered-looking tourists taking photographs. As she moved around to the second side of the square, she saw him. He was standing with his face close to one of the pillars and was staring at the carvings. Celestine walked towards him, taking out her mobile phone, tilting it carefully so as to include him in the pictures she took. He seemed to be completely absorbed, but as she came alongside him he looked up quickly, and from the corner of her eye she caught the intensity of his gaze. She saw that he had very dark eyes, a flat, thick nose and thin lips. Perhaps his face was a little plump, as Monsieur Lefebvre had suggested, but it was difficult to tell, as he had several days' growth of a very dark beard. Celestine stopped at the pillar at the end of the row and took another few pictures, each time she caught the man as he leant out to try a different angle of vision. She could sense him looking at her, then, when she glanced up again he was gone. When she moved to where she could see the exit, she saw his dark blue shirt as he pushed through the glass door. She went quickly to look at the pillar he had been studying and took a photograph. Then a voice called out - Catherine was ushering out the elderly tourists.

'Catherine. Tell me, this pillar, what does it represent?' Catherine came closer and touched shoulders.

'It's the Vision of Saint John at Patmos. See the angel tugging his wrist. Waking him up. It's from the Book of Revelations.'

Celestine nodded and smiled. 'You know so much about them,' she said.

'Now I do,' Catherine replied.

'As much as Monsieur Ducrozet?' asked Celestine.

'Maybe not quite as much. He has been studying this for years. And he wrote the guidebook, as I told you. I do think I know enough now to be the head curator. Then I could spend more time doing academic work and less on administration.'

'Do you think the position will become available?'

'Possible. Monsieur Ducrozet hasn't returned to work. Nobody knows where he is. He might not return.' She shrugged.

Celestine patted her on the shoulder. 'Oh, and Catherine, do you know who that man is? The one who left just now, blue shirt. He was quite rude. He bumped into me and just walked away.'

'Jean-Michel Palomer. He's doing some kind of study here, but I don't know what exactly. He's certainly not an academic. His family make contributions to the charitable funds, they're bigwigs in the town.'

'What do they do?'

'Wine. They own vineyards. The Rama Estate. Very rich, very bourgeois.'

'And this Jean-Michel, you say he's not a scholar?'

'No. Nothing like that. A dilettante. Too much time on his hands.'

'Has he been coming here for a while?'

Catherine paused and looked at Celestine, uncertainly. 'No, not really. I didn't really notice him until the last few weeks, when he's been in and out quite often. He has access at any time we're open you see, because of the society membership. Doesn't speak much. I asked him once if he needed any help with his research, but he just cut me short. So, I haven't offered since. Why are you asking?'

'He was rude to me,' said Celestine sharply, 'and I don't like that. Rich or not, I'd like to give him a piece of my mind.'

'Forget him,' said Catherine, linking her arm in Celestine's. 'We're closed now. Come and have some lunch, and we can bitch about the men who work in this place.'

Chapter Twenty-Four

Lena Visser confessed early in the afternoon. Confirmation came through to Grimard's team that the girl, Lena Jaskiewicz, had once been a resident at a Catholic school some ten kilometres outside of Krakow. A school for orphans or the children of single mothers, it had been run by nuns of the Carmelite order. Further enquiries with colleagues in Poland had confirmed that Sister Agnieszka had been one of the nuns teaching at the school at the same time. Thriving at the time of the Polish Pope, the school had been untouchable, despite many reports of harshness and abuse towards the resident girls. The authorities had finally closed it down nearly ten years previously, after an appalling catalogue of historic mental and physical violence and sexual abuse of the vulnerable girls had come to light.

Lena Jaskiewicz left the school after seven years of humiliation and pain. She survived an attempt to kill herself, more by luck than judgement; and so she turned her hurt into anger, and eventually into a lust for revenge. She fled Poland and moved to Holland, where she lived in a twilight world of prostitution, petty theft and squalor. Details of her criminal record and that of her partner Bram Visser arrived from Holland within hours. Visser had spent time in prison for drug-dealing and shop-lifting offences, and was currently a person of interest to the Dutch Police. They had met three years earlier; a chance meeting of two unfortunates swirling around in the undercurrents of society. For some reason, they had clung to each other, found a ladder, and had gradually started to climb out of the sewer they were living in. Bram continued dealing drugs, but at a higher level, helped by Lena's natural grasp of economics, and her willingness to threaten and use a knife with customers and suppliers when necessary. Financially, they stopped living from hand to mouth. They got married and Lena took control. She found a temporary job at a local café and opened a bank account - ostensibly to receive her wages, but also some of the proceeds of the drugs that Bram was selling, a little at a time. They bought a car and rented a getaway apartment on the other side of Amsterdam from where they were working. In two years, they looked like a different couple, both subject to violent or self-destructive outbursts, but they managed each other and came through the darkest times. Then two things happened, almost on the same day.

It was a mild August morning, a pale blue sky, and Lena was walking along the Keizersgracht, the Emperor's Canal, past the Catholic Mother of God Church of Our Lady. She had not been inside a church since she had left Poland, and never thought she would again. But this day, the twin doors were open, and she stopped by the railings and looked up at the towering pillars and great arched windows. She walked tentatively towards the opening and stepped inside the porch. The musty smell of old incense, cold stone and snuffed-out candles hit her. She shook violently and stepped back, almost falling against the door. She knelt down to steady herself and took hold of a metal rack containing leaflets of service times, church events and a small pile of catholic magazines. She picked one up, she didn't know why, but suddenly there was a dark shape standing over her. She looked up to see the black robes of a priest, and a young, bespectacled man peering down at her.

'Are you all right?' he said. She waved the magazine towards him and stood up. Unable to look him in the face, she mumbled a few words and walked quickly outside again and away from the church, her heart pounding and her face deeply flushed.

For some reason, she kept the magazine and took it home; sentimentality, keen to know whether she was now strong enough to face the almost forgotten world; for whatever reason, that was where she saw the picture of Sister Agnieszka. In an article about Romanesque church architecture in France, there was a mention of the Abbey at Lissac-sur-Tarn, and a photograph of Sister Agnieszka, arms out, in front of a group of school children, standing on the steps of the great portal of the church.

Lena went rigid. She closed the page quickly and sat back. But then she had to open it again and look more carefully at the picture.

It was definitely her, and ten years of buried hurt and fear came bubbling up to the surface, and she screamed as loud as she could. Bram came running and tried to calm her down. He saw the magazine lying open on the floor and picked it up.

'Is this it? Is this what you're screaming about?' he sneered.

She turned to him, and gasping and sobbing she explained to him who Sister Agnieszka was - one of the worst sexual abusers at the residential school. Not so violent as some of the others, but insinuating, calculating and devious. Lena had dreaded her the most, more than the ones whose violence was just born of stupidity, frustration and unlimited power.

'She,' said Lena, pointing to the magazine. 'She took away my innocence, piece by piece, dismantled my childhood, corrupted me, and left me with nothing but self-loathing.'

'What d'you wanna do? Where's this place?' Bram asked, his own anger rising quickly.

'France somewhere, South West France it says here.'

Bram grasped her shoulders. 'We could go there. Kick the shit out of her. Eh.'

She looked up at him, her wet eyes now hard and unblinking. 'I'll fucking kill her,' she said.

Two days previously, Bram had run into a new problem with his enterprise. One of his couriers had been caught near the port of Rotterdam, drugs confiscated and the woman incarcerated. An occupational hazard, but this was a particularly large shipment and Bram would still have to pay for it, as theoretically, he had taken possession of it through his courier. Without the drugs to sell it would be an exceptional cost, and one he would have some difficulty in meeting immediately. And these people only understood immediate when it came to payment. He and Lena had stashed quite a sum from the last few years' work, but he didn't want to use it all up to meet this shortfall. In addition, he was worried about the woman. She was facing some serious charges, and he knew pressure would be put on her to lighten her sentence by implicating others. She had been good up to now, but he had sensed that she was using too much and getting careless. He should have dropped her. She was weak, and she had made him vulnerable. He had thought that it might be a good time to disappear for a while, to let the heat cool down. So, after Lena's outburst, he suggested to her that they leave immediately for the South of France and that he would help her to deal with this Agnieszka.

The plan was straightforward, as she explained it to Grimard. They studied the area carefully, found out about the routes to and from the town of Lissac-sur-Tarn. They noticed that the route of the Santiago de Compostela Way came through the town, and Bram had come up with the idea that they join this route as pilgrims, a short way before Lissac, and leave the same way. No one would suspect pilgrims, he thought. They would buy a guidebook and put cockle shells on their rucksacks. Carry a religious book, maybe a small bible. A few days of walking, deal with the nun, then back to the car and head for Spain, where Bram had connections.

That is what they did. They had started in Lauzerte, then stayed in Lissac for two nights. But when it came to it, Lena claimed, she couldn't go through with it. She had seen the nun at the Convent - a tiny, ageing creature, pathetic really. Lena had realised that there was no fear there anymore, no terror, not even anger, just disgust, and a contempt for a contemptible little life; and the desire for violent revenge left her. She was hollow. She had decided that she would write a letter to the Mother Superior at the Convent, exposing Sister Agnieszka for the abuses she had been guilty of. That would be her revenge; and she was ready to move on, more now than at any time in the last ten years.

She had told Bram, who she said, had been relieved, although he still wanted to hurt her somehow. But he was ready to leave when she was. They had walked off that morning, following the Compostela trail, and then they had seen the corpse of Sister Agnieszka on the hill at Calvary. She had been so shocked that for a moment she had wondered if, in fact, she had done what she came to do, in a madness that she couldn't recall. Despite Bram's assurances, she had panicked, and so they had left the scene, acting the part of pilgrims one more day. And also, she said finally, there was something about the walking, the walking was starting to change her head.

Grimard glanced sideways then leaned forwards so that his face was directly in line with hers. 'So, let me be absolutely clear about this, Madame Visser. You came to Lissac with the intention to kill

Sister Agnieszka. You admit that?' Lena nodded, 'For the record please.'

'Yes.'

'But you changed your mind. Yet, two nights ago, she was brutally murdered. But not by you?'

'Yes.'

'Or by your boyfriend, husband?'

'Yes, no, not by him. He was with me all the time.'

Grimard shook his head and twisted up his mouth. 'You are asking a lot for me to believe this,' he said grimly. 'In any case, we have a lot of work to do and you will not be leaving Lissac-sur-Tarn for quite some time.' Grimard and his assistant Bedeau left the room. 'Jerome,' he said. 'We have to swarm all over this. There must be some physical evidence linking that woman, or her husband, to the murder scene. I want the scientific guys working double time. That story is unbelievable, there must be something. Find it.'

'Yes, Chief,' said Bedeau, and hurried off to the incident room, with the niggling thought that they were missing something, something vital, but he was dammed if he could place it.

Chapter Twenty-Five

Chantal Ducrozet kissed her husband lightly on the mouth, whispered to him and walked away from the café. Jacques watched her go. There was no energy in her shambling walk, so little confidence in the way she carried herself. He turned to Ducrozet, pricked with annoyance.

'You are very lucky, Jean-Luc,' he said. 'You have a woman there who would support you come what may. A woman who loves you. But it's time she loved herself a bit too. That's another job for you when you return to normality.' Ducrozet nodded but said nothing. He looked permanently like a cowed dog expecting to be hit at any time. 'Come on,' said Jacques, rising from the table. 'Let's take this boat back to Lissac, and mind you keep your bloody clothes on.' Ducrozet looked startled, but Jacques just grinned. 'Spies everywhere man,' he said.

They walked to where Ducrozet had left his boat, tucked in beside two larger cruisers. Jacques took the wheel while Ducrozet slumped down beside him. They passed through the lock to the river and out into midstream. It was a beautiful, September afternoon, and Jacques let the rhythm of the boat and the flow of the water seep into him. This was the calmest and most content he had felt for days. The trip took a couple of hours, and he was surprised by Ducrozet's ability to withdraw into himself to sit in silence and misery. He took no interest in the scenery they passed. A few times Jacques pointed out some sight to Ducrozet, like the two fishermen arguing volubly in a little boat.

'Arguing,' he said. 'Fishermen arguing. Isn't that exactly the opposite frame of mind you need as a fisherman?'

Ducrozet barely responded. Jacques noticed the changes in the landscape; some fields were bursting with the late summer crops, and others were bared, plough ravaged, waiting for the sowing of winter seeds, or the winter's rains. A buzzard floated overhead, surfing the thermals, keening its wild cry, mere twitches of its wing tips keeping it hovering above its prey two hundred metres below. As they neared the estate, Jacques nudged Ducrozet and asked him what he knew about the family that lived there.

'Wealthy. Monsieur Palomer is a hard, avaricious bastard. He's on the committee of Friends of the Abbey, and can't keep his opinions to himself. Bombastic, grossly overweight,' Ducrozet said with some relish. 'That's his big house. It's not a chateau, it was a vintner's house, but they've extended it over the years till it looks like a parody, a chocolate box.' He paused. 'What else. Owns miles of vines, good vines too. Makes a lot of very expensive wine.' He was warming to his subject now and he sat up in the boat. 'Plays Trictrac. Was in some kind of regional final a few years back. Won. Put it in the local papers. Trictrac; the preferred game of the aristocracy before the revolution. That shows how pretentious he is.'

'That's it, that's the name. Now it's falling into place. Monsieur Palomer, the guy who ordered the Trictrac table.' Jacques smiled. 'I play Trictrac,' he said quietly, enjoying the look of surprise and discomfort on Ducrozet's face. 'It's a very intriguing game, and one that, to my mind, is infinitely superior to backgammon.'

'I wouldn't know about that,' said Ducrozet dismissively. 'Anyway, he's the largest producer of Chasselas wine, and is relentlessly pompous, arrogant and a total shit.'

'Not so keen on him then,' said Jacques. 'And what about his family, does he have a son?'

'Yes. Another shit. Not as intelligent, or should I say cunning, as his father, but an abrupt, unpleasant man. He hangs around the Abbey sometimes, doing some kind of familial research.'

'Like Malraux?'

'Oh no, not like that. Not in the same league. Probably just trying to add to the family brand, to find some ancestral link to Lissac's past. I don't know. Anyhow, he has a blank look about him sometimes, like his features have switched off, and it's all going on inside his head.'

Jacques pondered this for a moment. 'Is he married? This son.'

'Yes. I've seen her in town and at the Abbey once, she didn't register with me too much. Although, the stench of her perfume, I swear, hung around for days.'

Jacques shook his head and laughed. 'So, Jean-Luc, would you like to say anything more about the family Palomer, before I write it up? There's not a lot of the milk of human kindness swilling around in that speech.' Ducrozet shook his head. Jacques brought the boat closer to the shore. He looked into the boathouse, only the black boat was there. 'Does that black boat belong to Palomer Junior?' he asked.

'I guess so. I don't really know. I don't think I've ever seen him in it,' said Ducrozet.

Jacques looked up the slipway towards the house. 'It's a very pretty setting, isn't it? For such an ugly crew I mean.'

Jacques really felt the need to tease this waspish, browbeaten, acerbic creature, with his eyes that looked like the glass burr at the bottom of an old bottle. He was sitting hunched up, arms around his knees. Definitely in the wallowing position, Jacques decided. He would need to pump some life into him. There were hard days and uncertainty ahead for him, that's for sure. Further down the river, Jacques slowed the boat down as they came close to Monsieur Lefebvre's residence. He eased the boat towards the rickety old jetty. There was no sign of the old man.

'Why are we stopping here?' demanded Ducrozet.

'I just want to check on a friend of mine,' said Jacques, and with that, Monsieur Lefebvre's head appeared out of the side door of the boathouse.

'Oh, it's you, Jacques. That's a different boat,' he said, smiling as he walked gingerly along the jetty towards them. 'Another piece broke away this morning,' he said. 'I shall have to have the whole place renovated.'

'You do that,' said Jacques, 'and mind you charge the owner. It's a disgrace expecting a man to live in a death trap like this.' Ducrozet was looking askance at the old man. Jacques introduced them. 'Henri, this is Jean-Luc Ducrozet. He is the curator at the Abbey in Lissac-sur-Tarn, a most prestigious position you understand. Jean-Luc, this is Henri Lefebvre, a retired engineer and master spy.' The two men looked at each other without enthusiasm. 'Now, Henri. Jean-Luc lives in Lissac. I will give you his address later, and you can also find him at the Abbey. If, when you come to Lissac in the future and we are not here, you must call on Monsieur Ducrozet if you are in need of anything at all, and it will be his duty and his privilege to assist you in any way he can. Won't it?' Ducrozet looked dubious, but the firmness in Jacques' look left him in no doubt that he had better agree.

'It will be a pleasure,' he smiled weakly.

'And of course, Henri,' Jacques continued. 'You have him at a disadvantage. You have seen him in his most natural, even naked state.' Jacques snorted with amusement. Monsieur Lefebvre giggled and smiled happily at Ducrozet.

'Oh yes. I won't forget that sight,' he said.

Ducrozet slipped back into his hangdog look and slouched down in the boat. Jacques and Monsieur Lefebvre spoke for a few more minutes. The old man told him about the call to Celestine, but that he had seen nothing else that day. Jacques thanked him and they pushed away from the jetty.

'Come on, Ducrozet. It's time you started your rehabilitation.' he said.

The police were very active in the Rue de Valence that afternoon. In the house of Krastyo Dacheva a team of specialist search officers were taking apart cupboards and lifting floorboards. Every item of clothing was being placed in bags and tagged meticulously. Nothing was left undisturbed, including the jars of preserves on the melamine shelves in the kitchen. Dacheva, meanwhile, was sitting restrained in the back of a police van, an agent ignoring his angry and largely incomprehensible complaints. A short thick body and a blunt face, lined and darkened by the sun, he sat as tears seeped out of his dark brown eyes and funnelled into the creases and wrinkles of his weather-beaten face. Unable to wipe away the tears, he hung his head and muttered to himself in his Slavic tongue.

In the other houses in the street, the police were going pointedly from door to door, demanding to know who lived there and if they were any relation to Dacheva. Had they seen anything on the night of the murders? What more could they tell about the accused Bulgarian and his private life, about the way he worked, his friends, his enemies? Two agents stood at each door and insisted that every member of the family come out to stand in front of them. The tone of the police was intentionally aggressive; they turned on any family member who was in any way uncooperative. One young man was hustled away to where another team was waiting by their vehicles. He had come to the door reluctantly and had demanded to know by what right they were harassing these people. He was cautioned to calm down and cooperate, or he would be booked for obstructing the police.

Many of the Bulgarians lived on the same street, or close by, in the poorer parts of the town, sharing the neighbourhood with North Africans and other immigrant groups. The police spent more than three hours there. Eventually, they left Dacheva's house; and the young couple, who rented two rooms from him, were allowed back inside. Krastyo Dacheva, however, was taken back to the police poste to be interrogated again by Grimard.

Chapter Twenty-Six

Celestine's lunch was a drawn-out and rather tasteless affair. Catherine Tallandier cooked the way she dealt with most day-to-day aspects of life, with a little disdain and not much interest. However, the good bottle of wine that Celestine had brought proved to be useful in unmooring her hostess' mental ropes, encouraging her to drift into the stream where Celestine could steer her towards the area most of interest to her. She learned more about the activities of Malraux and the head curator, and about their "delving in the cloisters," as she called it. At one point, Ducrozet had asked her if she could think of any connection between two very different carvings. Another time, Malraux had stretched himself over her desk and, in a wheedling voice, had asked if she was aware of the carvings of two doves on one of the pillars and if she thought they could represent a particular sign or portent. Celestine listened attentively. There was the merest germ of an idea starting to grow in her mind, and she wanted to gather as much relevant data as she could to help it emerge. When she left Catherine's house, after several hours, her hostess was quite garrulous, her face was flushed and she was slurring her words slightly. She kissed Celestine firmly on both cheeks as they said goodbye.

Celestine stood outside and took a deep breath. She looked around the road of small, but well-kept, respectable houses. She had drunk little except coffee, because she needed to stay sharp. It was time to increase the tempo and start leaning on the pressure points. It was also the time when she needed some space, to draw the patterns that had formed so far. She was excited, her brain was running with possibilities. She walked quickly through the streets of Lissac to the canal, expecting to see Jacques sitting on the bow deck, sketchbook in hand, looking out at the world through his startling, dark blue eyes. She felt more than disappointment when she realised he wasn't there. She felt a little uneasy, but more, she realised she had come to rely on him, on his earthiness, which was such a good balance to her own cerebral activities. She sat down with her notebooks and began to give her vague ideas a visual representation, the easier to spot any links or connections. When Jacques finally arrived, he found Celestine sitting on the floor of the salon surrounded by pages of diagrams, flowcharts and lists. She looked up at him and smiled, they touched hands and she gestured for him to sit down quickly.

'I have to work through this. Just give me a few minutes,' she said. Quietly, almost in a whisper to herself, she said: 'There are always patterns. Sometimes you have to come from a different angle, or perspective, to see the edge of a shadow or a link, and then when you see it, you can't unsee it again.' She let her mind wander over the pages spread out on the floor. They were carefully arranged so that from side to side was one line but also up and down and crossways too. 'You can't be rigid; you need order and rationality to gather the data, but then you have to let your subconscious mind take over and make the connections, see the unseen.' But she knew there were pieces missing, crucial pieces that would offer reasons, and explain some of the actions and the facts. It was hard to imagine what these pieces could be. She could hold complex equations in her head, she was meticulous and methodical, and once all the pieces were present she could shift them and juggle them in her mind without dropping or misplacing them. But what she lacked right now was a sense of where to go to get those missing pieces. What she needed was Jacques' uncanny intuition.

Celestine looked up, Jacques was sitting absolutely still, watching her with an expression of admiration, but with just a little wryness, shown by the slightly raised eyebrows.

'What?' she demanded.

'Nothing. You are the queen of the flowcharts. Magnificent.' He smiled. Celestine stood up and stretched. She leaned over and kissed Jacques on the forehead.

'I am so glad to see you,' she said. 'I have a nervousness in my stomach. I've had it since you left.' She sat back. 'I want to know what happened with Ducrozet today, but let me tell you first.' Celestine briefly described her lunch with Catherine Tallandier, and the information she had gathered, pointing to various papers where the details were noted. Then she described following the man from the boat.

'Jean-Michel Palomer,' said Jacques. 'The son of Monsieur Palomer, who owns that estate we were looking at yesterday.' When Celestine came to the point where she described how the man had spent five minutes looking at Ducrozet's house, Jacques interrupted again. 'Casing do you think? Waiting for someone?'

'I don't know. He had a very good look and he took some photos. It made me shiver, Jacques. I think I've been uneasy since that moment. All through the lunch I kept thinking about it.'

'Casing for what?' asked Jacques. 'To break in? Perhaps he thinks Ducrozet has some information, the letter for example. Or does Ducrozet hold the information and this guy is aiming to extract it by force?' Jacques stared intensely at the papers on the floor. 'If that's the case, then Ducrozet is in danger, and I've just brought him back to his family.'

Celestine held up her hand. 'That's what I thought at first. My blood ran cold when I realised what he had been looking at. But if he did try something at Ducrozet's home, with his family there, he would completely expose himself, and any other theories about the two murders would go out of the window. It would all be linked.' Celestine looked up at Jacques. 'No, I think Ducrozet is safe for now, but we can't be complacent. Anyone who can murder two people in cold blood, including a nun, is a psychopath and a risk taker.'

Jacques nodded, but he was still uncomfortable. 'Perhaps I should ask Desmarais to arrange a regular check on him.'

'If they have the manpower,' said Celestine. 'But listen, killing is "in extremis," it's the last resort in most cases, when other courses of action have failed, or when you are certain of the consequences of inaction. Our killer must have believed, without a reasonable doubt, that Malraux had information that was dangerous or detrimental to him. Likewise, with the nun. He, I believe it is a he, must have had some proof, acceptable to his admittedly warped mind, that the communication between them was at a level where the nun could also have proven dangerous. How did he ascertain that?' Celestine sat up on the bench, stretched out her arms and linked her fingers. 'There must have been some communication between Malraux and the killer, and it must have included enough detail to propel the killer into action.'

Jacques went into the galley and returned with two glasses of wine.

'Catherine told me that this Jean-Michel was a frequent visitor to the Abbey. Doing some family research, he said.'

'And Ducrozet knows more,' said Jacques. 'He's slowly thawing out, but he was frozen with terror, and shame. I believe we'll be able to get more from him tomorrow at the Abbey.'

'Tomorrow?' said Celestine surprised.

'Yes, after the services. I've arranged to meet him there. We need to find out exactly what Malraux was looking for, and why someone would see that as a threat.'

'What's your hunch, Jacques? What's your intuition telling you?' asked Celestine.

Jacques sat back and pondered for a minute or two. 'My intuition tells me that this murder, these murders, were planned, they're not random. They're a panel in a screen, like a rood screen. Panel one leads to panel two and suddenly panel twelve, or whatever, links right back to number one again. This is no petty vengeance or anger. This is cold. And cold can strike again. We must move quickly. If this Jean-Michel is our man, and although he feels very unclean to me, we don't know that for sure. He could just have been fleeing a jealous husband.'

Celestine scoffed. 'And his casing of Ducrozet's house? We need to find out everything we can about him, as soon as possible, and rule him in or rule him out. Tomorrow will be crucial, we must make progress.'

Just then Jacques' mobile phone rang. He reached for it and grunted.

'Yes, Paul.' He was silent for three or four minutes, only interrupting twice to confirm the details. He put down the phone and Celestine looked at him quizzically. Jacques appeared shaken, and his hand stroked the tip of his beard. 'That was Desmarais,' he said finally. 'He believes they're likely to formally place the Bulgarian under investigation for the murder of Malraux. Apparently, some new evidence came to light this afternoon.'

'What evidence?' demanded Celestine, sharply.

'He was killed with some kind of an agricultural knife; the forensic opinion has just been confirmed. They searched the Bulgarian's house this afternoon and found some more material. I don't know what else.'

'They're actually placing him under investigation? Which means they think he did it.'

'Not yet. Waiting for the Examining Magistrate, according to Desmarais.' Celestine looked stunned.

'There's more,' said Jacques. 'They have a woman in custody, a Polish woman. Apparently, she's admitted coming to Lissac to kill Sister Agnieszka, but she denies actually doing it. Says she chickened out. General feeling is, it won't take long to find enough evidence to place her under investigation too.'

They sat in silence looking at the floor. Jacques threw back the wine in his glass and went through to the galley to pour himself another one. When he returned with the bottle, Celestine was rocking backwards and forwards, muttering to herself. He couldn't hear what she was saying, so he leaned closer and put his head next to hers.

'They're wrong again. They're wrong.' She glanced up at him with a haunted look. 'Jacques, they're wrong again,' she said.

Jacques looked out of the window at the dark waters of the canal. Time to move on, he thought. Time to take Celestine farther away, time to let the gentle motion of the boat on the water soothe the old sores that still keep erupting. More time to heal. He rested his hand on her shoulder. 'Time to move on, do you think?' he asked. She looked up at him and glared, her expression was scathing, but she said nothing to him, nothing at all.

Chapter Twenty-Seven

Lissac-sur-Tarn: October 1943

Only a few hours left.

Samuel Joseph Steinbach climbed unsteadily down the wooden ladder. He stood momentarily on the stone floor and looked up. He moved his head slowly from side to side, it seemed well concealed. He had no more time. He carried the ladder back along the track and lifted it over the stone wall that edged the copse. He was breathing heavily; the thick winter suit and woollen overcoat were unseasonal for the time of the year, and he was sweating uncomfortably. With a silk handkerchief, he wiped away the beads of sweat that ran down his face from beneath his trilby hat. He started walking briskly along the track to the house. Leaning against the wall at the side of the house was a bicycle. On the pannier were strapped a small leather suitcase and a valise. He took a last look at the house, now shuttered up and silent, and he turned away and started cycling up the drive. A man was standing in the garden of the small cottage at the end of the drive where it met the road. Steinbach stopped and addressed him.

'You must look to the vines, Marcel,' he said. 'There's much to do.'

The man raised his head slightly and looked him directly in the eyes. *He knows*, thought Steinbach. The man's eyes didn't change and his face was a blank. He didn't speak, it seemed as though there was nothing there. 'Oh well. Au revoir, Marcel,' he said, and cycled out and onto the road.

He reached Lissac in less than an hour and stopped at the foot of the hill that led to the Convent. He decided to push the bicycle ahead of him up the hill, although by this time he was deeply red in the face, and his clothes were sticking to him with perspiration. He pulled the bell chain by the small door at the Convent, and after some minutes it was opened by a young, sturdy nun who hauled his bicycle over the threshold and leaned it against the wall.

'Leave that there, monsieur,' she said. 'It'll not go anywhere.'

Steinbach thanked her and made his way across the courtyard to the main building. He asked to see the Mother Superior, Sister Beatrice, and was shown down a long, musty corridor into a small enclave where there was a single, hard, wooden bench. He sat in the gloom, it was at least cooler here, and he could feel his heartbeat slowing. He looked at the wooden figure of Christ on the cross, attached to the wall opposite.

Such anguish, he thought. Religions, all religions, are moulded in such anguish. Yes, it was very hard for a man to believe.

The Mother Superior was very old and her back was stooped. She waved Steinbach to a chair and sat behind her desk facing him. She looked at him, not unkindly, but puzzled, there was a drawn, fixed look to her lined face. Like a sculpture in the making, he thought; the moment she dies the sculpture will be complete, and there will no longer be even the suggestion of a movement in her face.

He sat up, rigid, hands on his knees and his hat on the floor beside the chair. He opened his valise and took from it two packets, a larger one and a smaller one. He put the larger one on the desktop and opened it; it contained two cloth bags. He pulled open the drawstrings and let a small stream of gold coins tip onto the desktop. The Mother Superior looked at the coins, then up at Steinbach, indicating her surprise with only the slightest movement of her eyes.

'I wish, Reverend Mother,' began Steinbach, 'to make a donation to the Convent, to the sisters, to you.' He stumbled a little on the words. 'I also wish to make a donation to the sisters at the Convent in Auvillar.' And he picked up the second bag and placed it alongside the first. 'I am aware,' his voice sounded hoarse and strained, but the nun nodded very slightly to indicate that he should continue, that the timbre of the voice was of no matter.

'I am aware of the many good works you do, and that the sisters in Auvillar have done, in protecting the children in this time of ....

turbulence. I should like to thank you and to help you in your good work.'

'That is generous of you, Monsieur Steinbach,' said the Mother Superior.

'No, I don't think so. I think it is a duty,' continued Steinbach. 'The children are our future. A future that I firmly believe will be better than the one we are living through at this time.' He paused. 'I have also a request to make.' The nun remained silent and motionless, so he continued. 'I have a small package here. It's a letter, some simple keepsakes, nothing of value, but I would like you to keep it safely, here in your archives,' he looked questioningly.

'We retain many documents, mostly ancient, but others entrusted to us over the years,' affirmed the Mother Superior quietly.

'The package is for my son. I do not know where he is at this time, but I believe he is safe and therefore it is better that I do not know where he is. But I expect one day he will be able to join the wider community again, and that he will come here to collect this package.'

'Does he know of its existence?'

'Not specifically, but I hope to get word. He would expect me to leave something.'

'You are leaving us then, Monsieur Steinbach?' said the Mother Superior, a tinge of sadness in her voice.

'I fear it is inevitable,' he replied quietly. 'But I hope, sister, yes I hope.' He stopped. 'Will you take care of this for my son, David Samuel Steinbach, and let no other person have access to it.' He thrust it across the desktop. She rested her hand briefly on the package.

'You have my word, Monsieur Steinbach.'

Steinbach rose to leave. He put forward his hand towards the Mother Superior and she took it firmly in both her thin, bony hands.

'I will pray for you, Monsieur Steinbach,' she said. 'I will pray for you and your family.'

Steinbach smiled. He turned around as he opened the door and looked again at the package. The Mother superior was still sitting, quietly looking at him.

'Thank you,' he said and closed the door behind him. He crossed the courtyard, deep in thought, and as he reached the gate the young nun appeared beside him. He untied the suitcase from the pannier and stood it beside his feet. 'Sister,' he said, 'this bicycle, I find I have really no more use for it after all.' He put his hand on the saddle. 'It is a very sturdy machine. Would it be of any use to you or the sisters, perhaps in your visits to the poor or the market?'

The nun smiled, 'Why yes, monsieur, but you see, there is a slight problem. This bicycle was designed for a man. I am not sure that our vestments would fit very comfortably, or very properly, on either side of the bar there.' She laughed, and for the first time in a long while, Steinbach smiled.

'Of course, sister, foolish of me,' he said.

'But perhaps, if you have no further use for it, we could find someone who could benefit from such a bicycle and who, at this time, cannot afford to buy one,' suggested the nun.

'Yes, that's the answer, excellent. Please, dispose of it as you think fit.' He smiled again and the nun's broad, plain face beamed.

'Then thank you, monsieur. Bless you, and the Lord be with you.' She opened the door, and Steinbach, in some strange sense feeling lighter, almost unburdened, hurried down the hill to the town once more.

He had one more call to make. The office of Maître Vautour, the notary, was in a row of fine old houses just off the main square. Steinbach rang the bell, and after a few minutes a tall, thin man, wearing thick spectacles, and with a pinched, supercilious expression, opened the door and peered out.

'I wish to see Maître Vautour,' said Steinbach firmly. The clerk escorted him to a waiting area on the landing at the top of the wide stairs.

'Maître Vautour is currently engaged,' said the clerk. Steinbach thought quickly. He took another folio size packet from his valise. It was sealed with string and wax.

'Then no problem,' he said. 'I just wished to return this.' He held up the packet. 'I don't need to disturb him.'

'One moment, sir,' said the clerk. He walked along the corridor and tapped on the door of one of the offices. He disappeared inside for a few minutes and then emerged and walked back.

'That's all in order, sir,' he said. 'You can leave the packet with me. Maître Vautour says thank you for its return.' Steinbach handed the packet to the clerk.

'It's sealed,' he said. 'Perhaps it should remain so.'

The clerk smiled patronisingly. 'I can assure you that Maître Vautour will know how to handle it correctly, monsieur.'

Steinbach thanked him and walked slowly down the steps. Now everything was in place. Now, there was nothing more to be done. He crossed the market square and walked slowly, with his suitcase and valise, through the quiet, ancient streets down to the river. He looked long at the dark swirling waters; the rains had brought the first spate for many months. He sat down on a small wooden bench beneath a plane tree that was even now casting its long yellow leaves. He sat there quietly for half an hour, his heart beating a little faster than normal, as he watched the waters lap against the bank. He heard the footsteps first, clunky and brisk. He looked up. Two gendarmes in dusty, cheap-cloth uniforms, came on either side of him. They grabbed an arm each and pulled him to his feet.

'Pick up your case, Jew.' One of them said. He picked up his case. The other gendarme took hold of the valise and let go of Steinbach's arm to open it. He pushed his hand inside, then yelped in pain as something snapped on his finger ends. He drew his hand out, cursing. On the end of his bleeding fingers was a mousetrap.

'A rat trap,' said Steinbach calmly. 'They are such a problem at this time of the year, after the harvest.' The gendarme cursed again and eased the trap from fingers that were bleeding in several places.

'What's in it?' asked the other gendarme.

'Nothing, it's empty.' He put his good hand tentatively in the various pockets of the valise. 'It's empty,' he said, and with an anger born of pain and disappointment, hurled the valise far out into the river. Steinbach watched it float for a while, and then slowly sink into the dark waters.

'Come on, Jew,' said the injured gendarme, as he took hold of Steinbach again. 'We have a place just right for you.'

Chapter Twenty-Eight

Celestine crossed herself self-consciously with two fingers and sat down on one of the wooden chairs near the front of the church. She couldn't remember how many years had passed since she had attended a Sunday service. Funerals, a wedding, a memorial service, social and professional imperatives; but not since she was a teenage girl had she chosen to join the congregation of Sunday worshippers. She was trying to establish, within herself the reasons why she was here. Why had she chosen to do this? She was distraught, angry and frustrated. She was deeply concerned that these murders were slipping away, that the wrong paths were being taken; and she had had so much hard experience of that. But why had she felt the imperative to come to this service, on this day? She thought perhaps that in some way she was trying to commemorate and honour the two victims. Was it reverting to childhood, looking for innocence or perhaps certainty? She did not believe, not for a minute, in the idea of a God. But she was here, and she was disturbed, and she was searching for answers.

She looked around; nuns, dressed all in white, walked serenely up and down the aisles, greeting people, smiling at the children. Like holy cheerleaders, she thought. People kept coming in. She hadn't expected the numbers, she had thought there might only be a handful of diehards, but she calculated that there were more than a hundred people in the congregation. And they weren't all old; there were young and middle-aged, men and women, children and teenagers. Celestine was surprised, and she started to feel more comfortable, it had the air of a large family gathering. The priest entered, he was short, and from an Asian background, which was another surprise to her. All the priests in her youth had been tall, hairy, hook-nosed Caucasians, and had seemed stern and unsympathetic. Dressed in his wide purple robes, this priest walked slowly up the aisle before the service commenced, greeting people in the congregation. He said good day to her and smiled, and she felt included.

A few minutes later the organ music struck up, and there was a sense of anticipation as the small procession of candle-carrying altar boys, a server swinging a censer from which clouds of incense arose, and the priest, walked slowly down the aisle to the altar. The smell of the incense took Celestine back twenty-five years, to a time of relative innocence and security, and she could feel that, despite herself, she was being gently absorbed into the community, and it was comforting.

She stood, sat, lowered her head and replied automatically to the chants. The words came back to her as though she had never been away. There was a sombre mention of the two violent deaths in the community, and she could sense the ripple of tension, like a stiffening through the crowd. She dropped coins into the red cloth bag held out to her by a short round lady dressed in exactly the same colour red. But she couldn't stop looking towards the row of five nuns sitting in the choir loft, and wondering if there might ordinarily be a sixth.

When the congregation stood and started queueing to receive the sacrament, she remained seated. She looked towards the tableau of Christ being lowered into the coffin, and saw again Sister Agnieszka's face, saw the horror and the fear when she was told about the death of Malraux. She had certainly recognised the import of the news. At that moment, she must have gained a sense of the danger she was in. Malraux must have shared enough with her. Would she have helped him otherwise? He was hardly someone she would ordinarily be sympathetic to, you would have thought.

Celestine stared at the emaciated body of Christ, and in her mind, she saw the nun, her small, taut body, being lowered into her own coffin. She thought about Malraux, in all his promiscuousness and exuberance, and she saw him being lowered into his coffin. Jesus wept. She had listened to the priest encouraging the saints to intercede on behalf of the world's sinners. All of us, thought Celestine, all the world's sinners. But saints didn't intercede, a God didn't listen to prayers, humans interceded. We are all sinners apparently, but some sins are more than that. The sin of murder, that's more than sin, that is evil. Celestine was aware that her thoughts were being coloured by the atmosphere in the church, but it was actually helping her, giving her clarity, good and evil. Evil must be punished. God punishes, except he, it, doesn't. Saints intercede, except they don't. People intercede; they intercede on the side of those sinned against, the victims. Wasn't that why she had joined the police force all those years ago? To intercede, and where had that got her? No longer a police officer, no longer an official interceder. But she was damned, unfortunate choice of phrase, but she would be damned if she didn't try to intercede in this case now. She had seen in her mind's eye the coffins being lowered into the ground. There was someone out there, someone who had chosen to take the darkness, to take life, for their own selfishness and protection. She sat back in the chair and closed her eyes, she could feel the tears welling up. The priest was rounding things up with a story of Christ's intervention. The words meant nothing to her - just fairy tales dressed up in learning, stories given credence by centuries of repetition, given power by the drama of the architecture, and the dead weight of centuries.

But it was somehow relaxing, this giving up of personal volition, if only for a few moments. And when the young couple standing in front of her turned, shook her hand and offered a blessing, she forgot the words and mumbled at them, and smiled, and she felt this was a counterweight to her dark thoughts.

She let it drift over her, the intoning of the priest, the childlike responses from the congregation. She closed her eyes for a few minutes, then a loud thud woke her from her reverie. The great wooden doors had clattered as people were leaving. She looked around, she hadn't realised the service was over. She hurried away down the aisle, she didn't want to have any contact with the servants of the church. It struck her, as she pulled open the door that she felt like an impostor, an adherent of another religion or no religion. What was a Jew doing, studying in a catholic abbey? It wasn't religious, it wasn't a study of religious artefacts or doctrinal history. This was a Jewish quest, a search for Jewish documents and Jewish historical artefacts. Jewish answers.

Celestine crossed the street and sat down at a table in the café opposite. She ordered a coffee and took out her notebook and phone. She called Jacques.

'When are you bringing Ducrozet to the Abbey?'

'I'm not.' He sounded surprised. 'I thought... I've been preparing the boat.'

'No. Bring Ducrozet to the Abbey as soon as you can. I'm in the café across the street. I thought you told me you were bringing him here today.'

'I did, but then... but I haven't spoken to him.'

'Bring him here as soon as possible.'

'Yes, Capitaine,' said Jacques testily, and ended the call.

Twenty minutes later, Jacques arrived with Ducrozet who was looking as furtive and uncomfortable as on the previous day.

'Jean-Luc, this is my partner Celestine Courbet, former capitaine of police in Bordeaux.' They shook hands. Ducrozet looked at her curiously out of the corner of his eyes.

'Let's go to the Abbey,' said Celestine, without preamble. 'I want to talk to you about the Jewish connection.'

In the foyer, they sat down on the benches. It was cool and a little gloomy, but Ducrozet didn't want to switch on the lights as the abbey was closed to the public.

'They're like moths,' he said. Celestine shook her head impatiently.

'Tell me, Jean-Luc. Why was a Jewish scholar rooting around in a Christian religious building? What on earth was he looking for?' Ducrozet sat with his hands on his knees and his head slightly bowed and took a deep breath.

'The Jewish connection,' he said. 'I'm not sure that's the correct phrase. I would say it was a personal connection with a Jewish association, a colouring perhaps.' He paused. 'Malraux's grandfather died a few months ago, in Paris I believe, or near, in one of the suburbs. A deathly, dull place. Nevertheless, Malraux visited his grandfather shortly before his demise. His grandfather, and as happens at these times, as one reaches the cusp, the edge of mortality, secrets that have lain buried for years, surface. An urgency you understand, an urgency to leave everything in the open, a last chance before the gates clang shut, as it were.'

Celestine sucked the air in through her teeth, and Jacques nodded wearily. 'Please go on, Jean-Luc.'

'Well. Malraux's grandfather told him that, as a boy, during the war you understand, he had lived with a family, no, had been placed with a family, a gentile, farming family, near the town of Dunes, which is some thirty kilometres from here.'

'Placed there why?' asked Jacques.

'Why, to keep him from the Nazis.' Ducrozet looked affronted. 'After the fall of the Vichy government, the invaders began to round up Jews all over the country in greater numbers, in areas that had previously been considered relatively safe. Lissac-sur-Tarn, rather splendidly, played a large part in the saving of those children, protecting them, absorbing them into catholic families to keep them safe. Papers. The offices of the Maire at the time and the Prefecture in Montauban were found to have supplied false papers, ration books, and travel warrants for these children. It was quite marvellous. You must visit the museum in Quai de Vieux Port. The story is told there. There was a school, children, Jewish children and adolescents, from all over France and Europe came to Lissac-sur-Tarn. There they were taught to be farmers, blacksmiths, and bookbinders etc. It was the major centre in the south-west of France. Oh yes. Ten Medals, "Righteous Among The Nations", were awarded to citizens of this town and region. Ten; for saving the lives of five hundred Jewish children. Five hundred.' Ducrozet looked up, there was at last a light in his eyes, a flicker of enthusiasm.

'And Malraux's grandfather was one of those children,' confirmed Celestine.

'Yes. He was placed with this family and stayed with them for quite a few years, until well after the war. But then, as a young adult, he moved to Paris, became a businessman of some kind. Design business. Something. Anyway, as he lay dying, he told Malraux that his father, Malraux's great-grandfather, had lived at Lissac-sur-Tarn, and that he had helped establish some kind of a Jewish community here. This was of interest to Malraux of course, but the grandfather admitted that there was more. Within the family it was believed that the great-grandfather had left something behind for his son. He never came back you see. Taken to the death camps. Left something behind of value, great value. Although of course, these stories through the ages, through the different generations, tend to gain a somewhat excessive, exotic attraction, an excessive value. The patina of time, you see, gives old tales an attraction, a beauty that does not always survive reality when it is breached.'

'So, Malraux came here to find what his great-grandfather had left all those years before,' said Celestine.

'Yes.'

'Didn't any other members of the family come looking in the last eighty years?' asked Jacques.

'Perhaps they did. Perhaps they drew a blank, perhaps they became too busy with their own lives. Malraux's father was an accountant who died when he was very young. They do not seem to have had a very strong lineage. I don't think there were many uncles or aunts or cousins. Which is unusual, I think, fecundity being a recognised attribute of the tribe.' Celestine snorted.

'So why now, why Malraux?' asked Jacques.

'Malraux's grandfather left him a little bit of money, but not much. So, being of, what shall I say, a quixotic nature?'

'A tilter at windmills,' suggested Jacques.

'Perhaps. A restlessness or unease with standing still. And I think he thought, he hoped, there would be some major pecuniary advantage in it for him.'

'Money,' said Jacques.

'Quite so, but,' Ducrozet paused for effect and glanced quickly at them both, 'I think, yes I believe, that the search became more, a quest, a quest for more than money, for his history, and yes, for even more, for the history of the Jewish people.' Jacques looked dubious.

'Do you think perhaps you are being carried away a little by the fond memories you have of him?' he said.

'Let's stick to the facts then,' said Celestine. 'What did he discover?' Ducrozet looked down uncertainly, and brushed his knees with his fingers.

'Jean-Luc,' said Jacques sternly. 'We need to know, you agreed to tell. This could be vital information. We are not interested in money, gold or treasure. If we found it, it would surely belong to Malraux's family.'

'What there is left of them,' murmured Ducrozet.

'Ok. We want to find out who murdered Malraux and Sister Agnieszka and bring them to justice. This just may help.' said Celestine.

Ducrozet hesitated, and then with a deep sigh began. 'Malraux found a package, a letter and a few other minor items.'

'Where? At the Convent?' asked Celestine.

'Yes, at the Convent. The package had been left there. They have no record of when, but we can assume. They have a kind of archive, but I think it's quite disorganised, shambolic he called it. But then, even the convents were ransacked at different times, and items may have been left in the wrong era, or category. Anyway, after many days he found it.'

'Was it addressed to his grandfather?' asked Celestine.

'Yes, it was. And inside was a letter dated October 1943.'

'Did you see the letter?' asked Jacques.

Ducrozet shook his head. 'No, he wouldn't show it to me. He wanted my help, but he wouldn't trust me with that. He liked to play games you see. Cruel little games. It excited him.' His eyes dropped.

'What do you know of the contents, and where do you think the letter is now?'

'In reverse order; I would say that the letter is now sitting in some evidence box. Do they have such things?' he looked up at Celestine. 'Sitting among his belongings at the police station. They took all his things away.'

'Of course they did,' said Celestine.

'And your first point. What do I know of its contents? Well, let me think.' He paused again and looked, as if for inspiration, at the ground between his feet. Jacques tapped his feet impatiently. 'There was a code,' he said finally.

'A code?'

'Yes, seven sets of numbers; sixty-seven, fifty-three, forty-seven, sixty-nine, fifty-four, twenty-five, seventy-five.'

'You remember.'

'Oh yes. You see Malraux was convinced that the code related to something at the Abbey, more specifically to the cloisters. He told me the code so that I could help him to "crack it". In the cloisters, yes. I am the leading authority on them, as I'm sure you know.'

'Did Sister Agnieszka know the code and the contents of the letter?' asked Celestine earnestly.

'I think she must have done. I know she helped him at the Convent, even pointed him in the right direction in the first place. They talked a lot, you know. I think he trusted her. She was quite an authority herself on certain aspects of the Abbey. Though not of course on an academic level. Yes, they talked, but I got the impression it was as much for the company. That's strange isn't it, for a man who might engage himself with a dozen different companions at any one time. Yes, I think she was company, unthreatening, understanding, sexless, yes that's it.'

'And the code, did you make any progress on that at all?'

'He told me it related to a location, a geophysical location. But that was all.'

'And you spent how many days working on the code?' asked Celestine.

'Oh, no more than two perhaps. He was not very exigent in the searches, for a scholar. He was, as I say, restless. He would start with great vigour and enthusiasm, but if there was little headway made, he would storm off and leave me to continue the search. And I had a lot of other things to do.'

'In short, you made no progress in cracking the code, but you believe it relates to a geophysical position. The answer, yes? The information provided by the unravelling of the code, would lead to a geophysical position?' Celestine tried desperately to get Ducrozet to clarify his thoughts.

'No,' he said sharply. 'Code, not a code, a puzzle, an interpretation, that's what he said was needed. These numbers are a signpost, a prompt towards something, which, if interpreted correctly, could offer a solution. The solution being the location of something.'

Jacques stood up and walked heavily around the edges of the foyer. He couldn't tell if Ducrozet was being deliberately obtuse, or if his way of talking was just a result of his years in the academic closet. Celestine was more patient.

'Come on, Jean-Luc. You must have thought about these numbers, and how they are linked to the Abbey structure and artefacts. You must have.'

'Yes, well, yes we did. Initially, we followed a number of lines of research. As you say, how could these numbers refer to the Abbey and its architecture or its history? The simplest, the most obvious, too obvious I might say, is that the numbers, split into couples or pairs, relate to the pillars around the courtyard. You see there are one hundred and eighteen pillars, and if we number them, as we do, in an anti-clockwise direction beginning at the west gallery, through that door there - the entrance door. In the guide you see, that is how we number them. Well, perhaps you've seen.'

'So, fourteen could refer to the fourteenth pillar in this system of yours.'

'Just so.'

'And did you use this system to check each of the numbers against the pillars?'

'Well, yes, we did, only briefly you understand, briefly.'

'And?'

'And nothing. They are pillars. Each pillar has a subject matter carved into the stone capitals. A story, scenes from the bible. We didn't make a list. If I'm honest, it seemed, nebulous. It was a difficult time. It was hard to focus, to pin him down.'

'Despite the fact that this was the culmination of the work he came here to do?' said Jacques loudly.

'Yes, yes. He was not…. consistent.'

Celestine leaned over and placed her hands on top of his. 'Jean-Luc, this is very important. This system you have of numbering the pillars, is it a recent thing, or have they always been numbered in that way? Would it have been a system in use in, for example, 1943?'

Ducrozet raised his head, not looking Celestine in the face, but his eyes moved up to the right to stare at the ceiling. 'I cannot be sure,' he said. 'No, I believe not. I will need to look into this, you understand. There are sources; for example, Shapiro, Romanesque Sculpture. Henry-Claude….'

Jacques interrupted. 'Specifically. Was there a similar system of numbers? Was it clockwise or anticlockwise? Was it from the same starting point in 1943? That's what's relevant. That was when this puzzle was created by Malraux's great-grandfather. Do we agree?' Celestine nodded.

'I'll start right away,' said Ducrozet as he stood up.

'Good. Will you open up the cloisters for us please,' said Celestine.

Inside the quadrangle, in the cool of the cloisters, Celestine looked around slowly. The carvings and stonework were a tribute to man's skill and dedication to a religion - a religion to live or die for. Peace, tranquillity and a sense of permanence seemed to seep from the stones. Was it this sense of permanence that had attracted Malraux's great-grandfather to choose this place to set his puzzle? A place that had survived for eight hundred years or more. There would be an assurance in that, a certainty in a very uncertain time. When Jewish culture, businesses and people were being destroyed by the barbarism of the Nazis, the solidity, the constancy of this catholic edifice must have recommended itself, it would still be here whenever his ancestors came searching. Of course, he couldn't have known how long it would take, some eighty years or so. No, he would have expected it to be his son collecting the packet, looking at the code, smiling, because he knew what those numbers referred to.

'It cannot be so difficult,' she suddenly said out loud. 'We are talking about a puzzle created by a man for his son, his young son, to solve. There must have been some connection, some link, a clue or a key, something his son could have used, something from his past with his father.'

'That doesn't help us,' said Jacques.

'Yes, it does really, don't you see. We can't know what the father and the son did together, spoke about together. But it couldn't have been complex. If the son was unable to solve the puzzle, then all of it would have been in vain.' She paused, her mind was moving slowly through the patterns. 'We need to definitively identify the seven pillars. Seven pillars.'

'The seven pillars of wisdom,' said Jacques, surprising himself again with his reservoir of religious references.

'Perhaps that is also relevant. Ducrozet needs to confirm the numbering system. Then we need to look at each story, each representation, and the meanings. But, we need to see it all through the eyes of a child, not the world-weary eyes of two distracted scholars.' She turned in the direction of Ducrozet's office and raised her eyebrows. Jacques nodded in agreement.

'Ok, let's give it a go.' Celestine turned her head to look at him. She smiled at the slightly startled look on his face. He had been running his fingers repeatedly through his hair and it was standing on top of his head like silver furrows. He smiled back.

'You take point on this,' he said.

Celestine led them to one of the pillars at random. They stood in front of it and then to the side, looking at the intricacies of the pictures carved in stone.

'Once we know for sure what the system used in 1943 was, I want to take photos of them. We need to look at the imagery; are there clues in that? And I want you to sketch it from the photos. You've said before that when you draw you seem to go deeper inside the subject.'

'All right, we can start work as soon as we know,' said Jacques. 'But can I suggest we discuss it further over lunch? I am in danger of wasting away here.'

Celestine snorted. 'There's a bit to go yet,' she said. 'But yes, let's do that.'

They left Ducrozet in his office where he had several books open on his desk. 'Progress, I think,' he called to them, looking up briefly. 'One or two more sources for confirmation, but it looks very like the numerical system used not only in 1943 but indeed before 1930, when there were some major repairs done to the surrounding structure, was indeed different. I believe I knew that. Of course I did. Leave it with me. I'll complete my research, time is of the essence, isn't it?' Celestine waved.

'Time is of the essence. How long can it reasonably take?' whispered Jacques. 'I bet there's a single book that would give me a definitive answer in two minutes, but he's cross-referencing it with twenty other sources and writing a paper on it as we speak. The species academicus in its natural habitat.'

Celestine laid her hand on his arm. 'Gently, he's had a hell of a time. Cut him some slack.'

The café was busy with Sunday lunchtime patrons; whole families, from children to grandparents, were noisily eating, drinking and talking. Particularly talking. At times it was difficult to hear themselves speak. Jacques was expounding an idea that he had been considering for a little while.

'I ought to visit Monsieur Palomer. I need to know what kind of man he is, and his son. I want to know whether they are capable of committing murder. And I may pick up a pointer, some understanding of their concerns, if they have any. I feel it might be valuable.'

'How?' asked Celestine bluntly.

'As a dealer in antiques. We know Palomer has a taste for fine furniture.'

'And less fine.'

'Ok. But the point is, I can introduce myself as a former colleague of Monsieur Pelissier, and even mention that I helped him with the location of a few pieces. I still have some business cards. A courtesy call, since I am visiting the area.'

Celestine looked dubious. 'Don't mention you're living on a barge.'

'No, of course not. It would just give me a legitimate, believable reason to talk to him. See how the land lies. Know your enemy. If he is.'

'Enough. When were you thinking of going?'

'Today, this afternoon.'

'On a Sunday?'

'Why not. I can suggest that I'm having a weekend away, staying with friends.'

'And how will you get there?' asked Celestine.

'By boat,' said Jacques triumphantly, feeling that he was slaying each argument as it arose. 'I have the key to Ducrozet's boat. I kept it to stop him from running or sailing away again. I can motor up there, moor it near the boathouse, and wander up the lawns, cackling maniacally like a peacock.' Celestine wasn't smiling.

'You must be careful, Jacques.'

'Have you heard from Henri, today? Has there been any movement on the river?'

'He hasn't called.'

'I'll stop off on the way back. Check up on him.'

Celestine looked across the street to the Abbey door. 'Two hours ago, you were preparing the boat to leave,' she said, looking back.

'I thought this whole... investigation was over. But you clearly decided, sometime through the night, that it wasn't. So, I'm with you. Always. I'm not convinced either that there isn't a connection to these murders. I don't know what it is, but it could be very interesting to find out. A real live puzzle for you. If that's good for you then I'm on board.'

'And for you?' asked Celestine

Jacques looked pensive and his eyes hardened. 'Gut feeling. There's something bothering me about these Palomers. The guy running, the same guy staring at poor old Ducrozet's house. I want to put that to bed.'

'Then I'll say it again. Be bloody careful, Jacques.'

He smiled across at her. 'Earth belongs to the brave, but heaven to those who deserve it.'

'Basque proverb?' Jacques nodded his head.

Chapter Twenty-Nine

Jacques was dressed casually, but in his own view, elegantly, in light slacks and a blue linen jacket. He checked the fuel tanks in Ducrozet's boat. There were two jerry cans inside one of the lockers, and he topped the tank up to the brim. Laying his jacket down carefully on the seat beside him, he unhitched the painter and edged the boat gently out into the stream. The river was busier than the previous day, with families and weekend boaters meandering along the shallows on both sides. He moved further out into the mainstream and throttled up the engine. He wanted to arrive quickly; if this was a waste of time then he needed to minimise that. He had no clear plan as to his approach, but he did have a great deal of faith in his faculty of improvisation and of thinking on his feet.

 He passed Monsieur Lefebvre's boathouse, but he couldn't see him; - sleeping, foraging, or cycling perhaps. Although, Jacques didn't think he'd be far from his lookout post. He carried on up the river where the pleasure boats had thinned out, and he passed no one for nearly a kilometre until he saw ahead the smart, tiled roof of the Palomer's boathouse. Easing back on the throttle, he steered the boat gently alongside the jetty. He reached out, hooked the painter over a mooring post and pulled the boat tightly to the wooden sides. There was no one around. He felt a flutter of nerves now that he was actually there, but he took a deep breath and threw back his shoulders. He thought briefly of Celestine, and knew that in many ways he was doing this to impress her. Would this impress her? He tied the boat securely, and then very carefully opened the side door of the boathouse. The large white cruiser was there, gleaming as though it had never been out of its box. Cautiously, Jacques stepped around the bow of the cruiser to where he could see the outline of the black motorboat. In contrast to its larger neighbour, it looked grimy and marked. There were jagged scratches on one side, and a twig with leaves caught in the metal strip that ran along the top of the gunwale. There was a small puddle of water lying in the lowest part of the boat.

Feeling uneasy, he retreated and quietly closed the boathouse door. There was still no one in sight. He took another deep breath, slipped on his jacket and strode across the immaculate lawn towards the house.

The first person he saw there was a semi-naked woman stretched out on a cushioned lounger on the terrace.

'Good afternoon, madame,' he said and raised a finger in lieu of a hat.

'The fuck are you?' She sat up, raising her large sunglasses and glaring at him. She was wearing a flesh-coloured bikini, the only splash of colour being the startling red lips, toenails, and the ruby stud in her navel. Jacques stood stock still and looked straight back at her.

'I am Monsieur Jacques Lecoubarry, and I'm here to see Monsieur Palomer,' he said firmly and continued looking at her without wavering. Eventually, her eyes dropped as she waved a hand at him.

'He's in the, fuck knows, study, whatever,' she said and sank back on the lounger.

'Most helpful,' said Jacques, and walked towards the large French windows that led from the terrace. He looked briefly around: close up he could see the rows and rows of vines that were now clipped of their golden jewels, the amber grapes used to make the local, much sought-after wine. He realised that by coming up from the river he had arrived at the rear of the house, and was wondering whether to walk around to knock on the front door when the French windows opened, and a stern-looking, middle-aged woman stepped out.

'Monsieur?' She had a face like an angry bird; hair pulled back into a tight bun, and her face drawn forwards to a curved and beak-like nose. Slightly startled, Jacques nodded then smiled warmly.

'Bonjour, madame, I am so sorry. I realise now that I have come not to the main entrance of this magnificent house, but to the rear. But I came from the river you understand. Forgive me for this. I am here to see Monsieur Palomer.'

'You are?'

'Jacques Lecoubarry, madame.' He held out his hand, which she ignored.

'I am Monsieur Palomer's housekeeper. I was not expecting visitors today.' She looked past Jacques, as though there might already be a horde of day-trippers swarming across the lawns.

'No, it was unexpected for me, too, though I think it very opportune. I am staying in the vicinity for a few days and had the opportunity of using my friend's boat. When I was told of the location of Monsieur Palomer's chateau, I decided it would have been churlish of me not to call. We have had some dealings in the past you see. Monsieur Palomer and I.'

The woman looked suddenly wearied by Jacques' discourse. She held open the door and invited him in.

'Please sit, monsieur. I will see if Monsieur Palomer is available.'

Jacques remained standing and looked quickly around the room. It was a salon of sorts, although the ceiling was just not high enough, just a little too squat to be attractive. It was furnished with a mixture of antique pieces of different styles and epochs. He ran his hand along the underside of a large, oval, rosewood table, then looked quickly under the frame of one of the seats. The pictures on the walls were a mixture: with early, idealised landscapes in juxtaposition to portraits of stern, be-whiskered and tightly buttoned men. He heard a door slamming and the tread of heavy footsteps approaching. Monsieur Palomer walked into the room and stood directly in front of Jacques, looking at him intently.

'I don't know you,' he said loudly.

Jacques stayed silent for a moment, then looked at Palomer with a slightly puzzled expression, as though wanting to verify that this was actually the Monsieur Palomer he had been expecting to see.

'Ah. Monsieur Palomer. I am sorry that you don't remember. I do remember you. Certainly, I remember you.' He smiled and held out his hand.

'What? Who? Margot says you are Lecoubarry.'

'Jacques Lecoubarry. We met, oh some years ago. I don't recall if it was at Monsieur Pelissier's premises. No, I'm wrong. It was at one of the antiques fairs we attended.'

'Pelissier's dead.'

'I know. He was never strong. But he introduced us. You were looking for something, a piece, an exceptional piece, a Trictrac table, a Louis XVI Trictrac table. Pelissier knew of my contacts in other parts of France. I am in business in Bordeaux.' Jacques took out one of his cards and handed it to Palomer. 'The Trictrac table, very difficult to find in good, original condition. I located it for Pelissier. In Tours, I believe.'

'You found the Trictrac table?' demanded Palomer, his eyebrows inching slightly higher and lifting the hoods on his eyes.

'Yes, I did. I trust you still have possession of it?'

'Of course I have possession of it. D'you think I'd part with an item like that.' He looked down at the card again and then back at Jacques.

'I have no recollection of meeting you, Lecoubarry.'

'You are a very busy man, you meet very many people. Whereas I remember everyone in this business who has shown an interest in exceptional pieces.' Jacques waved his hands slowly around the room. 'So many fine pieces. Perhaps you might forget the introduction. I understand. Believe me, I am not put out.'

Palomer moved towards the centre of the room and placed his hand on the rosewood table.

'Ok. What're you doing here?' he demanded in a harsh, truculent voice.

'As I explained to your housekeeper,' began Jacques. 'I am visiting a friend in the neighbourhood, for a long weekend. I haven't been here since poor Claude Pelissier died. And I thought I would take it upon myself to visit you. To see, for example, if you still had the Trictrac table, and if so, whether you could be persuaded to part with it. I have a very motivated client you see. But also, I admit, to see whether I can be of service to you in the location of antique furniture. I am very well connected, more so even than in Pelissier's day. I wondered whether we could do some business together.'

'And you came by boat?'

'Yes. My friend lent me his boat for the afternoon.'

'Who's your friend?'

'Monsieur Lefebvre. A splendid old gentleman, retired engineer, a marvel at repairing mechanical devices. Lives in Castelnau. We share an interest in automata.'

Palomer stood motionless for a minute or so, neither his body nor his face moved in any way, although Jacques felt that behind the blank screen, the mind, like a scale, was weighing up the situation, calculating quickly the for and against. Finally, he said:

'I won't sell the Trictrac table, so you can forget that. But you can come and have a look at it and at a few other pieces. You can tell me what they're worth. Or what you say they're worth.' Palomer nodded to Margot, who had slid into the room and was standing behind Jacques.

'Bring us some drinks, M,' he said. 'Come this way.'

Palomer led Jacques down a well-lit corridor and opened the door into a spacious, light-filled room; a single-storied annexe at right angles to the main building, where arched windows opened onto the terrace and sunlight filtered in through stained-glass skylights. Jacques murmured appreciatively. Palomer walked over to the other side of the room and put his hand proprietorially on the polished top of the Louis XVI Trictrac table. Jacques stood silently, looking at it.

'I'd forgotten what a superb example this is,' he said shamelessly. 'It has everything. There are so few now. So many destroyed.' He moved closer. 'But you've been using the table for its original purpose.' He looked at Palomer as if he was seeing him in a new light. 'You play the game on it. You play Trictrac.' Palomer nodded.

'I do when I can find an opponent worth the trouble. My son plays, but he's useless, reckless. Trictrac is a game of thought and planning and decision-making. I excel at these.'

'Your son, I didn't know you had a son. Is he here?' asked Jacques.

'Somewhere, maybe in the vineyard.' Palomer appeared to suddenly lose interest. 'Anyway, the table's not for sale, so your journey's been a waste of time.' Jacques shrugged.

'How good a player are you?' he asked. Palomer looked at him, surprised.

'Of Trictrac? I am, I will say, the champion of Occitanie.' He laughed. 'Perhaps even further afield. I've won tournaments. I am rarely beaten. It is one of my passions. I find it a very suitable, what can I say, metaphor for life. It was rejected in the nineteenth century because it was seen as the game of choice of aristocrats. Foolish to reject something purely because of its associations, don't you think? But it is still the game of the elite.'

Jacques smiled. 'Indeed, it is. Then why don't we play a match and I will try to be a worthy opponent.'

Palomer looked surprised again. 'You know the game?'

'But of course,' said Jacques. 'I am a man who deals in antiquities.'

Chapter Thirty

Celestine sat in Ducrozet's office, watching him poring over the notes he had made. He reminded her of a fussy little rodent, scratching the earth to find a morsel to eat.

'Yes, as I thought - Schapiro,' he said, looking up at her. 'Schapiro.'

'Go on,'

'The system of numbering of the pillars included in Schapiro's exceptional work, although now dated, and subject to several revisions, or clarifications of my own. Meyer Schapiro's The Romanesque Sculpture of Lissac-sur-Tarn. This was the system of numbering commonly in use in the year 1943.'

Celestine stood up. 'Well done, Jean-Luc. We now have a basis on which to start. Let's look at the seven pillars referred to in the puzzle.' In order to be certain, Celestine asked Ducrozet to count the pillars with her. 'So, this is sixty-seven, according to the Schapiro system?'

'Yes, although by the current system number eleven.'

Celestine studied the capital - the flared, stone top of the pillar, which was carved with a delicate frieze of plants entwined and human figures. It was hard to make out at first sight.

'The anointing of David by the prophet Samuel,' said Ducrozet, and he stepped in front of Celestine and pointed to the carving. 'You see. Sometimes referred to as the Coronation of David. "Now he was ruddy and withal of a beautiful countenance and goodly to look at. And the Lord said. Arise, anoint him, for this is he".' Ducrozet smiled sadly at Celestine.

'Anointing, selecting?' Celestine queried.

'Literally smearing with oil; but ceremonially it applies or applied, to the conferring of an office, a holy office, or in this case, the King of the Jews.'

'This may seem a little obvious, or simple, but was Malraux's grandfather called David?' asked Celestine.

'Ah no, obvious but no. Sebastien, I believe. Sebastien.'

'Did Malraux tell you this?'

Ducrozet didn't answer; he was tracing his fingers along the outline of the figures on the frieze. Celestine tapped him firmly on the shoulder.

'Do you have any suggestion as to what this particular representation might mean?'

'Only that anointing is a kind of beginning, as I said, a confirmation of one who must hold high office, or in a less exalted sense, complete a sacred task or quest.'

Celestine stood quietly, looking at the intricate carvings on three faces of the capital. She leaned on the low wall between the pillars to look at the fourth face. She tried to imagine herself in the position of a man, eighty years before, attempting to create a puzzle, a message for his young son; a message not so obvious to the casual searcher but not too complex, so that a boy or young man, knowing his father's way of thinking, with his shared experiences, could understand.

They walked around to the North Gallery.

'Number fifty-three.'

'Three Hebrews in the fiery furnace,' said Ducrozet. Celestine raised her eyes again and looked at the tormented figures, arms in supplication, as the flames, like waves, flowed around them.

'Prophetic you might say,' said Ducrozet. 'Although, one must bear in mind that these representations, all of them in the Abbey, were intended to be educational for a largely illiterate population. The concept of the murderers of Jesus Christ being cast into the fiery pit, I am sure gave succour to many a Christian in the dark ages of the twelfth century.'

Celestine sucked in a deep breath. 'I think I shall take some photos of each of the seven pillars. And if I could borrow a copy of your excellent guide. I could use some air and an opportunity to work on this in my own space.'

Chapter Thirty-One

Margot arrived with a tray of drinks. 'Wine, pernod, Ricard, beer, which do you prefer?' she asked, as though they were selecting a method of self-harm.

'I think perhaps a glass of champagne would be the most refreshing,' said Jacques smiling.

'Champagne, yes of course. Margot, champagne. Now sit down Lecoubarry.'

'Jacques, please call me Jacques.'

'Very well. Marcel. Let us see if you are really a man of character or,' he made a dismissive gesture, 'fluff.' Palomer arranged the pieces on the board. He dropped a die into a beautiful, green, embossed leather cup, shook it and rolled it onto the table top. 'Five.'

He passed a similar cup in maroon to Jacques, who rubbed his fingers along the gold embossing.

'I don't remember these fine cups with the table, Marcel,' he said.

'No. I had them specially made. Now roll the die.'

'Four.'

'Very well. I'll start,' said Palomer eagerly.

'I see that you've set up the board so that you are white,' said Jacques quietly.

'Yes, d'you object?'

'It's just a fancy I have, it makes no difference, a question of guest's choice. But I would prefer it if you played black.' Palomer looked at him. Slightly aggravated he collected the checkers and set them up again on the opposite side.

'If you are happy now, I will start.'

He rolled two dice, a five and a one and moved a single checker to point six. Margot came in with the champagne. Breathing a little heavily, she extracted the cork with barely a whisper and poured out two glasses. Jacques took his with a smile towards the housekeeper. Palomer merely waved his hand at a small occasional table beside him. Margot placed the bottle in an ice bucket on a stand. Art Deco, Jacques noticed. A nice piece - Christophle or even Caillar and Bayard, silver plated.

Palomer rarely raised his head from contemplation of the board. He spat out the points each time and moved his checkers and tokens with a firm snapping onto the surface of the board, as if to say, this is Trictrac, the onomatopoeic source of the name. When he achieved the twelve points to win a game, he plunged the short pegs into the holes on the edge of the board. Each time, he looked up quickly at his opponent, but his face remained impassive. He scored points quickly and efficiently.

Jacques missed a couple of possible scores, a schoolboy's error, and was falling behind very early in the match. He was distracted, with his mind only partly on the game. He tried to engage Palomer in conversation as they progressed, but the man merely grunted and made it clear there was no time for anything but the contest. Jacques drew himself up; learn what you can about the man from the way he plays, but don't lose too easily, or you'll be dismissed and have little chance of taking matters further, he coached himself. He took a deep draft of champagne and changed his stance. He started to take points. He tried a brave but risky move and it came off. For the first time, Palomer sat up and took his eyes off the board. He reached for his glass of champagne and threw it back noisily. Then he continued to calculate, swiftly and accurately, assessing all the various options available to him. He rolled his dice, and immediately the numbers were displayed he called his moves and shifted his checkers to their new positions, almost as though it was pre-ordained. Jacques fought back, but he needed outrageous chance to get him to a position where he could accumulate enough points. Palomer stabbed the twelfth peg into the hole and sat back triumphantly. At last, his face moved into a tight smile and his eyes flickered. He looked Jacques in the face.

'You see, Lecoubarry. This game is how I am. I cannot abide loose thinking, prevarication, any weakness in fact. Not in a man.'

Jacques nodded. 'You play well, Marcel. No excuses. But I am a little rusty. It is, as you say, hard to find an opponent who stretches you. Yes, I am a little rusty.'

'Hah. If you were a well-oiled machine, I would still beat you.'

Palomer beckoned, and a taller, much leaner version of himself came over to the table. Jacques hadn't heard him come into the room, and as he walked towards them his feet made no sound.

'This is my son, Jean-Michel,' said Palomer. 'Jean-Michel, this is Monsieur Jacques Lecoubarry, an antique dealer from Bordeaux.' Jacques stood up, shook hands with the newcomer and looked at his face. The eyes moved once, to the side towards his father, but his face was stiff and unsmiling.

'I've seen you in the town,' said Jean-Michel.

'It's possible. I've been here for a few days.'

'Yes, somewhere in town.'

'Lecoubarry and I have been playing Trictrac,' said Palomer.

'I see that, and drinking champagne. You're an honoured guest, Monsieur Lecoubarry. I don't think I've heard you mentioned before.'

'He plays not a bad game, better than yours. It has given me some amusement, a little challenge to play him.'

'I don't have patience for the game,' said Jean-Michel, still looking closely at Jacques. 'I prefer more physical sports.'

'Monsieur Lecoubarry came here by boat, Jean-Michel. He's moored by the boathouse. Perhaps you could go and check that his boat is securely tied. We wouldn't want it to drift off down the river.' Jean-Michel turned on his heels and left.

'Another match, Marcel,' said Jacques, sitting down. 'This excellent champagne may have provided some oil for my rustiness. But first, tell me how long you have lived in this superb house? The setting is, well, remarkable. The vines which seem to stretch forever. Is that the source of your wealth?' Palomer seemed uncertain for a moment, but pride outweighed his habitual caution.

'My family has farmed the Rama Estate for generations,' he said. 'The terra, the soil, and the aspect of the land, the gentle sloping hills, south-west, are perfect for the cultivation of the specialist grape. My grandfather extended the area of cultivation of vines in his time - before that it was a mixed farm, cattle, sheep, even horses. But it was the grapes. That was the genius. As the market expanded, our production increased, the prices rose. I invested in new machinery, looked at improved care of the vines and, as you can see, we have been very, very successful.'

'Yes, I see that. And the house?'

'The chateau has been modernised over the years naturally. But it's our family seat. I've spent a small fortune on improvements to the structure and also on the furnishings.' Jacques could sense him puffing himself up. 'It's in a way my duty. The duty of the elite, the wealthy, the successful, to dispense some of their wealth in order to support people like you, antique dealers, craftsmen, artisans.'

Fortunately, champagne can be a good tonic against nausea and Jacques merely smiled. Through thin lips he said. 'Very noble of you, I'm sure. But let's play another match. For the title of the elite.' Palomer grunted. He set up the board again and handed Jacques his dice cup.

Celestine stepped out of the Abbey and took a deep breath. The cloisters were beautiful, a haven of peace and tranquillity, but the place had darkened for her in the last hour. There were secrets and there were horrors. She could see in her mind's eye the carved image of the Hebrews perishing in the fiery furnace. Ducrozet had said, half-seriously, that it was prophetic. Steinbach must have known what his fate was likely to be. He must have known he was on borrowed time, that the relentless Nazi slaughter machine would one day take him. So, he had left a message for his son - I was here, I had something of value and I want you to have it, I want it to survive, I want you to resurrect it after this time of carnage.

Celestine needed fresh air and physical movement. She walked briskly through the Sunday afternoon streets of this quiet town, slumbering in the warmth of a late summer's day. She had already determined that she would discover the meaning in the message and locate whatever had been hidden so many years before. She would do it not only for the memory of the father and of the great-grandson, but she was increasingly certain that this discovery would lead her to the perpetrators of this recent bout of evil in the town. She stepped onto the boat and threw open the doors and windows to let in the air and the sun. She slipped on some more casual clothes and made coffee. Then sitting down at the table on the bow deck, she took out her notes and began to look for the patterns and clues that would help her to solve the puzzle in the cloisters.

Chapter Thirty-Two

Jacques' early moves were more controlled this time and more deliberate. He watched Palomer's moves intensely and missed no opportunity to grab any points available to him. He was starting to understand a little more clearly how Palomer liked to play. He rarely made a quick move, but when he did place his checkers, it was rapid and decisive, as though the decision had been made definitively, after a consideration of all the possibilities available to him. There was a lot of strength in that way of playing. He was relentless and he made no mistakes. Jacques realised that he couldn't compete with that level of focus and consistency, so he would have to break up the play, wrong foot Palomer, and stretch his understanding of where Jacques' moves were going.

It started slowly in one game; Jacques threw a three and a six and made a move that appeared reckless. But, for the first time, Palomer shuffled on his seat, sat back slightly and turned his head to look at the board from a different angle. He took longer than usual, but when he did move, it was exactly what Jacques had hoped for. There appeared to be no threat in Jacques' move, and Palomer chose to ignore it. He was a little ahead on points, and he started clicking down his pieces more quickly, as though they were following a well-grooved path. Jacques was beginning to perspire. He could feel the tension on the side of his head as he held so many possible positions in his mind. And he waited, waited and hoped for the magical roll of the dice. Suddenly, Palomer snapped down two checkers with the clear sound of Trictrac. He raised his head, and for the first time in the game looked across at Jacques.

'Le Case de Diable,' he said. 'The Devil's Point.'

'So I see,' replied Jacques calmly and looked back down at the board.

The throw came. Jacques stared at the two ivory cubes as they tumbled out of the leather cup and rolled to a stop on the board. A double, and the key to unlocking the play. Palomer didn't move, he sat immobile, staring at the board, as though he might ingest it or alter it by his will. His move, when it came, was tentative. He touched the pieces like a child reaching to see if something is hot. Jacques moved again, quickly calculated the points gained, and placed another peg in the hole on his side of the board.

From that moment on there was more hesitation in the way Palomer played. Jacques continued to distract him with the occasional unusual and surprising move, which seemed to unnerve him, and he started to make small errors. Jacques rolled up the points relentlessly. Just then Jean-Michel came in and started to speak, but stopped mid-sentence when he saw the concentration in his father's face. He stood directly behind Jacques, so close that he could smell his scent. Palomer rattled his dice cup violently and the dice came bouncing out onto the table, but the numbers simply gave him more problems. Jacques took points from his opponent's moves as well as his own, and he soon led by three games. Palomer tried some desperate plays; but he was like a hooked fish, tiring and making increasingly feeble lunges to get away. The dice didn't support him and he left himself ever more vulnerable. After that, it was just a matter of accumulating points for Jacques, and Palomer knew he was beaten. Jacques placed the peg in the twelfth hole and sat back.

'Enough,' shouted Palomer, and slapped his fat fist down on the table.

'Well, that was a good match,' said Jacques mildly. Palomer looked at him angrily. He rubbed his hand over the back of his head.

'Very good, Lecoubarry. A remarkable and very lucky way to play.'

'There's always luck, Marcel,' said Jacques. 'But I think yours ran out when you kept stretching for that Devil's Point. Yes, I think that's when you lost your way.'

Palomer seemed to notice for the first time that Jean-Michel was standing behind Jacques' chair. He was looking askance at the board.

'I have checked Monsieur Lecoubarry's boat,' said Jean-Michel, in a voice as flat as his father's. 'That boat belongs to Ducrozet, the curator at the Abbey Museum.'

Palomer looked at Jacques, who said nothing. 'I thought you said the boat you came in belonged to a friend. What did you call him?'

'Lefebvre.'

'Lefebvre. But in fact, it belongs to Monsieur Ducrozet.'

Jacques shrugged and smiled. 'I don't know any Ducrozet. My friend told me he bought the boat a few days ago from a gentleman, who, he said, was having some difficulties. Lefebvre is a very sharp man, doesn't miss a trick. Asked me to listen to the motor today; he thought perhaps it was missing. He's an engineer, he worries. I noticed nothing.' Jean-Michel came around and stood over Jacques who looked up at him calmly.

'Are you saying that this friend of yours bought the boat in the last few days?' demanded Jean-Michel, his voice harsh with disbelief.

'That's exactly what I just said. But since you raised the query, I will ask him when I see him, which will be this evening. I'll ask him from whom he bought the boat. A Ducrozet you say.'

'You don't know him?'

'I know only a few people in Lissac,' Jacques replied. All this time Palomer had been watching every movement of Jacques' eyes, listening to every inflection in his voice. Jacques stood up and turned to face Jean-Michel, who didn't move, so that the two men were face to face, centimetres apart. 'It has been a most pleasant and entertaining afternoon, Marcel, and I must thank you for your hospitality.' Jacques spoke to Palomer but didn't move from his position, his eyes on Jean-Michel's, his arms loose by his side, fists clenched. 'I am disappointed that you don't want to part with the Trictrac table, but I'll leave you my card. If I can be of service to you in the future. I think I now have a better understanding of the quality and type of piece you prefer.' He then leaned towards Palomer, laid his card on the table and extended his hand. Palomer took it in a rigid grip and squeezed tightly, Jacques did the same, and they stayed like that for a few seconds. Then Palomer's face went blank, he released his grip and turned back to the board.

'Jean-Michel, show Lecoubarry out,' he said.

Jean-Michel took him to the French doors and opened one. He barely stepped aside so that Jacques had to manoeuvre around him.

'Au revoir, Jean-Michel,' said Jacques, as he walked across the terrace. Jean-Michel said nothing.

Jacques walked quickly over the lawned gardens down to the river. He looked at the position of the boat next to the slipway; was that exactly where he'd left it? He checked the mooring carefully and looked for any signs of damage. He checked the fuel gauge and opened the engine housing - all seemed to be in order. He cast off and reversed away from the slipway and into the stream. Then he turned the bow downriver and throttled up as high as he could. The boat shot forwards, and he sat down with relief. His shirt was damp with sweat and the palms of his hands were sore where the nails had been digging in. He decided to put some distance between himself and the 'chateau', so he kept the boat at its maximum speed, steering ten metres or so from the shore. Occasionally, he glanced backwards, but he couldn't see any other boats on the water. If the black boat was following him, he knew it would catch him very quickly. The sky was beginning to darken, and he thought it would be a good idea to get back on dry land before it became too dark to see clearly. A bank of clouds had built up on the western horizon and the setting sun had tinged them with red and gold. A wind was getting up as well, and the branches of the trees hanging over the river were beginning to rustle and shiver.

Relieved when he saw the lights on the bridge at Lissac, he pulled in and moored the boat further down the concrete jetty from where Ducrozet normally kept it. Just a subtle difference, he thought, but perhaps enough to help maintain the subterfuge. He knew that Palomer and his son had not believed him about the ownership of the boat. They would undoubtedly assume that Jacques knew Ducrozet well enough to be able to borrow it. They knew he had lied. Palomer would already be calculating what moves Jacques was making, why, and what moves he needed to make to counteract them.

He walked quickly along the streets, across the small bridge over the canal and along the towpath. There were lights on in the barge, and he stepped over the gunwale with relief. Celestine called out to him from the salon.

'There you are.' He walked to her and kissed her on both cheeks and then fully on the lips. Celestine could feel the tension in his body. 'Henri just called, just now. He said you came past and didn't greet him or wave.'

'No, I didn't.'

'Well, he also said that the black boat came down the river just a few minutes after you.'

'Damn,' said Jacques, and jumped up. He stepped out of the salon and onto the deck, keeping his head low. He looked around quickly. It was still and peaceful. But then he saw a movement on the other side of the canal; a figure, half-hidden by the cabin of another boat. It was almost fully dark and the figure was in the shadow between two street lights. He couldn't see a face, but he could tell, by the stance and the shape, that the figure was looking across at the *Incognito*. He called out and started moving towards the canal bridge, but he knew that by the time he reached the other side, the figure would have melted away. He waited in the gloom for several minutes. Celestine came to the door but he waved her back. Eventually, he went back inside and sat down. Celestine looked at him quizzically.

'I think we have moved onto another level in the game,' he said. 'And it's not without risk.' After opening another bottle of the dark Cahors wine, Jacques took Celestine through the events of the afternoon.

'And your conclusion after all that?' she said.

'My conclusion. My conclusion is that Palomer is a cold, calculating, pompous, ruthless, unemotional....'

'You said cold.'

'Ok then; without human empathy. He has massive delusions of grandeur. It's almost as though he's built an edifice around himself to show that he's in some way an aristocrat. The portraits of 'ancestors', the antiques, the Trictrac - a game of the aristocracy.'

'You play Trictrac, and obviously very well,' commented Celestine.

'Yes, but I learned to play working on the tables, restoring them. I became intrigued by the game, then I played for fun, and sometimes for money.' He stopped. 'But he's a peasant. He's cunning and narrow and coarse, and he gives absolutely nothing away. It's as though every conversation was a negotiation. You know the kind.'

'And the son.'

'The son. He's a fucking brute,' said Jacques and raised his hand in apology. 'Not as calculating, clever if you wish, as his father. But those dead eyes. And strong, physically I mean.' He paused and took a sip of his wine. 'That said, are they any more than an unpleasant family of rich, country bastards? The son has a wife straight from the Cruella de Vil School of Etiquette. So, I wouldn't be surprised if he was looking for more harmony in a duet somewhere else.'

'Ok, but why was he hanging around the Abbey, casing Ducrozet's house?' interposed Celestine.

'Ducrozet. We must phone him. Tell him he's sold his boat to Monsieur Lefebvre,' said Jacques.

Celestine looked at him in surprise. 'Really!'

'And tell him to keep his doors locked. Without frightening him of course.'

'Ok, I'll do that now,' said Celestine. 'You look as though you need to relax a bit. Go and get out of your maverick duds, then I'll tell you what I've been doing this afternoon.'

'What I need, apart from all those things, is to eat. I have never lived such a desert lifestyle. I need to come across an oasis soon,' said Jacques.

'There's food in the fridge - cold meats and salad. Then hurry up, I think I'm somewhere near solving the puzzle, but it seems a bit crazy to me. I need your opinion.'

'You think you can solve it? Of course you can.'

'Nearly. And if I have, it's very intriguing.'

Chapter Thirty-Three

The juge d'instruction, Maitre Drouillard, had spent several hours with Commandant Grimard, on a Sunday, which had made both of them particularly irascible. At the end though, after looking at what evidence there was and discussing the other circumstances of the case, the magistrate ruled that there was still not enough to formally place under investigation either the Bulgarian Dacheva or the Polish woman Lena Visser in relation to the murders.

'We know it's almost impossible to commit two such crimes without leaving some trace, however small. These were killings done in the open, in places where, at any time, a civilian could have walked by,' said Drouillard.

'Well, the hill at Calvary at night is not a place many would visit,' responded Grimard.

'No, but my point is this. To leave no trace, the murderer was likely to have been wearing protective clothing, gloves, headgear and…,' he stressed the point by shaking his finger, 'they would have had to destroy or dispose of the clothing very quickly. You've searched the Bulgarian's house and surrounding areas; the walker had only a rucksack. You've got a sighting of her walking through the town the day before, carrying only a rucksack.' He paused with his head on one side. He was a short man, with strands of dark hair straggling around the bald patch on the top of his head, but his face was neat, with even, regular features, and his eyes were gimlet-sharp behind his wire-rimmed spectacles. 'No, Commandant, there is something just too incomplete in this. Motive you have, of sorts. Opportunity, yes. Witnesses, none for the Polish girl.'

'She was seen visiting the Convent the morning before the murder,' said Grimard.

'And she has explained that. But no one saw her at the actual time of the murder. The Bulgarian: you have witnesses who state they saw him in the street near where the murder took place, but no one saw him with the victim or can place him at the scene.' The magistrate paused again and looked at his fingers, which were twitching, as though he were calculating the numbers for and against. He started again. 'The knife you found in the Bulgarian's house; too common, used by hundreds of people in this area, for pruning. It's not enough, Jean-Philippe. Do you not think you should cast your net wider? You have two murders within a few days, an incredibly rare occurrence in this town or any other small provincial town in France. Less rare if they are connected. Tit for tat, revenge, that sort of thing. They knew each other, the victims. Yes?'

'They knew of each other, but what possible link could they have? A youngish, homosexual, Jewish professor from Paris and an old, Polish, catholic nun. Strange bedfellows indeed.' Grimard was greatly exasperated but he knew the magistrate was right.

'Hold the Bulgarian until late tomorrow, just in case something else turns up, then release him. And intensify the house to house, someone, somewhere, must surely have seen something.' The magistrate looked down at his hands, now lying flat on the desk top. 'The Polish woman is different. She admits to coming here with the intention of killing or at least harming the nun - but she says she didn't do it. That sort of coincidence worries me. She left the scene of a crime, so you can hang onto her a little longer. The Dutch Police want the husband, let him go to them. If we need him back it'll be easy. Without his presence she may soften. Worth a try I'd have thought.' He was well aware that he was stepping on Grimard's turf with these suggestions. He believed in collaboration though, not the often-cited antagonism between the two services. He looked at Grimard and smiled briefly. Grimard shrugged.

'One of our problems,' he said, 'is that CCTV hasn't picked up anything. We don't have cameras in most parts of the town. Hardly any parts of the town, in fact. The murderer, in both cases, was unseen. We've had officers walk the possible routes to and from the crime scenes, and it's certainly possible if you know the town well. You'd have to avoid the main square, use the back alleys and side streets.'

'What about the road leading to the hill at Calvary?'

'It's a very quiet road. The houses are set back. There are two houses that are empty at the moment, they look as though they have security cameras. We're trying to trace the owners and get access. But I'm not optimistic.'

'Very well, let's leave it at that. Keep me informed. If you make progress I'll be with you immediately.' They shook hands and the magistrate left. Grimard sat back in his chair and steepled his hands. He sat like that for several minutes, then he picked up the phone.

'Is Desmarais here?' he barked into the phone. 'When? Tomorrow at eight. Ok, tell him to come and see me the minute he clocks in, understand?'

He sat back again. Desmarais had interviewed some tourist from a barge on the canal. Cast your net wider, Grimard. Mon Dieu. Ok, he would cast his net wider, but that wouldn't stop him from drilling down ever harder on the suspects he had. Something, someone, will break, it always does. He realised he was hungry, a long way from his family and home in Montauban, on a Sunday. Yes, this town was starting to get right up his nose.

He left the building and began walking towards his hotel, which was on a corner at the end of the bridge. He could hear a burglar alarm, shrill and insistent in the quiet of the evening. He stopped. Then he heard the sirens of two police vehicles coming closer. He wanted to resist, he was hungry and tired, but the alarm could only be a few streets away - everything was in this town. He retraced his steps and followed the sound, emerging onto the pedestrianised street just along from the Abbey. He kept walking, the sound seemed to be coming from behind the church. He turned the corner; two police cars were already parked diagonally in front of the lobby to the cloisters, and he saw three agents run to the door. The alarm was so loud that it was hard to think. The main door to the glass lobby pushed open and the agents went inside, shining torches all around the room. When Grimard entered the lobby, the sound was unnerving, it hammered at the brain like a physical threat. He held his hands over his ears. The agents were searching the administration rooms behind the counter of the lobby. The door into the cloisters was locked. One of the agents had switched on a light in one of the offices. It was a small room, with a desk, a bookshelf and a wooden filing cabinet. On the desk, the computer was lying on its side. The drawers of the desk had been riven open and there were papers and cards all over the floor. The filing cabinet also looked as though it had been opened with a chisel, and papers were hanging in sheaves from the half-open drawers. The noise was devastating, unreal and Grimard felt himself becoming a little unhinged.

'There's no one here,' said one of the agents.

'Let's wait outside until this bloody noise gets switched off,' shouted Grimard.

Outside, the agent by the car stepped forwards. 'The key holder, a Monsieur Ducrozet, has been contacted. He's on his way to disable the alarm,' he said.

Ducrozet! Grimard mused. Another coincidence. He felt he was starting to slightly lose his grip on reality. 'I'm going around the other side, agent,' he said. 'When Ducrozet arrives and he's switched off this noise. Keep him there, I want to talk to him.'

Chapter Thirty-Four

Celestine sat on the floor of the salon and arranged a series of papers around her. Jacques sat on the bench opposite and looked at her long brown legs.

'Ok. Firstly, we must remember that this was a puzzle created by a father for his nine or ten-year-old son. It wasn't designed to test the crack brains of the Sécurité or the Gestapo code breakers. I presume he wanted to hide the message from the casual observer. Perhaps he wanted to challenge his son, to play a game with him, but with a very serious intent. Perhaps this is something they did, the father and son.'

'A game from beyond the grave,' said Jacques. 'A bit morbid.'

'Monsieur Steinbach may not have been certain that he was going to be killed, perhaps only incarcerated.' She stopped and looked down. 'He certainly expected to be taken away. He must have feared the worst.'

'Ok, go on.'

'So, Steinbach left a puzzle for a young boy. But the trouble he took, the package left at the Convent, the cryptic numerical clues, suggests something very important was being hidden, not something trivial. This was not a time for trivial things.' Jacques nodded and Celestine continued. 'So, trying to think like him. He imagines the boy, Sebastien, visiting or being contacted by the nuns; we don't know if the boy had been given instructions to visit the nuns after the war, when it was safe again to assume his real identity. At that stage, Steinbach had no idea when the war would end or indeed what the world would look like afterwards. But he must have had hope. He must have hoped that eventually life would return to normal and that his son would be able to collect the letter.' Celestine paused and took a sip of wine. 'So, in his mind, Sebastien opens the letter. Ah, he says, Papa has left me a puzzle. These numbers, what could they refer to? Perhaps there was a hint in the letter, perhaps together they had explored the cloisters, and immediately the boy grasped that the numbers referred to the pillars there. It would only have taken two words in the letter, meaningless to anyone else, to point Sebastian in that direction.'

'But Sebastien never came,' said Jacques.

'No, he didn't,' said Celestine. 'But who did come was Sebastien's grandson, with no common experience with his great-grandfather, but with the highly-trained, academic mind of an adult. He realised, Malraux, after some time that the numbers referred to the cloisters. But then he addressed the problem with that same academic, adult mind, partially distracted with drugs and his chaotic lifestyle, and he was frustrated. Given time, he might well have solved the puzzle; perhaps he solved enough of it to start seeing the end position, and that's what got him killed.'

They both sat quietly for a few minutes; Jacques stroking his beard, letting his mind run through Celestine's ideas, looking for flaws or weaknesses in the argument. That was his role, he knew.

'So, I'm Sebastien, Papa has left me a puzzle. He's done that before. The pillars in the cloisters; of course, the numbers refer to that. Sebastien goes to the cloisters, and checking the numbers with the corresponding carvings, writes down the sequence. One. The anointing of David. Why this one to start? David anointed King of the Jews, the chosen one. But the boy's name is Sebastien. That's the name he lives under for the rest of his life, the French name he was given when he was placed with the catholic family. He kept that identity. Perhaps after such a long time it was easier to blend in. He had papers…. But what if, just if, his name was really David.'

'That's a big leap,' said Jacques.

'I know, and it doesn't really matter. The anointing, the giving of a task, the assuming of a role, that's what's important. The start of a quest. But I am going to the Jewish Museum tomorrow morning, and if they have records I will check. Meanwhile, bear with me. I read the passage in the bible. On Google, don't look so worried. Bear in mind that Steinbach was Samuel Steinbach. I made notes. Book of Samuel 16: 1-13. 'Samuel took the horns of oil and anointed him in the presence of his brothers etc. etc. Samuel then went to Ramah.'

'Rama!' exclaimed Jacques.

'Yes, Ramah. R a m a h,' she spelt out the letters. 'Close isn't it.'

Jacques sat back slowly, shaking his head. 'There's something a little uncanny about this. Do you think we're reading too much into it? Maybe you're imagining patterns, like … Rorschach ink tests.'

Celestine looked up at him angrily. 'It was literal. This puzzle was literal and metaphorical. His father Samuel was giving him a task, metaphorically anointing him.'

'Ok, ok, but the quotation from the bible. Would a ten-year-old boy know that? That line about Ramah. And what would he make of the anointing? He was ten years old. Are you thinking like an academic adult now? When I was a ten-year-old boy, I didn't know shit about anointing.'

'You were a heathen,' said Celestine, matter-of-factly.

'Basque. There's a difference.'

She smiled. 'I think for a Jewish boy of that generation, close to his father, it would be a big deal. And the Old Testament bible stories would have been part of his education. They must have been close. His father let him go into hiding to save him, while he remained in danger and maybe to complete the work he had to do.'

'Ok. So, Sebastien has been given a task and he's all bigged up for it; what next?' asked Jacques, settling down again.

'The next one is pretty scary,' said Celestine. 'Three Hebrews in the fiery flames of hell.'

'There's a carving of that?'

'Yes. Ducrozet explained it. He said some Christians at the time quite relished the idea that the murderers of Christ should be consigned to the eternal flames.'

Jacques blew out his cheeks and took another deep drink of his wine. 'Could this be a warning, a statement of some kind?' he asked.

'No, I think it's more an explanation, a reason why Samuel needed to set Sebastien this task, and an apology, an apology for not being with him at that time.'

'For being sent to the gas chambers. This is getting dark.'

Celestine looked at him unmoved. 'Of course, it's dark, these are dark matters. If you just want light, stay on deck and draw pretty pictures of the trees.' Jacques looked stung, but said nothing. 'The message is: this is a serious task and you will know now the reason why I am entrusting you with it. I think these first two clues, pictures, are effectively setting the scene. This is the situation, I want you to do this because I can't. The next ones, I believe, are the directions for finding whatever was hidden away. Here I'm more unsure. As I say, I need to visit the Jewish Museum tomorrow. I think there might be information there that'll help. But so far, I have the following, again bear in mind these are directions to a boy.'

Celestine picked up two of the pages from the floor. 'These clues could be very simple, and I'm assuming almost literal, at this stage. I'll run through them quickly. You look deadbeat.'

'Unfortunate choice of words, but yes, I'm feeling the pace. This afternoon drew on a lot of my resources.'

'Ok. Three. The calling of the Apostles. It's one of the clearest of the carvings.' She handed Jacques her phone on which there was a picture of the frieze. 'I've taken a few photos of the other sides. What do you see?'

'Boats,' said Jacques. 'Men in boats, fishermen presumably. If I remember rightly, and as you know, I am so far lapsed that I am almost pre-Christian, Jesus recruited a couple of fishermen as apostles. Come I will make you fishers of men.'

'That's right. But boats.'

'Ok.'

'Number four, a carving of birds and beasts. No bible story, just birds and beasts.'

'So, fields, countryside,' suggested Jacques.

'Countryside certainly.'

'Five is the Miracle of Saint Martin. Martin shares his cloak with a beggar who turned into Jesus Christ.'

'We've all done that. Figuratively at least,' said Jacques.

'Seriously. You must tell me sometime. I don't know the reason behind this one. But, there are a lot of places in France, in this area, named after Saint Martin. We may need to pour over a map. You're good at that,' she looked at him, unsmiling. 'Number six is the washing of the feet. Again, it could refer to a place. If this puzzle is to give directions to a location, it has to start with the broader picture and gradually narrow it down to a specific spot. I need to clarify the earlier indications and then I hope these later ones will become more apparent.'

'And the last one. The seventh number.'

'The seventh is the Ascension of Alexander.' She looked at Jacques. 'I don't know. I just think that these are veils. You have to get nearer to one clue, or veil, then you tear that one.'

'Asunder.'

'Ok, asunder, and that gives you a hint, a push towards the next one. And when you get there and confirm its location, you can see the way forward to the next one. I think the clues have to be followed on the ground.'

'But which ground?'

'That's the first move. We need to establish where the initial location is. But don't you see, this would be fascinating for a boy, wouldn't it? Fun, a challenge?'

'Yes, I see that, and you need to gather a lot more information. Go to the museum tomorrow. I may go with you. But, as the only boy aboard this vessel, I have an approach I would like to follow.

Celestine looked at him curiously. 'It's been a few years since you were a boy, Jacques.'

'I know. But I feel I have retained that freshness of thought, that enthusiasm for the game.'

'Clearly, if this afternoon is an example.'

'Yes, but, Celestine.' Jacques' voice took on a new level of seriousness. 'This is getting dark. Someone doesn't want this information to come out, for whatever reason, and at this stage I am completely baffled. But we must take precautions, personally, and here with the boat.'

'Are you worried about Jean-Michel? You're convinced he knows where we are?'

'I'm sure of it,' said Jacques. 'But I don't think he can see us as a threat just yet. An annoyance, and his father is vindictive enough. I'm sure he'll want to hit back. He didn't take it well this afternoon and he knows I haven't been truthful with him.' He paused and placed his hands on Celestine's elbows. 'We must be careful, and we need to solve the bloody thing quickly. I miss those carefree days of wandering down the canal, the greatest excitement being, apart from you of course, the choice of food and wine. I miss those days.'

Celestine smiled, but only with her mouth. 'Let's just focus on this right now,' she said. 'I can't think about the future.'

It was almost eleven o'clock before Ducrozet was permitted to leave the Abbey. The phone call from the police had shaken him badly, so at first, he hadn't been able to comprehend what was being said. Behind the voice, he could hear the searing noise of the alarm, and he'd finally realised what was required of him. He grabbed his car keys and drove the little Renault Clio to a parking place in a narrow street behind the Abbey. The street was dark, and the sound of the alarm was echoing between the buildings. As he rounded the corner he caught the full blast of the noise and he felt as though he was walking into madness. Outside the lobby, Grimard took him by the arm and hurried him to the keypad inside the building. He quickly tapped in the numbers, and in the sudden silence, Grimard felt the tension draining from him. The other agents of police also visibly relaxed and began talking again as Ducrozet looked around helplessly.

'Thank Christ for that,' said Grimard. 'Monsieur Ducrozet come with me, but tread carefully, and don't go anywhere or touch anything unless I say so.'

More than an hour later, Grimard indicated to Ducrozet that he could go.

'The Abbey must remain closed tomorrow. I want you to come to the commissariat, the police poste, at ten a.m. D'you understand? When the techs have finished, I will want you to look more closely again at all the items in your office.' Ducrozet turned to leave. 'And, Monsieur Ducrozet, I want you to think very seriously about what reasons there could be for this break-in. Think really hard. And you should contact your staff. We will want to see them in the morning, as well. But they're not to enter the building. Men will be here all night.'

'Fine. Yes, I will. Can I go now, Commandant? I am very tired.' Grimard waved him away.

Ducrozet walked around the corner into the dark street where his car was parked. His brain was dull with exhaustion. He climbed listlessly into the little car and drove through the quiet back streets of the town. He was utterly drained. He had suffered a great nervous upheaval in these last few days, and he sensed that he was balancing on the edge. Yet, a thought, which had been gestating in his mind for some time, just then rose to the surface. It is time to move somewhere else, he wondered? A new job, a new start, for him and

Chantal and the children. A start away from the memories and the traumas of the last few weeks.

He parked the car beneath the plane trees in the little parking plots for residents. He felt a little easier, the idea was out in the open. He would talk to Chantal tomorrow, look at alternative places. He knew he would find work; France was full of medieval sites, wonderfully preserved for the people, the tourists, and of course the scholars. It would be interesting, a challenge, to begin a new study, perhaps write a new book.

He partially opened the door, but hesitated, loath to let this new, comforting, more optimistic feeling dissipate. He looked up, slightly euphoric, and then he saw the movement - a black shape coming swiftly from behind the tree on the passenger side of the car, coming towards him, a man dressed all in black. Ducrozet screamed and jammed the key back into the ignition. The dark figure was coming around the bonnet, was grasping for the door handle. The engine fired and the car shot backwards, Ducrozet gripping desperately to the steering wheel. The car mounted the curb on the other side of the lane and grazed the wall, the door slammed shut. The black shape was still hurtling towards him. Hair on end, screaming constantly, with one last vestige of reason, Ducrozet managed to put the car into first gear and press hard on the accelerator. The car bumped off the pavement and shot off down the street. Looking fearfully backwards in the mirror, he saw a black figure, bent over in the middle of the lane.

He drove recklessly, shivering, his head shaking, his tongue slipping in and out of his mouth. The engine was screeching for the gear to be changed but he couldn't take his hands from the steering wheel. Where? He swerved around a corner, keeping in the light. He looked back fearfully, expecting the dark shape to be there, somehow pursuing him. Across the square, a one-way street, it doesn't matter, get away. Over the cobbles, around the corner, dead end, slam on the brakes. I'm at the Abbey. There's a police car, there's a police agent. Switch off the engine, slump over the wheel, stop screaming.

Agent Lavigne jumped out of his car, and fingering his belt strode quickly towards the Renault. He pulled open the car door angrily, and shouted, his hand grabbing Ducrozet by the shoulder.

Ducrozet squealed and sat up, rigid. He turned his tear-streaked face to the agent, who recognised him instantly.

'Monsieur Ducrozet,' he said. 'What the hell?'

Chapter Thirty-Five

Jacques and Celestine knew just after seven o'clock. Desmarais called them.

'He's in a hell of a state. Says he saw a black man, coming for him, coming to murder him. He was parking his car, smashed the wing. There was a break-in at the Abbey. Yeah, he got called, he's a key holder. Grimard was there. He's in a hell of a state, can't get much sense out of him. Sedated now.' Black figure, thought Jacques, a black figure. 'Grimard wants to see me first thing. Think he'll want to talk to you,' affirmed Desmarais.

'Is his family all right?' asked Jacques.

'Yes. Protection's there. I'll call you.'

Jacques looked at Celestine who was sitting up in bed, arms folded, her head was moving slowly from side to side, her eyes hard with anger.

'It's time,' she said. 'We need to move quickly now. I knew they'd have a go at Ducrozet. We should have warned him.'

'We did. He got called out. There was a break-in at the abbey. Our man is smart.'

'Not as fucking smart as we are,' said Celestine, and she jumped up, naked, and stepped angrily off the bed. She kicked a shoe into the door frame and strode into the small shower room. Like a Valkyrie, thought Jacques, aroused. But he called out to her.

'Put your running gear on and go to Henri's boathouse. We need to know if he saw the boat return last night.' Celestine came back out and started dressing quickly. Jacques went into the galley to make coffee. He called out. 'And, Celestine. Tell him to pack up his stuff and come to stay here on the boat. It's not safe for him to be there now. Celestine, stay with him until he's on his bike and heading this way.' Celestine came into the galley and took the coffee offered to her. 'I should have done more. I knew he was in danger. I thought he'd be all right in the house,' said Jacques.

'I'm going to get Henri, then I'm going to the Jewish museum. We need all the pieces in place now. What are you going to do?'

'I'm going to buy some more detailed maps.'

'Are you going to speak to Grimard?'

'No, not unless he asks for me.'

'The third number, Jacques,' said Celestine. 'We need to find the location. They're linked, the attack on Ducrozet and the murders. What we're working on, the puzzle, that's the link. But until we solve it, there's no motive. Without a motive, the police won't do anything. They certainly won't accuse an important citizen like Palomer or his family.'

Celestine ran quickly, her heart pounding. This was not a morning jog. She felt the bile rising in her throat, and she spat and kept running. She thought of Ducrozet and his wife, and her scalp felt like it was burning. Her feet hit the ground hard with every step. She stumbled, and grabbing at the undergrowth with her hand, tore the skin on the thorns of a bramble. She almost relished the pain, and kept running, sucking the blood from the palm of her hand and spitting it out. She covered the distance quickly and called out as she neared the boathouse. There was no answering call. She had half expected to see Monsieur Lefebvre sitting on the jetty, mobile phone in hand, waiting patiently for a boat to pass. She looked into the boathouse, his bicycle was leaning against the back wall, and a few of his belongings were lying on the wooden platform above the water. She suddenly had a terrible fear. She edged closer to the water and looked down. The river lapped gently at the wooden piles. She called out again and stepped out of the boathouse. She heard a rustling in the bushes on the other side of the path. Stupidly, she reached quickly to where, in a past life, she had carried a gun. A figure burst out of the bushes and rushed towards her. It was Monsieur Lefebvre, his yellow shirt flapping and his hair sticking up like a thistle top.

'Celestine, I heard you call, but I was… engaged.' he said sheepishly.

Celestine put her arms around his shoulders and squeezed him. They stood like that for several minutes, Monsieur Lefebvre patting her arms gently. Eventually, Celestine stood back.

'I'm so relieved you're all right. Monsieur Ducrozet was attacked last night. We fear, we feel, it was the same man. But you're all right.' She sank down onto her haunches. She explained what Jacques had said, and asked him if he would come with her now. 'Please.'

The old man looked doubtful at first, but then suddenly said: 'Yes, I'll gather my belongings together.' He disappeared into the boathouse and emerged just a few minutes later pushing his bicycle, the panniers bulging with all his goods and chattels.

'One more thing, Henri. Did you see the black boat go past, upriver, last night? I don't know what the time was but probably late, very late.'

Monsieur Lefebvre thought for a moment. 'See. I didn't see a boat. I stayed watching all day, you know, and I tend to sleep early when the night sets in. So, I didn't see anything. But I did hear a boat, sometime in the night.'

'Did you look at the time on the mobile phone?'

'No, I'm sorry. I was asleep. The boat must have woken me up. I didn't see it, but I did hear it. It was the black boat, I'm sure of it, I know the sound. Quite sure. But at the time I didn't think to look. I went back to sleep.'

'That's Ok, Henri. Let's go to the *Incognito*. I'll run a little ahead, but I'm sure you won't be far behind.

When Celestine returned to the barge, she saw that Jacques had spread two maps out on the table on the bow deck. He was eating carelessly.

'He's just coming,' said Celestine, 'He heard a boat last night, and he's sure it was the black one.'

Jacques nodded. 'There's bread and croissants in the galley, and coffee,' he said and lowered his head again to the maps. Monsieur Lefebvre cycled up to the boat, breathing heavily, his tattered straw hat hanging on his head at an unlikely angle. Jacques lifted the bicycle onto the boat and patted him on the shoulder. 'We'll put your bike undercover in a few minutes. There's breakfast in the galley, please help yourself.' Monsieur Lefebvre stood for a moment and looked hard at Jacques.

'You are very considerate, Jacques,' he said. 'But you must look after yourself and Celestine. If I can help, I will. But you must look to yourselves.' He turned and walked down the tight steps into the boat.

Chapter Thirty-Six

After a quick shower, Celestine left to visit the Jewish Museum. There was a small group of schoolchildren, with a very severe-looking teacher, waiting outside the door. Celestine looked at their animated faces and she remembered the little nun, waving her hands, entrancing the children. She hesitated, but the door of the museum was open so she stepped inside.

The interior was furnished like a school, with old desks and benches, and slate blackboards on the walls. The era depicted was the early 1940s, and there were artefacts from that time, and black and white photographs of groups of strong-looking children and more serious adults. Celestine felt very emotional. She just sensed that there were, if not answers, then at least pointers or clues in this place, and she was determined to find them.

At ten o'clock Jacques received a call from Desmarais.

'Grimard wants to see you.'

'It's a bit fucking late,' snapped Jacques. 'I'm busy now and I've got nothing more to tell him than I had the other day. I may have soon, but don't tell him that. I'll make myself available sometime later. Anything more on Ducrozet?'

'His office was ransacked. Grimard's called him in there this morning to have another look.' Desmarais paused. 'And, Jacques, don't do anything foolish.'

Jacques ended the call and sat back. What had they been looking for? The letter, Ducrozet's notes, or was it just a ruse to get him out of the house in the dark? Jacques pictured a dark figure waiting for Ducrozet's return. He phoned Desmarais back.

'Paul, what time was the break-in and when exactly did Ducrozet set off home?'

'It was recorded at nine o'clock. As I say, he left shortly before eleven.'

'Two hours. Grimard kept him there nearly two hours.'

'I guess.'

'Ok, another thing. There should have been a letter, an old letter in Malraux's belongings. I need to see it.'

Desmarais hesitated. 'I don't know Jacques, it's not public property.'

Suddenly he sounded so young to Jacques. 'Paul, if Grimard wants my help, he must let me see that letter. Do you understand? You're being a great help mate. I appreciate it.' He rang off again.

So, the assailant must have waited, hidden, for nearly two hours. That certainly suggested someone of cold nerves, focused, fearless even. Surely someone must have seen something in those two hours. But Lissac-sur-Tarn was such a sleepy town after nine o'clock; most citizens were indoors, watching television or talking with their families. Dog walkers possibly, lovers. Anyway, that was Grimard's work. We need to act now, he thought. It won't be easy. He just hoped that Celestine had garnered what she needed from the museum. He had drawn a small pencil ring around a point on the map. The difficult part would be locating it in reality, and not being seen while doing so.

Celestine left the museum after nearly two hours of studying old photographs, documents and contemporary narratives. She was shocked and enthralled by the information she had discovered there, and not simply in relation to her own quest. There were details of a community, an organisation of education, assistance and even resistance. She felt humbled when she read some of the histories of families fleeing from persecution to temporary safety in the small town in South West France. By the confluence of two great rivers, Jewish children had been secreted, housed by ordinary families, but not really ordinary, saved from the Nazi barbarism, more than five hundred of them, including Malraux's grandfather. The museum had been a school preparing young people for a new way of doing things, new skills for a different way of life. Then she read a passage that started her thinking in another direction. The passage gave details of the communal farms, established by local Jewish associations, farms which were similar in aspiration and inspiration to the Kibbutz movement in Palestine, at the time.

Celestine waited until the schoolchildren had completed their tour and had clattered out of the building. She approached the guide, a tall, angular woman with a no-nonsense look and lively, piercing eyes. She asked if there were any details of where the farms had been located in the region.

'Unfortunately, many of the records were destroyed. We know of two sites for sure; these were traced by descriptions left in letters and documents, and by matching photographs to landmarks. But we believe there were more. The records, you know, much was destroyed.' She directed Celestine to a section of exhibits, and on an old faded map, she pointed out the boundaries of two farms known to have been owned and run by the Jewish associations. Celestine looked carefully; one was near Auvillar, and the other further east on the road to Castres.

'But you believe there were more?' she asked.

'Most certainly. At least two along the valley of the Tarn.' She shrugged, and her sharp eyes became wistful. 'Given time, we might be able to cross-reference exhibits we have. But it would be a lot of work, and we are not well-staffed, or funded.' She smiled at Celestine. 'May I ask, why you are interested in this matter?'

'This is difficult to explain,' replied Celestine. 'I have a puzzle to solve. I felt, I hoped, there might be some clue in the material here. In fact, there has been.'

The woman looked at her closely; it was an intense weighing-up. There was silence for a few moments. 'A puzzle,' she said. 'That sounds a little light for research into such serious matters as these. The last visitor we had whose research might have been described as "being done with the intent of solving a puzzle", was a young man who only a few days ago met a horrible and disgusting end. The young man who was murdered.'

Celestine felt the hairs on the nape of her neck rise. 'He came here?'

'He did,' replied the guide. 'He came here on several occasions. He was so full of life, extraordinary really. Very quick, oh yes, very quick, sharp you know and knowledgeable.'

'Specifically, what was he looking at?' asked Celestine. The woman again stopped and looked closely at Celestine.

'He was looking for information about his family,' she said. 'And he was looking, like you, at information about the activities of the Jewish associations like the Scout Movement, and the placing of Jewish children in gentile homes. And,' she paused, 'at the location of Jewish farms in the region.' The guide walked to her desk and sat down. Celestine followed her.

'I hope that this puzzle, when solved, will bring some kind of resolution,' she said.

'Resolution and retribution,' replied Celestine, more fiercely than she'd intended.

The woman nodded and closed her eyes. 'Good luck with your puzzle,' she said. 'If there is anything else I can help you with, do not hesitate to ask.'

'Just one more thing. Did Monsieur Malraux find what he was looking for, about his family and the farms?'

'I think he found out just what you have found out. So many records were destroyed. I know I keep saying that. But we must piece together history as we can, from fragments left to us by luck or forethought. We are lucky to have what we have to tell these stories.'

'Yes, you are right, and I thank you so much for your assistance.'

'You are welcome. Good luck with your puzzle. You will let us know the outcome of your efforts, successful or not?'

Celestine hurried through the streets, unaware of her surroundings, thoughts racing through her head. She leapt onto the boat and put her hands on Jacques' shoulders. He turned his head. 'Good?'

'Good, yes. Listen.'

'I am, sit down. I will listen to you, then you can listen to me, and then we'll blend our listenings. Proceed.' Celestine described what she'd discovered at the museum.

'Nothing about Malraux's great-grandfather?'

'Not specifically, but there's a mountain of material to go through. I did find out about the farms. I never knew this history, quite recent history really. It happened here, just a hundred and fifty kilometres from my home.'

'And Malraux knew about the farms?'

'He found out. Maybe he knew beforehand. There are Jewish archives in Paris, and other places no doubt. He was an academic, after all. There were farms owned and leased by Jews and Jewish associations. But why would he be particularly interested in that? He didn't seem to have been the agricultural type.'

'No, but perhaps the family legends had suggested that something was hidden on one of these farms,' mused Jacques.

'Money, gold, jewellery?' questioned Celestine.

'Maybe. Some of the Jews who came here were undoubtedly rich, and they had to carry their wealth with them. Perhaps things were buried before the Germans could get their hands on them. Buried to be collected later. Buried with clues left for the next generation to follow.'

Celestine looked up as a solid-looking Dutch barge eased past on the way to the first lock. The driver smiled and waved, a woman was lounging on a deck chair, smoking and fanning herself with a magazine. It wasn't that hot. Celestine suddenly jumped up and stared at the boat. The man's mouth dropped and he turned away, touching the wheel lightly to correct his course. The barge passed and Celestine sat down again. Jacques looked at her with concern.

'It's just a pleasure boat. They're just ordinary people, doing ordinary things. Calm a little,' he said. Celestine shook herself and looked up sharply.

'Ok, what did you find out?' she demanded.

Jacques picked up one of the maps and spread it out on the table top.

'There are two maps,' he said. 'Would you believe it? Part of the river is on one map and where it curves away is on another one.' He shrugged.

'Maps of where?'

'Maps of the land alongside the river for about ten kilometres.'

'A map that covers the Palomer's estate?'

'Yes, and look.' He drew an imaginary line along the surface with his finger. 'The maps are really detailed. They show a lot of small features; historical buildings, but also fountains, ruined shelters and chapels.' He took his pencil. 'This is Palomer's land, see how it goes along the riverbank, not so far, but then spreads out like a fan up the hillsides, and up to the road at the top.'

'And these woods. Are they a part of it?'

'I don't know. I imagine so, but there are no boundaries shown on the map.'

'So, you don't know, for certain, which is the Rama Estate?' asked Celestine.

'No. But remember I was there. I saw the fields and fields of vines; that's those fields there, see, leading up to the brow of the hill. Then it's trees. Traditionally, the trees and the oak woods were on the top of the hills, and on the slopes where the soil was poorer, and it was harder to work. So, it's likely that this wood is also part of the Palomer's land. It's probable, ok.' Celestine nodded her agreement. 'I looked at the features in this whole area, to see if there was anything that could link to those clues you described.' Jacques paused and looked up.

'And?'

'Here, in the woods at the brow of the hill, or actually, by the contours, in a little dip behind the hill, there's a fountain, a spring. Look at the name of the fountain.' He pointed and Celestine followed his finger and peered down at the map.

'St. Martin. The Fontaine of St. Martin,' she said.

'Yes. Mind they're very common. Saint Martin stuck his appellation on a million fonts, churches, streets, villages, car parks. Not car parks. But you know how popular he was.'

'The patron saint of vintners,' said Celestine.

'And alcoholics.'

'Figures. But this spring, how far is it from the house?'

'I would say it can't be seen from the house, but there is a track running past it and down to the buildings beside the house. It must be five hundred metres away, I would guess.'

'Are there any other buildings around it?'

'Nothing named, but there are ruins, some form of old habitation, just along the way. If there was a source of water, it's likely that there were houses somewhere nearby. People gathered around water.'

'Yes they did,' said Celestine. 'I need a cup of coffee.'

'Henri is resting in the salon. I'll go and make some coffee, but you just sit there and think. Is this just a long shot, or does it potentially fit into your quest?'

Celestine took a long breath and settled back in the chair. Could it really be that simple, not simple, just so literal? A boy given a task, the reason why, the destruction of the Jews and of the father. A quest for the boy to go to a place that he knew. It had to be somewhere he knew well, where he would recognise the landscape. The boats on the river. Did the boy and his father travel there by boat? A boy would love that, and remember it for sure. A place in the countryside, a farm with beasts, cattle, sheep, birds. And the Miracle of St. Martin. St. Martin's Fontaine. Was it possible? It was like a child's treasure hunt. But two people had died in this hunt. She didn't know for sure that this had led to their deaths but... she stopped. Malraux had not found out more at the museum than she had, but he must have known more. He must have had other information, from his family, his grandfather, the archives in Paris, but he didn't pull this together, although someone thought, or assumed that he had. If the Palomers were involved, how could they know he was looking into matters that related to them, matters that could hurt them in some way? Jean-Michel had spent some time hanging around the cloisters, which in itself seemed unusual. He must have gone there for a reason, something must have raised their suspicions. Where could the Palomers have got that idea from? She ran through the possible sources in her head: she imagined each of the characters, as if in a scene, with Malraux on one side and the Palomers on the other; the nun, Ducrozet, her friend Catherine Taillandier, Desmarais, Monsieur Lefebvre, the lady in the museum. She couldn't see it. She had seen Jean-Michel at a distance, but she hadn't met his father, only seen his head under a hat in the boat. Jacques returned with the coffees.

'Jacques, describe Monsieur Palomer, the father, to me; physical characteristics, height, build etc.'

'I've drawn him,' he said. 'Just a minute.' He returned with his sketch pad. 'Not Albrecht Durer, I know, but this is as close as I can get. I might ask him to model for me someday.'

'Don't hold your breath.' Celestine looked closely at the drawing of a slobbering, fat face, with side whiskers and flat, dead eyes. 'Flattering,' she said.

'Doesn't do him justice, he looks worse than that.'

'And the main feature, the thing that really stands out when you look at him?'

'His face doesn't move. There are no expressions, his eyes look at you like from a dull pool. It's quite animal-like.'

Celestine looked again, there was something, some small link, a hook that had caught, and then it suddenly dropped into place and she saw it. 'The Deacon, the Deacon at the Abbey. Flat face, unemotional. Do you remember when he whispered to the nun and then led her to her seat? It was just a gesture, a proper action, but it wasn't caring. And when we spoke to him the next day, did he leave the impression on you of someone who was interested in you having a good experience from the visit?'

Jacques thought back for a moment. 'You could be right, but what…?'

'I saw him in the service too. I was watching him, absently. But now I realise, he was just going through the motions.'

'There must be an element of that every week,' said Jacques. 'It's just repetition for them, isn't it? They're probably thinking about football, or dinner, or women, or….'

'Perhaps, but this man. I'll tell you where I'm going with this. Someone had to alert the Palomers that Malraux was asking questions. Someone inspired Palomer to send Jean-Michel to the Abbey, to keep an eye on Malraux. He must have seen it all.' Celestine picked up her laptop. 'There'll be a list of personnel at the Abbey on their website.' She searched for a few minutes then looked up and passed the laptop to Jacques. 'Look, Deacon André Palomer. '

Jacques looked at the photograph of the Deacon of the Church. Now he could see the resemblance. 'Brother maybe, cousin?'

'I don't know, but we're going to find out. That's how they knew, the bastards.' She drank her coffee in one gulp and poured out another.

Chapter Thirty-Seven

Ducrozet arrived at the police poste at midday, two hours later than agreed; but the sedative had finally knocked him out just as the sun was rising. He was grey and dishevelled, his nerves shredded and his stomach twisting and knotting inside him. His fear of Grimard was only slightly less than his fear of the man in the dark clothes. He couldn't see the faintest glimmer of light ahead, only catastrophe.

Grimard waved him to sit down. 'So, Monsieur Ducrozet, my officers tell me that you came back to the Abbey last night. You thought a man was waiting for you at your home.'

'Yes, he was, I came back. I thought you might still be here. I was terrified you see. I knew I was in danger. I mean, that's why I went away, well partly, and other things.' Ducrozet stumbled on wretchedly.

'You thought your life was in danger. You didn't mention that to me last night.' Grimard's voice and face oozed disapproval.

'No, well you were occupied,' said Ducrozet faintly.

'Monsieur Ducrozet. Now, not next week, not when you think it's the right time, now. Now you're going to tell me everything you know. And if you leave anything out, and I discover that, your life will be in bloody danger. Go on, talk. No wait, let's record this. If this is a confession, I want it written up.' He nodded to the junior officer sitting at the end of the table.

For nearly an hour, Ducrozet took Grimard laboriously through the events of the previous weeks and up to the activities of the weekend. He was very thorough, and Grimard, biting his lip at times, allowed him to continue at his own pace without too many interruptions. He eventually stopped speaking and looked pleadingly at the Commandant. Grimard started several questions in his own mind but finally said:

'And you don't know who this man is, who you think was going to attack you, but you think it was the man behind the murders?'

'Jacques Lecoubarry knows,' said Ducrozet.

'Jacques Lecoubarry!' snapped Grimard, 'Jacques Lecoubarry.' He picked up his phone. 'Jerome. Get Monsieur Jacques Lecoubarry in here now. Yes. He lives on a barge. Get down there and take Desmarais, he seems to know him. Now.' He looked across at Ducrozet and shook his head. 'Monsieur Ducrozet, I am speechless. I want you to go away now, not far. Have a coffee, no, and some lunch. But don't go far. I want you back in here in two hours. Do you hear?' Ducrozet began to speak and then stopped himself. When he had gone, Grimard began to make notes on the pad in front of him. Could this even be possible? 'God, I hate these little towns,' he said out loud.

Monsieur Lefebvre looked neither surprised nor alarmed when a uniformed police officer and another, older man, in a dark suit, came up to the side of the *Incognito*. He was sitting on a seat in the bows, on an old handkerchief spread on the table there was an assortment of fruit, which he was slowly devouring. He stood up politely and smiled.

'Gentlemen?'

'Jacques Lecoubarry,' said the older one. Desmarais held up his hand.

'This is not Jacques Lecoubarry.' He turned to Monsieur Lefebvre. 'Monsieur, is Jacques Lecoubarry here?'

'No,' replied Monsieur Lefebvre. 'No, not on the boat?'

'And Celestine?' asked Desmarais.

'No, also.'

'And you are?'

'I am Henri Lefebvre, a friend of Jacques and Celestine. Staying with them as their guest. And,' he added, 'I am looking after their boat.'

The older man stepped onto the boat and pushed past Monsieur Lefebvre. He opened the door and stepped down into the salon, calling, 'Lecoubarry, Jacques Lecoubarry. Police.'

Monsieur Lefebvre stared after him, then turned and glared at Desmarais. 'That is wrong,' he said. 'I stated that Jacques was not here. I am not a liar. You cannot just barge in. What is his name and what is yours?' Desmarais attempted to calm him down.

'Look, Monsieur Lefebvre. My name is Desmarais, I know Jacques, he....'

'Desmarais. And the other person?' demanded Monsieur Lefebvre.

'Capitaine Jérôme Bedeau, Police Judiciaire. But look, do you know where Jacques is? It's very important.'

Monsieur Lefebvre just stood looking at him, and then down into the interior of the barge. Eventually, Bedeau emerged up the steps and found himself face to face with an angry Monsieur Lefebvre blocking his way. He looked across at Desmarais.

'What is this? Out of my way, old man,' he said, but Monsieur Lefebvre didn't move. When he spoke, his voice was a little shaky, but he kept eye contact with the man.

'I told you that Jacques was not here. You have no right to enter people's property. No right at all. You are Capitaine Bedeau. I will inform Jacques when he returns. He may wish to complain.'

Bedeau looked again at Desmarais.

'Monsieur Lefebvre, please. Do you know where Jacques is?' Desmarais pleaded. Monsieur Lefebvre stepped aside and Bedeau eased around him.'

'No, I don't.'

'Well, when do you expect him back?'

'I don't. I mean, I don't have a specific time to expect him.'

Exasperated, Desmarais finally said. 'Jacques has my number. Can you ask him to call me? He's not picking up his phone at the moment.'

'No, he wouldn't,' said Monsieur Lefebvre. 'Not on a bicycle.'

'He's on a bicycle?'

'Yes. He and Celestine. Electric bicycles. They left perhaps half an hour ago.'

'And you don't know where they were going?'

'No.'

'Direction?' Monsieur Lefebvre pointed vaguely towards the town centre.

As the two police officers climbed back into their car, Bedeau turned to Desmarais. 'This Jacques Lecoubarry, he's a piece of work no? And who the hell was that, really? Dressed like a tramp, talking like a lawyer.'

Desmarais grinned. 'Jacques Lecoubarry is definitely a piece of work. We'll just have to drive around. We should spot them on the roads somewhere, and I'll keep trying his phone.'

Jacques and Celestine had turned off their phones shortly after they had reached a small track leading diagonally off the main road, some seven kilometres east of Lissac. A chain hung across the entrance to the track; the notice on it said - Défense de Chasser - No Hunting. There were other notices nailed to the trees on either side; Private Property, Entrance Forbidden. Jacques lifted the bicycles over the chain and leant them against a broad oak tree. He took out the map.

'Is this it?' asked Celestine.

'Yes, I'm sure.' He pointed to a place on the map. 'Look this track goes past the Spring of St. Martin. It's an old mule track, possibly older than the road that is used now. It goes past the fountain, to water the animals and the humans. We'll hide the bikes behind these trees.' He looked down at the surface of the trail. It was hard and parched where there was no tree canopy, but in the shade of the oak branches, some tough grasses and weeds had kept their tinge of green. There were also the dried-out marks of footprints and hoof marks in the hardened clay. Jacques knelt down and put his hand on the earth. 'It's a well-used path,' he said. 'Horses and people. Quite recently too.'

'Who are you? Tonto,' said Celestine. 'Put your ear to the ground and tell me how many horses are coming?'

Jacques grinned. It was good that Celestine could joke at this time. Her nerves were good. 'You mock, Hiawatha, but it means we have to be careful. We must appear to be just a couple of walkers enjoying the landscape.'

They were both dressed in shorts, t-shirts and robust canvas boots. Jacques carried a small rucksack. They tucked the bicycles in the undergrowth behind two tall trees. The woods were predominantly oak, some hornbeam, with a few shorter shrubs of hawthorn and elder. As they walked along the track the woods became denser; small oak saplings, their spindly branches straining for sunlight, filled in the gaps between the larger, older trees. There was less light and it was noticeably cooler as they moved deeper into the woods. It was very quiet. There was no road noise, and with only a gentle breeze, the trees themselves moved only slightly and without sound. No birds were singing. It was late summer, and it seemed as though all the energy had been drained from the natural world - exhausted in growth, procreation, flowering, fruiting and surviving. The undergrowth at the side of the track was a tangle of brambles, blackthorn and dog rose; the tentacles of the brambles forcing their way through the branches of the trees. The track began to descend slightly, and on one side an old, low, stone wall appeared, broken down, with dislodged stones lying where they'd fallen on the ground.

'Signs of human endeavour,' said Jacques quietly. Celestine nodded.

A little further along the track the land on the right-hand side fell away sharply, and in a clearing, they could see rows of vines in the fields below. In the distance, they could see the line of trees that marked the river. They were not yet level with the house, and after the clearing the woods thickened again. A pheasant suddenly flew up from under their feet and clattered away, squawking hoarsely, outraged, into the higher branches. One of its tail feathers drifted slowly down and Jacques picked it up. He poked it gently into the hair on the back of Celestine's head.

'Now, Hiawatha, you look like the real thing,' he said. 'But don't go scaring up any more pheasants.'

'It was hardly intentional. How far are we from the fountain do you think?'

'Not far. The wall is getting higher here.'

Just then they heard a sound on the track ahead of horses cantering, clopping on the hard ground, and rapidly coming closer. Jacques looked at Celestine.

'Hide,' she said. 'We don't need any complications, so close.'

'Over the wall.'

Jacques pushed his rucksack over a broken part of the wall, and using the jutting-out, lower stones to stand on, rolled over the top and stumbled down on all fours behind the wall. Celestine took one quick stride, placed her foot on a stone and hurdled it easily. She crouched down a few feet from Jacques. The horses were getting much closer, moving easily, they were almost at the point where Jacques and Celestine were hiding. Jacques was kneeling, his legs completely entwined with brambles, and Celestine could already see blood seeping out from scratches on his arms and shins. She had been luckier; she had landed on a mound of stones covered in coarse grass and ivy. Jacques was biting his lip but he remained still and silent. Celestine leaned her head against the wall. The pace of the horses had changed, transitioning from a canter to a trot and then to a walk. They could hear voices, two horses, two women's voices. Jacques recognised one of the voices as that of Jean-Michel's wife, the other voice was younger, more high-pitched and excited. They were almost alongside, and they heard the younger woman say something like:

'She never feeds them properly.' And then they were gone; and they heard the clip-clop sounds retreating up the slope of the track. Celestine stood up carefully and peered over the wall. She watched the horses move into the clearing, where the colours were more obvious - a grey and a chestnut. The girl on the right had her head turned permanently to the other rider, chattering relentlessly. Celestine moved over to Jacques and helped disentangle him from the brambles. One was in his hair and had scratched his right cheek, his arms and legs were crisscrossed with scratches and deeper cuts. She pulled him up.

'Two women, or a girl and a woman.'

'The woman was Jean-Michel's wife,' said Jacques. 'I know what she would have said if she'd seen us. They may come back this way, or they could go back along the road and the drive.'

'If they do come back this way they won't canter downhill, so we'll have a little bit more time to hide.'

'Good. I may choose my landing place more carefully next time.' He wiped the drops of blood from his face and arms and they clambered back onto the track. 'I reckon the fountain should be just down here.'

They walked another fifty metres. The ground on their left began to rise until there was a face of fractured, white rock, with only a few small trees clinging to it. Then the track widened, and the wall, now well preserved, curved around to stop at a stone arch, some two metres high. On the wall was an old brass tap, green with verdigris, and encrusted with age. Below it was a grill, built into the stone, and below that a stone trough extending a foot or so out from the archway. Celestine looked at it, unimpressed.

'That's not what I was expecting,' she said. 'I thought the water would be gushing out of the rock into a pool.'

'To catch the moonlight,' said Jacques. 'Traditionally, I expect, this water was thought to have healing properties, or tasted good or was free. People would have gathered here to fill up their cans and bottles. A tap is much more convenient for that.'

'Yes, I suppose.' Celestine stood back and looked more carefully at the fountain. She had been hoping for something clearer, something that matched the pattern in her head. The clues formed a narrative for her, and now that they had reached St. Martin she wondered what was next. There didn't seem to be anything clear. She looked at Jacques who was closely examining the stones and the stone sink.

'Have you found something?'

'No. Just some of these stones were not originally here, they were used for some other purpose. Look at this one, the groove there, that's where a bar was slotted in, it was part of a gate post or a small outbuilding. And this one's the same. They came from another building.'

'Yes, but what does this tell us?' asked Celestine.

'We know there were other buildings, ruins now, along the track, and in the woods behind them. We also know that the original stone sink here was broken, or didn't exist, and there was an earth pool of water. So probably, when the water was piped and the tap installed, stones were taken from somewhere down the track and used to build this sink.'

'When do you think?'

'Hundred years ago, more possibly, late nineteenth century.'

'So, it would have looked like this in Steinbach's time.'

'Almost certainly.'

Celestine looked down and pondered. 'It's just a signpost,' she said, 'a waymark. When you reach this clue, then you look for the next one. What troubles me is that we are going in the wrong direction.' She paused to collect her thoughts. 'If Steinbach left this trail for his son to follow, wouldn't he expect him to be coming from the direction of the house? In which case, when he reached the fountain, the next point would be beyond that, but we've just walked that way and I didn't see anything but trees.'

'Perhaps, or perhaps not,' said Jacques. 'The ruins further down, you might not be able to see them from the track. The fountain here is on the track; so, you find that first, which gives you the approximate location to start looking for the next clue.'

Celestine twisted her mouth. 'Ok, let's see. The next picture was the washing of the feet.'

'Remind me, what did it look like?'

'It was a bit bruised and battered, but you could pick out a number of characters. Jesus looking down, getting ready to, well, wash the feet of the disciples, I guess.'

'Anything else in the carving?'

'Two horizontal figures holding a wreath in the frieze above.' Celestine shrugged and looked for a moment rather uncertain.

'Right, let's walk on. Think about Monsieur Steinbach; he wouldn't hide something where lots of people were moving around, would he? He'd be more careful than that,' suggested Jacques.

They walked on as the land began to flatten out on both sides. The trees were thinner, and as the track curved a little, they suddenly caught sight of the roof of the house through the canopy of leaves. Jacques motioned for Celestine to move closer to the left side of the track. He stood behind a tree and looked down the hill. He could see the gravelled drive as it opened out in a circle in front of the main entrance to the house. There was a car parked there. He could only see a part of the front elevation and the roof of the house. He listened carefully, but there was no sound coming from it and no sign of anyone around. They were still some four hundred metres from the house, so he felt relatively comfortable, but they would need to be even more careful now. They walked a little further, alongside the low wall which was no more than a few stones high at this point. Then there was a gap in the wall, overgrown with brambles and other creeping branches, and partly blocked by fallen stones; but the sides were of square, dressed stone. It was about two metres wide, and the wall continued at right angles to the track.

'This should lead to the ruins,' said Jacques, quietly. 'More bloody brambles.' He stepped over the fallen stones and pushed aside the lower branches. Celestine followed him, lifting the branches carefully back into place behind them. The track was completely overgrown and almost impassable, except for a small path where the grass had been trodden down and the bushes pushed aside. 'This is an animal trail,' said Jacques. 'Wild boar and deer. Not humans, I don't think, not now.'

In fact, they came across animal tracks dried in the hard earth, in places where there would be mud and water when the rains came. They had to push aside low branches where animals could run easily beneath. There were piles of stones, lichen and moss covered, at places along the side of the path; hardly recognisable as a structure now, they were the ruins of buildings, hovels and animal shelters. The path fell away down to a dried-up stream bed, striations in the clay showed where animals had slid down the banks before crossing the narrow stream. It opened up into a wallow, dry now, with tufts of meadow grass and wild carrot growing out of the baked earth. There were some stones left in what must have been a causeway across the mire when the path was well-used. They crossed it and started up a slight incline. Jacques could hear the sound of running water. On the left, he saw a thin stream of rusty-looking water trickling out of a fissure in the rocks, and running down through the undergrowth to the stream below. He stopped, and Celestine nearly bumped into him. She looked at the water trickling from the rock face, and she thought of the stone carvings. She shook her head, trying to clear it, trying to move into the narrative of Monsieur Steinbach and his son. Thinking aloud she said.

'The washing of the feet is biblical. But, what if in this context it's much more prosaic than that,' she sighed. 'Ok, Steinbach and his son have visited these places, that's the only way it makes sense, shared experiences. They visit the fountain of Sainte Martin, they see it often, and it's a landmark. An easy clue for Sebastien, or whatever his name was. But boys like to explore. They turn off the track to explore the ruins; the boy has imagination, ruins are a source of fascination for him. He wants to come here often. They walk up the path. It's winter or early spring or late autumn; there's been rain, lots of rain. What would that track be like, back there in the hollow?'

'A quagmire,' said Jacques, looking intently at Celestine as she sketched out ideas with her hands.

'Yes, muddy, very muddy. There must have been stepping stones or a wooden bridge at some time; but those stones would have been flat, and maybe taken for other purposes once the dwellings here had been deserted. So, they cross the muddy dip in the track. Monsieur Steinbach steps carefully when he can, onto stones or branches thrown down. Sebastien steps gleefully into the mud and enjoys the mess of it. He's wearing sturdy boots, part way up his calves. They climb up from the hollow. Sebastien's boots are caked with mud, he can barely lift one foot at a time. But that's ok, it's part of the fun, because they come to a source of water, a cleaning place. In the winter, the water gushes out of there, it doesn't trickle. Sebastien holds on to his father's arm and sticks his muddy boot into the flowing water. He washes the mud from his boots, one, then the other, laughing, his father smiling. They have done this before. The washing of the feet. Light-footed now, Sebastien clatters on up the track.' Celestine stopped and shuddered slightly, as though emerging from a trance. Jacques looked at her askance.

'Maybe, just maybe,' he said.' It's not an infallible proposition, but perhaps a working hypothesis.' To himself, he sounded dry and unconvinced.

'I think it's more than that Jacques. I feel as though I am inside the minds of Steinbach and his son. Ever since I visited the museum this morning, I have felt, I don't know, close to them. I saw the photographs, I thought about their lives at that time. This was one, just one, little story played out, and I feel that I have joined it. I have become a part of the story. To me, this feels right. This is what Sebastien and his father would have shared, no one else, so no one else could follow the trail.'

'Except you.'

'Yes, but only because the murders have given a huge impetus to the quest. The search for the meaning of these killings has forced us to look deeper, with more urgency, more creativity. I feel it, Jacques. This is the story. I am in the story and it's in me.'

To Jacques, she looked a little messianic and it troubled him, but he said: 'Ok, Hiawatha. Then lead on. If this was the washing of the feet, what was next?'

'The next and last is the Ascension of Alexander.'

'And the picture, the carving?'

Celestine lowered her head and briefly closed her eyes. 'This is the last clue. I spent some time reading around this one. Bear with me, Jacques.' She hesitated and then shivered, as though there was something more going on inside her. 'Alexander, who, despite being a Macedonian, heathen and bloodthirsty conqueror, became in the medieval mind, an example of "extra man, superman" if you like, a demi-god. That's what I read. He was depicted as ascending, rising, trying to reach heaven. In one of the carvings, there is a man, Alexander, being lifted upwards by large birds, eagles or griffins, I think. I remember one side has a figure with a rope attached to the birds. I've got the picture on my phone.'

'Don't switch it on. Electronic noises carry a long way.' Jacques blew out his cheeks. 'Let's keep walking, see if anything strikes us. You stay right there in the zone, in 1943, I'll take care of the present.'

The path wound around a large unruly tree with wide leaves like three, fat-fingered palms.

'Fig tree,' said Jacques. 'Must have been planted deliberately, a long time ago. Look at it, all the children have grown up around the original old tree.' In fact, there were dozens of individual trees, some thick as fence posts, others thin as a whip

'It's a colony, a colony of figs,' said Celestine.

'Good sweet food and good shade for people.' said Jacques.

There was still a definite path, overgrown in parts, but still bordered on both sides by low stone walls. It was starting to slope gradually back down the hill. They passed a flat area, a ten-meter circle of stones, covered with thin grasses. Jacques stopped. 'A threshing floor,' he said.

'What?'

'A threshing floor. It'll be stone under the grass and weeds. It's where the corn was threshed and later winnowed; probably with a donkey or an ox dragging a heavy log round and round the circle, crushing the straw and separating the grain. You see them all over Europe. I've seen them in Spain, in Portugal. Same model.'

'So, there must have been quite a community living in these buildings that are now ruins.'

'Yes. It's a good place. Plenty of water, access to fields below, grazing in the woods, up from the river which transported goods and produce, but also brought trouble.'

The path was slowly descending, the trees thickening again. Around a gentle curve in the path, they looked up to the left. There were more stone ruins, but also a taller building which looked to be in better repair.

'A pigeonnier,' said Jacques. They stepped over a small pile of stones and walked up to the building. It was more like a small tower, with a wooden door hanging off its hinges. It stood about six metres high to the front eaves, built of blocks of dressed white stone at the corners, filled in between with random boulders and small stones of all sizes. On the upper walls, there were several small openings with stone sills and arched tops. 'Pigeon holes,' said Jacques, pointing to the openings. He walked around to the side. 'The roof is still intact. This must have been in use long after the people left their hovels. Probably to provide meat for the house. Every settlement around here had a pigeonnier.'

'What's it like inside, do you think?' asked Celestine.

'They often had two sections. The lower part was used for storage and the upper part for pigeons. Wooden floors, but they often rotted; pigeon shit is not a great preservative.'

'I want to see in,' said Celestine, with a firmness in her voice that made Jacques look back at her. He pushed at the door which creaked but didn't move.

'It's a bit jammed.'

'Keep trying. I want to go inside.'

Jacques pushed harder and then reached around the door to pull away some detritus that was jamming it. There were tendrils and creepers wound around the hinges and clinging to the lintel above the door. He pushed harder again and the door splintered where it hung on one hinge. He was able to step on it, and it broke from the hinge with a loud crack which echoed through the trees.

'Shit, that'll wake the neighbourhood.'

'Go inside,' said Celestine, and came up close behind him. 'I want to go inside.'

Jacques stepped over a pile of splintered wood and took Celestine's hand to steady her as she came in. She shook it off, and moved past him to stand in the centre of the floor. Although covered in dust and pieces of rotten timber, the floor was flagged and still sound. Above, there was half a floor of rotten timber, supported on round joists of rough branches. On the side away from the door, there was no upper floor, just the broken ends of joists jutting from holes in the walls.

Celestine was looking up. The roof sloped from the front to the back of the building, and they could see the underside of the clay tiles. 'The roof is in decent condition,' said Celestine.

'Protestant.'

'What?'

'The shape of the roof. They say, I don't know how true it is, pigeonniers in catholic steadings were built in the shape of a steeple. You'll have seen them, they're the most common type. Protestants, being altogether plainer folk and less ostentatious, built their pigeon towers with a simple, one-angled roof; much cheaper in tiles, wood and carpentry, but still brought the pigeons closer to heaven.'

Celestine leaned her back against the wall. She hung her head in deep thought. Finally, she said: 'What did you just say, Jacques, about the pigeons?'

'What? That whatever the style of roof, the pigeons were brought closer to heaven; because they were kept here to be killed; housed comfortably, according to their religion, but when the pot needed filling, the doors were closed and the reaper moved amongst them.'

He looked at Celestine's face, she was scanning the wall, up and down and side to side. Her lips were moving as she muttered quietly to herself.

'The carving on the pillar - the ascension or flight of Alexander.'

'Yes.'

'This was a really complex allegory. It was said to represent, amongst other things, an apotheosis... a,' she struggled for the words. 'The highest point, a culmination, the limit of human abilities, a kind of vanity in trying to reach heaven by earthly means. In the carving, Alexander is attached with a rope to large birds, probably eagles, which raise him to the sky.'

'Pigeons ain't eagles.'

'No, listen,' she snapped. 'There's more. I read a lot about this yesterday, about the ascension of Alexander. There was a legend of two eagles, flying boy masons, on ropes, to build a palace between heaven and earth - man's vanity. But this appeared in Talmudic texts also, it was a well-known story. Ancient rulers built towers to try to reach heaven. Sebastien would know these stories. Who knows how often Steinbach and his son visited the cloisters? Sebastien set up in business as an illustrator, we know that. He learned that here, in Lissac-sur-Tarn, maybe copying the works of the carvers of a thousand years ago. Like those school children we saw the other day, sitting on the wall and copying the pictures from the Old and New Testament - Jewish stories, not just Christian ones.' She paused. 'I missed it. I was trying to find a link with Alexander the Great, but that's me, an adult, an outsider. But a child, a Jewish child, his link is the birds, the rope, the rising up and the allegory - building a tower to heaven. And this is the final clue, the culmination. For Sebastien to solve this final clue he has to raise his abilities, but he also, literally, has to raise himself.' Celestine sagged at the waist, drained.

'So, you think that the Ascension of Alexander is here, in this pigeon tower?'

'Where else could he raise himself up? In a tree? There are a million trees in the woods, and trees get cut down, branches break off.'

Jacques looked up. 'OK, but I can't see anything,' he said.

Celestine stood upright and stepped into the centre of the building. 'It won't be obvious, we need to get up there, as high as possible, you won't be able to see anything from down here.' They stood silently, looking up at the rough stone walls of the pigeonnier.

'I could get onto the platform on this side,' said Jacques. 'I'd be able to check all of this wall.' He took hold of the broken door and dragged it to where he could lean it at an angle against the wall, next to the nearest joist. He put his foot on the wooden brace of the door and started to lever himself up. Celestine placed her hand on his arm.

'I think I'd better do that. None of the wood looks very sound, and I'm a lot lighter than you.'

'A little, certainly,' said Jacques.

'Give me a hand up.' Jacques put his hand on her buttocks and pushed as she levered herself up the door and rolled onto the wooden half-floor.

'Try to stand where there are joists,' said Jacques, 'the floorboards could be completely rotten.'

Celestine stepped gingerly onto the wooden floor and moved carefully towards the wall. She stood on the side above the door and scanned each stone and crack, pushing her fingers into the holes where the mortar had fallen away. Suddenly, there was a flapping of dark wings, and two bats flew out of a space between the roof joists and skimmed over her head, their membranous wings twitching the ends of her hair. She squealed involuntarily and brushed at the top of her head. The bats swooped once around the pigeonnier and then flew out through one of the gaps. She took a deep breath, she had controlled herself very well. She hadn't stepped back which might have sent her crashing through the floor. She glanced down at Jacques, who was looking concerned, but with a thin smile on his face.

'Funny?' she asked. He shook his head, smiling more widely. 'Well, you come up here instead if you like. Van Helsing.'

'You handled it really well,' he said. 'I'm taking notes.'

Celestine continued to edge carefully along the wall, checking every nook and cranny, expecting at any moment to be assailed by some furious, outraged creatures which had been left undisturbed for half a century. She came to the middle of the wall where the opening was at eye level. She looked out. She could see over the trees that sloped down to the valley, and could make out some of the rows of vines surrounding the house. But then she heard a sound. She listened carefully, she could hear the definite clip-clopping of a horse walking slowly up the track, coming from the direction of the house.

'There's another horse coming up from the house,' she whispered. 'Don't make any noise.'

'Can you see the trail?'

'I'm not sure. If I look at an angle I think I might see part of it. Keep behind the stone wall.' Jacques moved carefully towards the door, crouched down, and listened, uneasily.

Chapter Thirty-Eight

Monsieur and Madame Briseau returned early from a visit to their daughter and her children in Montpelier. Several messages and finally, a most insistent call from the police in Lissac, had convinced them to return to their house on the Route de Calvaire. They arrived home just after three in the afternoon and a police car pulled up shortly afterwards. The agent explained that they were looking for camera footage from a particular night, and it had been noticed that they had a camera that pointed down the drive towards the road.

'Yes, it records,' said Monsieur Briseau. 'I've looked at it before, to see the animals that cross the garden at night - foxes, badgers, a deer once.'

'And a snake,' said Madame Briseau.

'Yes, a snake.'

'How long does it keep the recordings?' asked the agent.

'I'm not sure. I think perhaps a week. Maybe more.'

'And how long have you been away?'

'It would have been two weeks next Friday when we planned to come home, except for this….'

'I'm sorry you've had to change your plans. But I would like access to the recordings, please.'

'Of course, in the back room, on the computer,' said Monsieur Briseau. Ten minutes later the officer had the data downloaded and sent by email to the poste de police.

'It's probably nothing, but we have to….' he said. 'Thank you for your cooperation and apologies again for disturbing your holiday.'

Monsieur and Madame Briseau watched the police car turn and edge out of the drive and onto the road. Slightly excited, Madame Briseau took her husband's hand and squeezed it gently.

Desmarais and Bedeau had been driving around for nearly an hour.

'Could be anywhere. This is wasting my time,' said Bedeau.
'Try his phone again.'

Desmarais pressed the button to call Jacques, but it went instantly to his messaging service.

'Jacques, call me back now. Desmarais. Seriously, we need to speak to you. Now!'

Capitaine Bedeau looked at him. 'Drive us back to the station. And if you've got nothing better to do, go and visit that old git on the boat again. I don't believe for a minute he doesn't know where they've gone.' As they rounded the corner to the police station they had to pull up quickly, as a large group of people, men, women and children were standing in the road and milling around the entrance. 'What the hell?' snapped Bedeau. Desmarais looked more closely. He recognised some of the faces, but more, the clothes and the physical appearance of the crowd.

'Bulgarians,' he said. 'Bulgarians. They are really pissed. Jacques said there would be unrest.'

'Jacques. The same Jacques we've been chasing all afternoon. What is he a fucking oracle now as well?'

'I can't get past them, and I'm not going to drive into them.'

'Is there a back way in?'

'Not for the car, but we could park and get in that way.'

'Do it,' said Bedeau.

Desmarais reversed, swung the car around and drove in a wide circle through some smaller streets, before parking in front of the doorway of an old boarded-up garage. 'Just down here,' he said, and they climbed out of the car and headed down the alley. Desmarais pressed the intercom beside the door, and after a short wait a voice sounded and they were let into the building. They met Grimard at the head of the stairs. He looked at them with distaste.

'Couldn't find him, sir. Lecoubarry. Looked everywhere. Gone off on a bicycle,' said Bedeau.

Grimard looked at Desmarais. 'You don't know where he is?'

'No, sir. We've been looking for him.'

'Great. They want me to release the Bulgarian, that crowd out there. The Magistrate agrees, says we don't have enough.'

'It seems like a good idea, sir. It'll quieten them down, for sure,' said Desmarais.

'Oh, you, municipal police agent Desmarais think that's a good idea. Well, that's all I need. It must be a good idea then mustn't it.' Desmarais stood his ground and looked straight back at Grimard.

'It is a good idea. You have nothing to hold him on, just a bit of hearsay.' He was raising his voice now. 'Someone murdered Malraux, and then the nun, and chased Ducrozet. It wasn't the Bulgarian who did all three things, he was in here half the time.'

Grimard stepped back. Bedeau placed his hand on Desmarais' arm.

'That's enough, police agent. You're speaking to a commandant. You have no say in this.'

'No say?' said Desmarais, unable now to stop himself. 'No say. This is my town. These people outside live here, you don't. You've got a Bulgarian who you think killed one guy; a Polish weirdo you think killed the other one; and a mystery stalker.' He turned away and started walking back down the stairs. 'Get a fucking grip. I'm going to find Jacques Lecoubarry. He knows, I'm sure of it.' Desmarais left the two senior officers, apoplectic, at the top of the stairs, and hurried out of the building. He was going to talk to the old man again.

Chapter Thirty-Nine

Celestine listened to the sound of the horses, trying to pinpoint their location. Down and to the left, about two hundred metres away, was a small clearing where a logging track ran up the hill at right angles to the trail. There were trees on either side, but there was a chance she would be able to catch a quick view of anyone passing there. Then she heard another horse, this time coming along the trail to the right. She whispered to Jacques: 'There's another horse coming down the trail.'

'One or two?'

'One, I think, just the one.'

Jacques slipped out of the door and moved towards a pile of stones surrounded by small trees. He crouched down there, well-concealed, and listened.

Celestine pulled her head back from the opening, the lower horse was definitely coming nearer and must be almost at the clearing. Suddenly, a tall, dark bay horse came into view. She had only a few seconds to see the rider, but she knew instantly that it was Jean-Michel Palomer. Horse and rider passed through the clearing quickly and were lost behind the trees. She could hear the other horse coming closer, down the trail. She moved to the other side of the opening and leant back against the wall. It would be very difficult to see her through the trees, but she was taking no chances. By the sounds of the hooves on the hard ground, she could tell that the two horses were slowly converging. Then the sounds stopped and she heard muffled voices She couldn't make out the words.

She wondered what Jacques was doing. If someone came along here she was a sitting duck, whereas in the woods and the ruins, there were lots of hiding places. She wasn't afraid, she just wanted to finish what they had started. She was certain that the solution was here, somewhere; and unless they had been seen coming this way, there should be no reason why someone would be looking for them. No one had been this way for a long time; so they just needed to sit tight.

She turned away from the opening, resting her head against the ancient stones. She looked across at the wall on the other side, and she saw something. At first, she was unsure, but then she looked harder. There was a slot, not quite a niche, almost at the eaves where the roof beams met the top of the wall. She blinked her eyes, looked away and then back. She ran her eyes backwards and forwards across the wall to see if there was anything similar; a pattern inserted by the original builder, a structural facet, but there was nothing like it. The base of the slot seemed to project a little from the wall, which would make it impossible to see from the ground. Even from here, she could have easily missed it if she hadn't been so intensely engaged. It might be nothing she told herself, just some architectural feature, something for the birds to retreat to. And how the hell could they reach it? It must be five or six metres from the ground. They would need a ladder of some kind. She turned back to the window. She could hear nothing now, neither horses nor humans, but she suddenly felt very vulnerable. She sat down on the half floor and waited.

Jacques could hear the voices, muffled by the vegetation. He looked down and realised he had picked up a small, pointed rock, and was clenching it in his hand until it hurt. He waited, expecting to hear the sound of movement, pushing past branches, stepping over stones. Instead, he heard the jingle of a bridle as a horse shook its head, the noise of a slap on leather, and then the clear sound of two horses trotting away, both travelling in the same direction towards the house.

Celestine stood up to look out of the small opening. She could clearly hear the two horses heading back down the trail. She focused on the clearing, waiting to see them pass. The sound seemed to flow into the clearing before the horses did, and then they passed quickly through it. She had a brief view, but it was enough for her to realise that there were indeed two horses, but only one rider. One of the riders had dismounted, and might even now be moving towards them.

Jacques relaxed a little when he heard the horses moving away. He laid the rock down carefully and stretched his fingers and then his legs. He was about to stand up when he caught the slightest of sounds coming from the direction of the trail - the sound of a cigarette lighter being struck. Within a minute he caught the smell of burning tobacco. Whoever was smoking a cigarette couldn't be more than fifty metres away, closer than the trail. But, were they standing still or coming towards them? Then he heard the crack of a broken twig, and he knew someone was heading that way. He quietly edged further behind the low wall and nestled into the branches of a straggling cypress tree. Through the branches he could see the door of the pigeonnier and wondered if Celestine was aware of the threat.

Inside, Celestine had heard the sounds coming closer. She lay down on the half floor, as tight to the wall as she could get. If someone came into the pigeonnier, they wouldn't see her unless they climbed up onto the platform. She lay absolutely still.

Jacques smelled the smoke before he saw the man. There was a curse as someone stumbled over a fallen stone, then pushed past a low-lying branch, snapping the dry end of it. A figure walked into the clearing in front of the pigeonnier. Jacques peered out. In his mind, he was certain this would be Jean-Michel Palomer; but this man was short, with a careless, shuffling walk. Wearing a felt cap and green gilet, he took a deep draw on the cigarette and threw the end on the ground, stamping it out with his foot. As he did so he turned to face exactly where Jacques was concealed. He seemed to be looking straight at him and Jacques was certain that they would lock eyes, but the man turned his head away and looked lazily around. He looked up at the pigeonnier then walked over to the gaping hole where the door had been. Jacques readied himself to jump up and rush at him with whatever he had to hand.

Celestine heard the noise as the man scraped his boot on the old stone threshold. She willed her muscles to be stilled and her breath to be shallow and silent. The man put one foot inside and looked casually up and around, then stepped back out again. He leaned his back against the stones at the side of the door and took another cigarette from a packet in his gilet. He was looking in Jacques' direction. Jacques could feel every stone that was sticking in him, in his back, his buttocks, his elbows; his legs were cramped and desperate to stretch out, and branches prickled the back of his neck and his cheek. If the man decided to smoke out his cigarette there, Jacques knew, he would be forced to jump up quickly and rush at him out of the bushes, hopefully taking him by surprise. But after lighting his cigarette, the man stood up straight and started walking along the path which curved back towards the main trail.

Jacques waited until he was out of sight and then gradually uncoiled himself. Looking nervously down the path, he stepped cautiously out of his hiding place and tip-toed across to the pigeonnier. He called very quietly to Celestine.

'Ok. He's gone, he's out of sight. We need to leave now,' said Jacques.

Celestine crawled to the edge of the floor and looked down. 'No, we don't. Look.' She pointed to the slot high up on the wall.

'What? I can't see anything.'

'About halfway along, right at the top, nearly at the roof beams. There's a flat stone that juts out a little. No?'

'I guess.'

'Well, there is, and above it there's a cavity, a niche. Thin but definitely there. We have to look inside it. I'm coming down.' She climbed down using the old wooden door. Jacques put his head carefully outside and looked down the path. There was no one there. He stepped back in and faced Celestine.

'Firstly, who do you think that was? Where did he come from? And why did he come this way when no one has been here for years?'

'We must have left some sign, a broken branch, a stone dislodged.'

'They're looking for us. But where did he come from?'

'From one of the horses. There was only one rider, Jean-Michel, with the two horses.'

'So, this guy must work for the Palomers. Jean-Michel must have sent him to check out the path. Maybe someone saw us. It's difficult in the countryside. You think it's easy to hide, but it's easy to be seen.'

'He didn't look very thoroughly, did he? He hardly came in here.'

'I don't know,' said Jacques. 'I am anxious, there's something not right. If they thought we were here, wouldn't they both have come and really searched the place? Or was it just an idle worker, he looked listless.'

'Or did Jean-Michel want us to know that he knew we were here, and that he'd be waiting for us?' She moved close to Jacques and laid her hands on his arms.

'We have to move fast. We need to look in that niche,' she said firmly.

Jacques looked up and shook his head. 'It's five metres up. I don't see how we can get up there. We need a ladder.'

'We don't have a ladder. Think.'

Jacques looked out of the door, there was no sign of anyone. He stepped outside and walked around the clearing, peering at the pile of stones and fallen timbers, most of which appeared to be rotten rafters from the old buildings. Behind one of the stone outlines of a ruined building, there had been a small landslide. The earth was sharply cut away and raw, and a few trees had toppled over as their roots had been torn out. They lay there inverted, their bent trunks head down on the slope and their dead roots standing stark in the air, like the tangled hair of a thin giant. Jacques poked at them with his boot, then he spotted the long pole of an ash tree, snapped off at the base. It must have been tackled and brought down by the other trees, but its roots had remained in the soil. It was trapped beneath the branches of another tree, but as Jacques tugged at it, he felt there was some movement. He hurried back to the pigeonnier where Celestine was still staring up at the wall. He grabbed her arm. 'Come and help me,' he said.

The pole was wedged between the branches and part of the trunk of two trees. They tried pulling, but it only moved a little way and jammed again. Jacques climbed down between the branches and the earth. 'I need to lift these two up, while you slide out the ash pole,' he said.

Celestine looked at him doubtfully, but she took a strong grip on the pole. Jacques braced himself on his haunches and put his arms beneath the overlying trees. With a grunt, he heaved and lifted them slightly. Celestine pulled as hard as she could and there was a sudden release of pressure on the pole. She pulled it further out. It took them three attempts; each time Jacques grunted and lifted, and Celestine pulled it a little further, until finally, it was free and Celestine fell back on the grass. Jacques let the branches fall and shook out his aching arms and shoulders. He clambered over to where Celestine was sitting. 'A ladder,' he said.

The ash trunk was about four metres long, straight as an arrow, with only a few thin side twigs. The top branches were hanging off where they'd been broken in the fall. Jacques twisted them backwards and forwards until they came away completely.
'Come on, we have to hurry,' he said. They carried the pole into the pigeonnier and manoeuvred it under the half floor until they could prop it up, at an angle, against the wall beneath the niche. Jacques looked Celestine up and down with approval.

'You, Celestine, were made for this - lithe, strong, balanced, motivated,' he added. 'I'll hold the tree firmly, you lean towards the wall and slide up slowly. You should be able to reach, but you'll have to stand up at the end.'

Jacques braced himself at the bottom of the pole, and Celestine used his arms and shoulders to push herself up so far. She climbed it like a rope, hooking her feet around and pushing herself up while also pulling with her hands. She had reached three-quarters of the way there when her right foot slipped. She dropped quickly, her left foot landing heavily on Jacques' shoulder, and her hands scraping off skin as she tried to break her fall. She yelped with pain. Jacques put his full weight on the pole, and with his right hand reached up to steady her. He took hold of her right leg and pushed his head under her buttocks. She lifted her hands momentarily off the surface of the wood to ease the pain. Her palms and fingers were badly scraped, and there were little drops of blood appearing where the cuts were deepest.

'Push off from my shoulders,' said Jacques. 'Grip with your knees. You know this position.' Celestine almost smiled.

'Ok, I'm going to get there,' she said. She placed both feet on Jacques' shoulders and pushed herself up as high as she could. Then, despite the pain in her hands, she hauled herself higher. Her hands were burning, and she was blinking away the tears, but she stretched up higher again, gripped the pole, then released her knees and hauled herself up to a new position. This way, she made slow progress until her fingers touched the top of the pole. Above the pole there was still a metre of white stone, with the niche a little to the right. In order to reach it she would have to stand up, and that meant releasing the grip with her knees. About fifty centimetres from the top of the pole there was a slightly raised nodule, where a branch had broken off; it wasn't much and the other side was smooth, so she would be completely reliant on the soundness of the nodule and of her own leg's strength to hold her there. Jacques sensed her hesitation.

'If you think you're going to fall, push away from the wall and try to land on the lump of human flesh standing below you. Trust me. I'm made for a soft landing and I promise I won't sue you for damages.'

Celestine gathered herself. She walked her hands slowly up the wall, trying to find a purchase in the crumbling mortar joints between the stones. She moved her legs up until she could feel the rough protuberance against the top of her right foot. Leaning into the wall, she slowly eased her foot onto the nodule and tentatively pushed against it. Centimetre by centimetre she managed to straighten her legs as she walked her hands gradually upwards across the surface of the stone. She felt as though her left foot was just dangling there, waiting for the other one to slip or the foothold to give way. Her face was almost touching the wall, and she could smell the dry age of the stone and the lime mortar. She twisted slightly to look up and get her bearings. Her right hand was no more than thirty centimetres from the stone that protruded below the niche. She felt her right foot slip and she tensed the muscles in both legs, willing them to stay in place. She felt terribly exposed, fine margins keeping her clinging to this bare stone wall. She expected to plunge to the earth at any second, but things held.

She inched her hands a little higher; the stones were rougher and smaller, used to fill in the spaces before the roof. Then her finger ends touched the bottom of the protruding ledge. She didn't look up. She slowly walked her fingers higher. She touched the top and immediately her fingers involuntarily grasped the horizontal surface. She felt her limbs stiffen and she gripped hard and felt more secure. The handhold was strong, as strong as she was. She straightened her legs to the fullest as she hauled on the ledge with her right hand.

'I'm there,' she whispered. Jacques said nothing; he was braced with all his weight and strength against the pole so that it didn't move or slip. Braced also for the sudden plunging of the woman above onto his head and shoulders.

Celestine inched her fingers further into the niche, and to give her balance, moved her left hand higher and out a little, digging her nails into the mortar joints between the stones. The fingers on her right hand went deeper, her whole hand was now inside the niche, there was nothing there. She felt a deep dread. What if this was just a colossal waste of time? She felt her left foot relax and slip a little. She tensed her legs quickly; her right foot was rigid and she could feel the hard nodule digging into the sole of her boot. She realised that she was hardly breathing. She took a deliberately deep breath and pushed her hand deeper into the niche until she was taking her whole weight on her wrist. Then she felt something. Something gave slightly as her fingers pushed in. She tried to grasp it, but it felt greasy, and wouldn't stay in her fingers. She looked up, her left hand was no more than fifteen centimetres from the top of the wall where the roof timbers rested. She couldn't go deeper into the niche, she would have no grip with that hand, but if she could get her left hand up to the top of the wall, she would be able to hold herself there. The problem was that she would have to stand on the very top of the pole to push up to that height.

'Jacques, there is something in the hole, but I need to get higher. That means standing on the very top of the pole and grabbing the wall with my left hand. That's going to put a hell of a strain on the pole, and you'll need to hold it absolutely rigid. And apart from that, I don't know how I'll get down from that position.'

Jacques grunted. 'Do it, grab it, drop it down, then let yourself fall. I'll catch you. I'll catch you. Go for it.'

Celestine put all the weight on her right leg and gripped the stone ledge firmly with her right hand. Leaning over she quickly raised her left leg, jammed it on the top of the pole, and at the same time pushed her left hand over the surface of the stones until her fingers slipped over the top of the wall and gripped tightly. Her right leg was dragged up by the movement and dangled uselessly. As the balance of her weight swung to the left she plunged her right hand deeper into the hole in the wall. Her fingers settled on top of what felt like a package, greasy, but firm. She flipped it backwards with her finger to the front of the niche. She wanted to look, but she was clinging on, defying gravity with the flimsiest of holds. She pulled the package out of the niche and heard it fall onto the stone floor. Then her muscles gave out; the searing pain in her hands was too much, and she released her grip and pushed off from the top of the pole. She pulled her head back so as not to hit the wood on the way down, and dropped.

Jacques sensed the release of tension in the wood. He was standing, straddling the pole, arms and legs bracing the wood. He flung his arms outwards and hunched his shoulders. Celestine hit the pole, painfully between the legs, and her body started to arch backwards. Desperately, she gripped with her thighs and turned upside down. Her head missed Jacques' head by millimetres and her neck banged into his shoulder. She felt her thighs open and her legs swing outwards, and then she felt the arms wrap around her hips, and strong hands grab her knees. For a second, she felt suspended, but then Jacques buckled beneath her, and he fell backwards, still holding her legs, and forcing her, through his shoulders, to land above him. He sprawled on the ground and she landed heavily on top of him, her elbow crashing on the stone floor. They lay there motionless.

Slowly, Celestine untangled herself and rolled gently off Jacques' body onto the floor. He didn't move, but his eyes were open, and he was breathing in sharp gasps. She put her hands on his shoulders and ran them down his arms. His legs were bent under him, but not unnaturally. He started to gasp noisily, trying desperately to fill his lungs with air. Celestine forced him into a sitting position. His breathing was tortured and there was panic in his eyes.

'You're winded,' she said. 'It will pass. Don't get tense. Relax and concentrate on slowly deepening your breath. You're just winded.' She felt her own arms and legs. Her hands were scratched and torn, and her thighs were burning. She felt as though she had been kicked in the groin. Jacques' breathing was slowly coming more easily. He stretched his legs awkwardly out in front of him, rolled his shoulders and felt the muscles in his arms. There was blood on his neck and face, and his knees were scraped and bleeding.

'Better than a trampoline,' he said and started wheezing badly.

'Shut up, and don't try to talk. Just let your breathing get back to normal.'

She looked around at the floor. The pole was lying jammed, low down against the wall. Beside it lay a green package. She picked it up in her tortured hands. It was a kind of waterproof canvas, thirty centimetres long, twenty wide and perhaps fifteen centimetres thick. She turned the package over in her hands, wincing at the pain. It was very firmly packed, and sealed tightly along one edge. There were bird droppings on one side, and what looked like the marks of pecking from a sharp beak. But it was well wrapped, and the outer cover was thick and intact. She held it up towards Jacques.

'Gold?' he asked, still gasping.

'Not gold. I don't know. Not so heavy. But, Jacques,' she turned to look at him. 'We have it. This is what was hidden. This is what the code, the puzzle was leading to.' Jacques managed a wan smile.

'Good oh,' he wheezed, and then they both heard the sound of horse's hooves, clattering along the trail, coming closer.

Chapter Forty

Driving through the narrow streets to the canal, Desmarais picked over the embers of his career. He was clearly not destined for higher office if he couldn't keep his mouth shut. Insubordinate, rude, actually swearing at a very senior officer. He shook his head. What was that phrase? Your bright future is now behind you.

He parked near the canal and walked along the towpath to Jacques' barge. Late afternoon was softening into evening, the intensity of the light had faded and the air was soft. The scene by the canal, with its colourful, quirky, different-shaped boats, seemed a peaceful world away from the harsh realities of violence, mobs and arrogant bosses. Jacques' boat was around twelve metres long, painted green and a rich, wine-inspired burgundy colour, with four garish murals painted at intervals along the side. Desmarais stopped to look more closely. The first one appeared to be of a woman on a flying horse in flames, with mountains behind. The second was of a man jumping over high sheaves of grain. The third was of a red bull with fire coming out of its nose and mouth, and the last one was simply of a flower - a flower that looked something like a sun. The paintings were primitive but well executed, with strong bold lines and colours. They looked mythological, and Desmarais wondered if they had been painted by Jacques; who was himself becoming something of a legend to the young police agent.

When he reached the bow of the boat, he saw that Monsieur Lefebvre was sitting in the identical place. He waved to him and stepped onto the deck. Monsieur Lefebvre didn't stand up, but he gestured to the other chair.

'Monsieur Lefebvre, you've not heard from Jacques or Celestine?'

'No. Have you?'

'No, I've been trying his phone and spent a lot of time looking for him. But no, I haven't seen him.' He paused. 'But I have just blown up my career as a police agent, for better or for worse.' He sat down opposite Monsieur Lefebvre and looked at the murky waters of the canal. The old man said nothing. 'I've just sworn at a Commandant and walked away. That's not a good move, believe me. These people don't take things like that lying down.'

'I suppose it depends on your reasons for acting in this way,' said Monsieur Lefebvre slowly. 'I dare say, commandants, like senior engineers, like politicians, are all quite capable of acting like complete arseholes. And, in my opinion, sometimes they need to be told, whatever the consequences.' Desmarais looked up at him surprised. It was very hard to weigh up this old man.

'Is that what you did, Monsieur Lefebvre?' he asked.

The old man smiled. 'Oh no. You imagine that I did that and that's why I ended up living like this? Oh no, no, no, that was something completely different. Don't worry, I'm sure your actions this afternoon will not be the first steps on the slippery slope to destitution,' he chuckled and beamed at Desmarais. They sat looking at each other. Desmarais removed his cap, put it on the table and vigorously scratched the back of his head.

'You know, monsieur. I am trying to figure you out. Jacques, Celestine, you. I'm trying to find a link, but I just can't place you precisely.'

'No,' said Monsieur Lefebvre. 'Complicated'

'Complicated, I'll say.' He shook his head. 'But listen, I think Jacques is right about the murders. It makes much more sense to me. And I think, I heard in Bordeaux that Celestine was a brilliant police officer. Was. She's quite….'

'Yes, she is.'

'Exceptional.' Desmarais swallowed. 'There must be a connection. Three people looking for something, two of them dead, one frightened half out of his wits. Can you tell me anything, anything at all about what Jacques and Celestine have found out, and where they might be today? It must be something to do with the case. Must be. But are they doing things on their own? Are they taking risks? If you're pursuing a murderer, I guess you can very quickly turn into the pursued.'

'Predator turned prey.'

'Precisely. This guy has murdered twice to keep a secret, secrets. Why wouldn't he do it again if he was threatened? I'm worried, Monsieur Lefebvre.' The old man looked at the young man and was silent for a short while.

'I will tell you all I know,' he said. It took some time. He liked to gather each line of his thoughts before he expressed it. But finally, he lifted off his old straw hat and waved it in front of his face as if to fan himself. 'That's all I know. Celestine asked me to come here to stay, she was worried about the man in the black boat. And I will stay here and look after the *Incognito* until they return.' Desmarais sat back and stared at the darkening waters of the canal.

'So, Jacques is convinced that this man in the black boat, Jean-Michel Palomer, is involved,'

'Sure.'

'Phew. The Palomers are very big fish in these parts. You don't go stirring up their pond unless you are well prepared for the fight back.

'I think that Jacques would stir up the pond of the devil himself if he thought it would do some good.'

'I expect so,' said Desmarais and he stood up. He shook hands with Monsieur Lefebvre.

'What are you going to do, Agent Desmarais?'

'I'm going to the Palomer's place. I'm looking for two people. My commanding officer wants to interview Jacques, and I want to see if they are there.'

Chapter Forty-One

'Can you move, Jacques?' Celestine wrapped her arms around his shoulders and started to ease him up. 'We need to go now, we can't be found in here.'

Jacques was still panting, taking short gasps of air, unable to draw down a full breath. 'You go, take the package,' he wheezed. 'Head further back into the woods and try and make your way to the road. When you get there, switch on your phone and call Desmarais to come and collect you. Or call an Uber,' he gasped.

'An Uber, in deepest rural France. But I don't want you to get caught here, that man is a killer. Come on, we have to hide.'

Jacques slowly raised himself. He was hurting in a dozen places, and his breathing was fitful and shallow. Celestine hung his arm over her shoulder and they limped towards the door. She picked up the rucksack and stowed the package inside it, then she hauled it onto her back. Jacques brought his mouth close to her ear.

'Celestine, if necessary, you run. You're fast and fit,' he wheezed. 'Let's go outside and find a place to hide, but if they come this way, run, just run. It'll be dark quite soon. Run and hide.' He started to cough and Celestine put her hand over his mouth. They stumbled outside and listened. They could hear the sound of horses' hooves moving quickly, covering the ground. They stood still and strained their ears. The clip-clop stopped suddenly, and they heard a snort and the jingling of a bridle. Jacques pointed to where he had hidden before.

'Put me in there,' he said, 'then leave. Head up the hill, keep in the trees, give yourself a good start. Once it's all clear, I'll make my way up to the bikes and head back to the boat.'

He gently pushed the branches aside and tucked himself in beside the broken wall. Celestine pulled a few small branches over the front. It was certainly not easy to see him. He blew her a kiss and mouthed 'Go.' She listened; she could hear the stomping of horse's hooves, then a few words spoken in a hard, abrupt voice, then ominously, nothing. She turned and moved quickly up through the trees to the right-hand side of the pigeonnier. So many of the branches were dry at this time of the year and the forest floor was littered with twigs which snapped when she stood on them. She moved as quietly as she could, knowing it was vital to get distance between her and the horsemen. At least, they couldn't follow her on horseback here, the ground was too steep and the trees too dense and overgrown. She thought about the loggers' track she had seen further down the trail and wondered if she cut diagonally towards it, she might cross it and it provide an easier path to the road. She pushed on uphill, fighting against the pain in her hands and groin. Each time she grabbed hold of a branch to haul herself up a slope or to work around a tree or bush, she flinched, as the rough bark scraped against her raw flesh.

She stopped to listen; there was no sound from below, from near the pigeonnier. This almost made it more eerie. She shivered. In her imagination, she saw two men, one dark, deadly, Jean-Michel, moving somehow silently and effortlessly towards her in the woods. She shook herself. No one could move that quietly or that quickly. She started climbing again, her focus on making little sound but moving swiftly. And strangely, she started to feel a vague pleasure in exerting her muscles, pumping up the slope, hauling herself through the thin gaps between trees. She wouldn't be easy to follow. And the light was dimming, evening was coming on. It would be good to get to the road before it was truly dark because she could easily lose direction, or trip and fall. She had a sharp stab of anxiety in her stomach when she thought about Jacques in his vulnerable hiding place. But somehow, she always imagined Jacques extricating himself from any difficult situation. She had no choice; one of them had to open the package she carried, to discover what this was all about. She had to keep going.

Jacques could hear the approaching footsteps. The horses were still shuffling in the distance, but they hadn't shifted, and the sounds of men walking over rough terrain were coming closer. He reached down to take hold of his rock, but it wasn't there, and he didn't want to make a noise in feeling for it. His breathing was slowly getting back to normal, but he still couldn't inhale deeply, and he felt a little light-headed. He was hurting badly in his shoulders, back and knees, and he told himself to use the pain to stay alert. He stared out between the branches. The sounds were much closer; there were definitely two people, and Jacques could hear the hoarse breathing from one of them. He heard them as they pushed past the fig tree, and he pictured them walking by the threshing floor, and now on the slight slope down to the next group of ruins and up through the clearing to the pigeonnier. They brushed past the cypress tree, and stepping over the fallen rocks, came to a stop a few metres in front of him. They stood looking at the pigeonnier. One of them was the short, slovenly man, with the cap and the green gilet. The other, taller, straighter, dressed in black trousers and sweatshirt, was Jean-Michel Palomer. What was more alarming was that they were both carrying shotguns, broken at the barrel. Jean-Michel gestured to the other man to go into the pigeonnier, while he stood outside and snapped close his gun. The man went inside, called out, came to the door and then disappeared inside again. Jean-Michel went to the door and bowing his head, stepped inside. For one mad moment, Jacques thought about scrabbling from his hiding place and making a run for it, but that would be foolish; he was short of breath, and they would catch him in no time. He heard Jean-Michel raise his voice and something smash against the wall. He came storming out of the pigeonnier, his face contorted with rage. He marched a few steps forwards and looked around desperately. And then his gaze came back to stare directly in front of him, and he stopped. He craned his head forwards a little then looked straight through the branches into Jacques' eyes. Jacques thought he had never seen such a horrible, mirthless grin, his lips bared back from his teeth and his eyes wide. He shuffled the shotgun into his right hand and pointed it straight at Jacques.

'Three. Three seconds to crawl out here, or I'll blast you a new arsehole,' he snarled. The other man stumbled out of the pigeonnier to stand beside him, also raising his gun, although not pointing it directly at Jacques.

'Monsieur Palomer, Jean-Michel,' said Jacques as he pulled the branches away and clumsily extricated himself from his hiding place. 'Thank heavens it's you. I thought you were bandits, poachers or something. I was afraid I'd stumbled on something.'

Jean-Michel lifted his shotgun and pushed the end of the barrels up to Jacques's heart. 'Monsieur Lecoubarry. Well, well. What the fuck are you doing in my woods? And where's that woman of yours?'

'No woman,' said Jacques. 'I came here to look for something, alone.' Jean-Michel lowered his gun and moved it to his left hand, then suddenly snapped his hand up and cracked Jacques across the face. Jacques staggered back but righted himself quickly and made a move towards Jean-Michel. Both men brought their guns around and aimed them at his belly.

'You were seen, you dumb bastard. You were seen, you and a woman, coming down the track.'

'No, she turned back. Didn't agree with what I was doing.' He spat blood and spittle towards Jean-Michel's boots. 'And if you hit me again, I'm going to get really angry. If I'm trespassing, then sue me. But you and your monkey here, get your fucking guns out of my face. I'm leaving and I'll see you in court.'

Jean-Michel gestured as if for him to leave, but as he turned away, jabbed down savagely behind Jacques' knees and he buckled and fell forwards. Jean-Michel immediately sat on his neck and pushed his face into the earth. The other man pulled Jacques' hands together behind his back, and pulling out a roll of duct tape, quickly bound his hands together. Jacques couldn't breathe, his nose was blocked with grass and soil and his mouth was jammed tightly on a stone that was cutting into his lips. He tried to push his head back, but the full weight of Jean-Michel was too much. He was starting to lose consciousness when the pressure was suddenly released and he felt his head being jerked back by a rope around his neck. He choked and gagged as he was pulled up, first onto his knees and then onto his feet. He could barely see; soil and dust filled the corner of his eyes and he spat out the grit and earth from his mouth. His breathing was laboured again as the rope dug into his windpipe.

The smaller man was holding the rope behind him and Jean-Michel came to stand in front.

'Where's the woman?' he hissed. Jacques spat again, trying to get blood and spittle on Jean-Michel's clothing. The man behind jerked the rope, and his head snapped back as he gasped for breath.

He murmured something, very quietly, twice. Jean-Michel leaned forwards to hear.

'There's no woman, you ape. And I'll finish you.' Jean-Michel lashed out again with his hand, but Jacques ducked away sharply and it caught the side of his head, making his ear ring. Suddenly, Jean-Michel held up his hand and raised his head, listening.

'Is that her? Is that the little girl lost in the woods? Oh dear, dear. Anything could happen to a little girl lost in the woods.' He taunted Jacques, coming close to his face. Jacques felt the rope tighten on his throat.

'There's no woman you fucking moron.'

Jean-Michel turned to the other man. 'Pierre, let's put a piece of tape on Monsieur Lecoubarry's mouth, he uses dirty language. Take him to the grey shed. If he causes you any trouble, hurt him, again and again.' The man named Pierre looked dubious. 'Do it. He's dangerous. He's a murderer. He's the one who murdered those two people in Lissac. I suppose they were after the same thing so he killed them, him and that woman. So, hurry, take him to the grey shed, and don't take any chances, do you hear? Hit him, knock him out if you have to, drag him behind the horse. Just don't let him get away, or I'll tear you apart as well. Understand?' Pierre nodded and passed the duct tape to Jean-Michel, who roughly stuck a length over Jacques' mouth. Jacques bent his head away to resist and widened his mouth so that the tape caught in the corners. He yelped as it stuck on the open cut on his lips. Jean-Michel slapped him hard again across the face, and the man Pierre pulled his head back viciously and jabbed the shotgun in his back, forcing him to move forwards on the path down to the trail. Jean-Michel turned and headed up through the trees on the right-hand side of the pigeonnier.

Without his hands to balance and push branches out of the way, Jacques stumbled and fell a number of times. It was hard to negotiate the path. The man pulled relentlessly on the rope, choking Jacques each time, and blood from his lips built up behind the tape and caught in his throat as he tried to swallow. At one point he swivelled round to face Pierre and looked him hard in the eyes. He saw the flicker of fear there, and it was clear that Pierre was neither physically strong, nor very courageous. Jacques knew that if he had

had his hands free, he could have taken him easily, gun or no gun. Pierre jabbed the end of the shotgun into Jacques' ribs.

'Fucking walk,' he said.

They stepped over the last stones and stood by the horses. Jacques could see that this was a dilemma for the other man; a gun, a rope and a horse to hold. They stood for a moment beside the horses, Jacques catching his breath and taking in the sweet smell of the warm horses as they shuffled around the tree they had been tethered to. The deep, earthy smell filled his nostrils and revived him. Wonderful, powerful, graceful creatures, he thought, so much better than the miserable humans who rode them here tonight. Eventually, Pierre realised he couldn't control everything from the back of a horse, so he prodded Jacques forwards, to walk down the trail towards the house. He could move more easily now and kept lunging forwards, even though it hurt, to throw Pierre off balance. Meanwhile, he was nibbling on the tape around his mouth, and pushing it gradually lower with his tongue. They passed the junction where the logging track pushed up into the woods; there the trees thinned out on the downhill side and there were glimpses of the house below. They came nearer, and Jacques could see outbuildings which were tucked in behind the main residence. Calculating all the while, he could tell that Pierre was starting to relax a little as they neared their destination.

They approached a wooden gate with a top latch, the kind that could be lifted from the back of a horse, without dismounting. Beyond the gate was a yard. Jacques stood directly in front of the gate latch, and although Pierre tried to push him aside, he resisted and pushed back. Pierre jabbed him with the gun and tried to pull him away with the rope, but he couldn't do that and lift the latch at the same time. He struck Jacques viciously with the shotgun on the back of the shoulders and then swung the gun away and attempted to use it to lift the latch. As he did so, Jacques turned quickly around and buried his forehead in Pierre's face. Jacques felt the nose break, and Pierre crumpled to the ground, dropping the gun but holding onto the rope, which pulled Jacques down after him. Jacques dropped knees first onto Pierre's belly and the man gasped and his head flew back. He let go of the rope and Jacques stood up and jammed it between his elbow and body. He stamped down on Pierre's right hand, who screamed in agony. Blood was smeared all over his face, his eyes were rolling and he was trying to raise his knees up over his groin. Jacques kicked him hard again in the face, his head jagged back and he lay spread-eagled on the grass. Jacques could do nothing about the shotgun, so he kicked it further into the undergrowth. Then, to slow the man down further, he swung a boot into his ribs and stamped hard on the inside of his knee. Tucking the rope tightly under his elbow, he stood on one of the bars of the gate and pushed the latch up with his head. The gate swung open into the yard and he stumbled and nearly fell. He looked up. The yard was a rough rectangle, with a stone-tiled building attached to the house, and on the other side an open, corrugated-roofed barn, where various agricultural implements and a small tractor stood. He was breathing heavily, the tape on his mouth was tearing at the cuts in his lips and he could taste the blood gathering there. His head, where he had butted Pierre, and his shoulders were aching terribly. He needed to free his hands and mouth, otherwise, he was still a sitting duck in that place.

Chapter Forty-Two

Celestine reached the top of a ridge and leant against the bole of a huge oak tree to catch her breath. She had not come across the logging track or any signs of a footpath or trail. The light was fading rapidly and it was getting harder to pick a way forward. She tried to remember the line of the road from the map they had studied. She was unsure, but she thought it ran at an oblique angle, turning eventually towards the north but she was not certain how far down the road that was. The map was in the rucksack and she didn't dare shine the light from her phone on it. A sudden noise from below stopped her thoughts. She went rigid and strained to hear the slightest sound. She edged around the tree, held her breath and listened. She had heard what had sounded like muffled voices when she had been scrabbling up the slope, but she had not stopped to focus on them. Now she heard two sets of sounds; one below, where she estimated she had left Jacques, the other, a lighter sound, came from a different location, higher up the hill, nearer to her. She was being pursued.

She looked around quickly. She could still make out the way she had come, although the trees were now blending into the dark mass. She needed to go straight, not diagonally, away from the house and the horses on the trail. She listened again. It was faint, but she could definitely hear a scuffing noise, as of boots on hard earth, and twigs and undergrowth snapping underfoot. The breeze that had carried the cigarette smoke was helping bring the sounds to her, but she needed to be quieter and yet move more quickly than her pursuer.

She settled on a direction and started walking again. At first, the ridge was reasonably flat, with lots of smaller trees, bushes and the stumps of larger trees. Clearly, this land had been cleared some little time ago, and the saplings were still establishing themselves.

It was noticeably lighter there without the dark canopy of leaves overhead, and the trees were planted in rows, so that for a while it was easier to navigate. But this provided little cover, they were not thick enough to hide behind. She hurried on across the ridge, and it struck her that this was where the logging track had ended and that it did not continue to the main road at all. The undergrowth soon thickened, and she had to push her way painfully past the spiky branches of shrubs and brambles where they grew in the stronger light at the edge of the wood. Then she was in deep forest again and the ground began to rise. It was difficult to see now; the trees were dark shapes in a dark grey background. She walked with her hands in front of her, climbing steadily, pulling herself through and around the trees with her scarred hands. She sensed that the land to the left was falling away, and realised that she was on the edge of a ravine, the deep bank of a stream. She peered down but could see no further than a few metres. She tried to edge away from the ravine, but it was starting to curve to the right also, forcing her to move in that direction. It narrowed her options and could make her easier to track.

She moved forward carefully. The ravine could be perilously deep, and if she fell into it she would make a lot of noise and potentially hurt herself badly. She was trying to think clearly, while still focusing on every step she put down, when a sudden ear-bursting noise wrecked the silence - a shotgun blast. It sounded as loud as a cannon, in the dark stillness of the forest. Then a man's voice screamed out, she had no doubt that it was the voice of Jean-Michel. She could not make out the words clearly, her ears were still ringing from the blast. The voice called out again, and this time she did hear the words; ugly and violent, taunting words, tainting the air, and sending a shiver down Celestine's spine. More helpfully, she could place the direction and estimate the distance from her pursuer. She figured he was a little to the left of her and must be somewhere on the ridge. With luck, he would take the other side of the ravine. The sudden violence of the shot had shaken her for a minute, and part of her just wanted to stop, to sit down beside a tree and wait for the inevitable. She was exhausted, sore and in pain in every limb. But she would not give up. She took a deep breath and started moving forward again.

She rounded a tree and nearly fell headlong into the ravine, only saving herself by grabbing at a low branch. The ravine was now almost directly in her path, forcing her to move at right angles to the way she wanted to go. She stumbled on. The earth was softer here and she clawed at it as she moved on all fours. The soil worked into the scratches on her hands, and she bit her lip with the pain. She could hear a noise below but it was impossible to tell which side of the ravine it came from. She could see so little ahead that she felt it was all starting to close in on her.

Then she suddenly sensed that the ravine was no longer on her left hand. She stepped forwards cautiously. The land was almost level and the trees were thinning. It seemed to be a little lighter. She could sense something ahead but kept her eyes on the ground as she edged between smaller trees, holding on to them in case the next step could be into the abyss. She fell over a stone lying beside one of the trees, jarring her knee and digging her tortured hands into the earth. She eased herself forwards, stretching out a hand, and suddenly she touched solid air, rock. She stood up and raised her hands; on either side she touched rock, sheer and cold. She looked up, trying to fathom what this was. The rock was grey in what was left of the light, and she could just make out its outline against the sky. It was solid as far as she could see, perhaps twenty-five metres high. She looked to both sides, it seemed to stretch, right and left, to at least the same height. A wall of stone.

She gasped in anger and frustration, and fear. She listened; she could hear quite clearly the sound of someone moving through the woods below her, moving as quickly as possible in the gloom, unconcerned about keeping quiet or hidden. They were on her side of the ravine and in five minutes they would be here. She could move along the rock face and try to hide. It might be difficult to find her in the dark, but they could just wait until daybreak and she would be flushed out for sure.

Chapter Forty-Three

Jacques looked back at the man lying moaning on the ground. His head was turned away and his knees were pulled up in protection. His eyes were closed, and he kept snorting hoarsely through his fractured nose. Jacques felt no sympathy for him. He turned and made a beeline for the large implement shed, looking for something sharp. At the back of the shed was a bench, with various tools hanging on pegs on the wall. He tried to lean over the bench but his tied hands could not reach so far. Then the rope slipped from his elbow and snagged on the mudguard of a quadbike, jerking his head back, choking him and scraping the raw skin on his throat. In a frenzy of fury and pain, he staggered around the building until his eyes lighted on a cultivator, resting on the ground. He knelt beside one of the metal tines and turned around, placing his hands, as best he could, on either side of the curved metal edge. He began to rub the thick duct tape backwards and forwards. His shoulders were in agony, but he forced his arms back and kept rubbing. Eventually, it started to give, one strand at a time, but even with only a thin thread left, it was impossible to pull his wrists apart. It finally broke and he gasped with pain as he brought his arms forwards. He pulled the rope off his neck and took hold of the edge of the tape on his mouth. He knew this was going to hurt like the devil when the tape ripped away at his torn lips. Bracing himself not to shout out, he eased the tape from one end and then tugged. It felt as though half his mouth had been ripped away with the tape, and he hopped around, shaking his head, and bending over to hold himself against crying out. He drew in a deep breath and threw back his head to silently howl.

He went to the tool bench and picked up a large claw hammer and an adjustable wrench, about fifty centimetres long. He moved cautiously between the large machinery, and crouched beside the wheel of a tractor, peering out. He saw the man Pierre staggering across the yard, bent almost double, using the shotgun as a walking stick. Jacques eased back behind the tractor wheels just as a bright, white light flooded the yard. Pierre must have triggered an infrared detector on the wall of the shed where he was now leaning against the door. It was dusk and Jacques suspected there would be detectors on all the buildings; as soon as he stepped into the yard the lights would go on and he would be seen. He watched Pierre closely, he seemed to be fumbling with something in his gilet pocket. Then he suddenly sat down, his head fell forwards, and he let the shogun slip from his hands.

Jacques made a quick decision. The bright light faded and the yard seemed much darker than before. He edged around the implements until he was by the wall nearest the gate. He had seen that there was a road leading from the yard on the other side, which he assumed would lead to the house and the drive. He wanted to get onto that drive, then hide somewhere, and call Desmarais.

He looked across to where he could just make out the slumped figure of Pierre. For a second, he wondered if he had killed him, but he put that thought quickly aside. He laid down the wrench, then stood up and ran. The light came on almost immediately and he expected to hear a shout, or worse, the blast of a shotgun, but nothing came, and he reached the edge of the building and passed behind it. Although he had run as quickly as he could, he had felt that he was moving in slow motion, his limbs stiff and aching and his breathing shallow and weak. He didn't want to go too close to the house, so he headed towards a group of ornamental shrubs near the edge of the drive and dived into them. He sat behind the thickest shrub, where he was hidden from the house, and reached into his pocket. There was no phone. He patted his other pockets but there was nothing. He could not call anyone. He closed his eyes in frustration, and it was then that he heard the sound of a car coming down the drive.

Headlights swept across the grass as he crouched down near the base of the small tree. The car was coming fast, tyres crunching through the gravel. The drive curved before reaching the house, and the lights passed directly over where Jacques was hiding, before resting on the front of the building. The lights went out and the engine was cut. Jacques heard a car door slam, and he crawled between two of the smaller bushes to peer out. A figure was walking up to the house. Suddenly, there was a burst of whiteness from floodlights on either side of the door. Jacques saw the figure raise his hand to shield his eyes, and the badge on his uniform and the fluorescent strip on his cap flashed in the light. A police agent. Jacques staggered to his feet and called out. The figure turned sharply, as a man waving a hammer burst out of the bushes and rushed towards him, yelling in a harsh and strangled voice.

'Desmarais, Jesus, Desmarais, you have to help her.' Jacques ran right up to him, still waving his arms and the hammer. Desmarais put his hands up to protect himself but Jacques grabbed him. 'Come on,' he said. 'No time to lose.' Desmarais was looking at him, wide-eyed. There was a noise of bolts being drawn behind the house door. Jacques caught Desmarais by the arm again and started dragging him towards the car. He looked as wild and deranged as anyone Desmarais had ever seen, but despite that, he hurried back to the car with him and jumped in.

'Just drive,' said Jacques. Desmarais spun the car around, and Jacques looked back at the house. A tall, stiff woman was standing there, looking out of the half-open door. 'End of the drive then turn right,' said Jacques, and sank back exhausted in the passenger seat.

Chapter Forty-Four

Celestine hitched the rucksack up tighter to her back. She moved her hands from side to side across the rock face about twenty centimetres above her head. The fingers on her right hand dug into a small crack, and she cupped her left hand around a small bulge in the rock above. She slid her right foot up until she could feel a small horizontal ledge, and then with all her strength, she hauled herself up, pushing with her feet and clinging on with her hands. She knew this kind of rock; large chunks of chalk, calcareous bedrock, exposed by land slippage or erosion. A little rough, not like harder rocks, the surface dissolved and broken up by rain and wind. Not perfect for climbing, a little crumbly, but laced with cracks and crevices. She had climbed it before, maybe fifteen years ago, before she was married, when all her leisure pursuits were adrenaline-charged activities in mountains, lakes and wild country. She told her hands to stop hurting and to just grip. The ache in her legs was good, she told herself, it kept her focused. With her nose millimetres from the rock face, she began to ascend. She couldn't see anything except the stone dimly in front of her, and she relied solely on her sense of touch and her instincts. Handholds were easy, footholds were harder to find, and the boots she was wearing were thick and clumsy. She pulled up more than pushed and had climbed about six metres when she heard a sound below her, not at the rock face yet, but not far away. Her fear was that her pursuer would have a torch and would shine it up the face of the rock, where she would be pinned like an insect, helpless. But, if he'd had a torch, surely, he would have used it to show him the way, it would have been much quicker.

Her hands reached up and there was nothing there. There must be a ledge or at least a sill on the rock, she thought. She pulled hard and lifted her left elbow onto it. She stretched her right hand forward and touched rock a good sixty centimetres from her face. She pulled herself up as quietly as she could. It was a ledge, at least wide enough to be used as a resting place. She lay down on it, tucked up her legs, and lay still. Afraid almost to breathe, although her lungs were desperate for air, she listened intently. She heard branches breaking, a curse and then the definite sound of a hand slapping on stone. And then, to her horror, a light came on; pale, a mobile phone, it moved and was being shone in every direction. She flinched, were her legs far enough in, could she be seen? The light flooded up the rock face and Celestine glanced upwards to see what was above her; there was more rock, at least another eight or ten metres, but above that, she could see the branches of trees leaning out. The light was suddenly extinguished and there was silence. Celestine could hear her own breathing in her head. If he started to climb after her she knew she would attack him, while he was on the rock face, high up so that he would fall far enough to be injured. She would find a stone, a rock, anything.

There was a movement below. She listened for the sound of hands fumbling on the rock face. She heard footsteps, the rough sound of a boot scraping against stone, a branch being pushed aside. The sound was moving away, slowly. Then a devastating blast rang out again, bouncing off the rock face and rolling through the trees He had fired another shotgun round in the air. Celestine started and nearly rolled off the ledge, almost crying out. She could hear the detritus of broken twigs and branches raining down. The silence after the thunder was almost as scary, as if the whole natural world was waiting for the next assault. Celestine closed her eyes. She sensed the hard rock under her body.

'I'm going to stay here,' she thought. 'I will outstay you. You will not get me.'

She lay inert, drawn in on herself, holding her limbs so they did not slip, mentally holding her nerve. She listened for every faintest sound. She started to imagine herself waiting there with the patience and stillness of a small animal, knowing there are predators, but knowing also, that at some stage, you will need to move, for life. She thought she heard the light crunch of a foot pressing down old leaves, snapping a small twig. It was still close, and after each sound, there was silence for several minutes.

Predator listening for the tell-tale rustling in the undergrowth of the prey. Thank heavens humans did not have the same intensely developed sense of smell, she thought. She was starting to cramp in her legs, a sharp rock was burying into her shoulder, and the stinging pain in her hands was a constant. She took shallow breaths and tried to concentrate on only one thing - sounds.

She lay like that for twenty minutes. Vague, insubstantial noises seemed to come at intervals, they could have been farther away, or that could be just the impression, the trees distorting and muffling the sounds. The discomfort and pain of continuing to lie absolutely still finally decided her. She pushed herself onto her knees, and then with hands on the rock face, she stood up. It was a relief to stretch her limbs, her hands above her head, her legs apart. She stood for a minute, leaning against the rock, listening. She looked up, but could only see the slightly lighter space, which was the night sky. She could just distinguish the darker shapes of the branches hanging over the cliff top. She began to run her fingers along the stone above her. There was a crevice, which seemed to be running vertically, it was wide enough to jam in her right hand. She fumbled until she found a purchase with the left one and she started to slowly haul herself up the cliff.

The first few metres were relatively easy climbing and she moved steadily higher. She reached a slight overhang and edged along it until it narrowed; there she was able to use it as a handhold and then a foothold, which took her more than halfway to the top. The face was more or less vertical, but there were small cracks and fissures where the great blocks of chalk had split over time. Her hands felt pulpy now, and each time she gripped the stone it sent a sharp burning pain through the raw nerve ends. She had reached a point where her arms were at full stretch, and she was about to raise her right foot to search for a foothold when the light came on. She stiffened. It was the light from the mobile phone, pale and wavering, moving methodically from left to right, then higher and lower. She moved her head slowly to the right: the light seemed to be about fifty metres from her, although it was difficult to judge. It flashed against tree trunks, then flickered as it swung around under bushes. He was clearly looking for her, assuming that she was now in hiding somewhere. Suddenly, the light was on the rock face, and Celestine watched in horror as it slowly traversed the white, chalk cliff, like a searchlight on a screen. She cleaved to the rock as though she could melt into it. And the light moved closer. It stopped moving and stayed focused on a spot some ten metres to the right of her. It seemed for an age. Then the light went out, and Celestine closed her eyes, desperate to recover her night vision for the next part of the climb. She listened; there was that noise again of someone moving across the forest floor, brushing aside branches, stumbling, moving as quickly as possible in that terrain, not moving away any longer but coming towards her again.

'Focus now,' she told herself, 'one last effort, think only of the rock face and how to climb up it safely.'

She started to climb again; handhold, foothold, handhold, foothold, her hands caressed the hard chalk stone. She climbed faster, taking less time to test her holds, moving from one to the other as soon as she felt purchase enough. A small part of her mind heard the sounds in the woods below. The light came on again, although not on the rock face, he was searching the trees and the undergrowth, but she knew he was coming closer to the foot of the cliff that she was climbing. He need only shine the light upwards, she was not so high. Well, keep climbing. Then her right hand touched something softer than calcareous rock, wood, and the exposed roots of a tree. She wrapped her hand around it and dug her fingers into the softer shale above. She pulled herself up further, trying to gain a solid base to push on in the crumbling stones and thin earth. Then, she was over the edge of the rock face and onto the cliff top. She sensed, rather than saw, the thin tree trunk ahead, grabbed it with both hands and dragged herself into a horizontal position, just as the light flashed on again. It was almost directly below her and lit up the trees leaning out above. But she was deep in the shadows, and the light moved on, further towards the ravine. Then the light went out, and all was darkness again.

She lay there breathing softly, letting the tension seep out of her arms, legs and feet.

Chapter Forty-Five

Desmarais drove slowly as he listened to Jacques' breathless narration. He picked up that Celestine was, in Jacques' view, in great danger, that she was in the woods being pursued by Jean-Michel Palomer, the son of one of the wealthiest and most prominent citizens in the area. And with a shotgun. The avowed reason was that they had discovered an article in the woods, which was in fact, the catalyst for the killing of two people in Lissac-sur-Tarn.

'So, I'll go along with you,' Desmarais said. 'I want to see you and Celestine in a safe place. And I want to know what's in the package you found. That's all we can do right now. Where do you think Celestine will be? How do you expect to find her?'

'She'll make it to this road, somehow. Through the woods. She'll get to the road and then she'll start back towards where the bikes are hidden. And she'll call you, once it's safe to use her phone.'

'Does she have my number? Won't she call you?'

'Lost my phone. Somewhere in the woods.'

Desmarais stopped the car in a small pull-in under the trees. He switched on the central light and looked at Jacques. 'You're bleeding from your mouth and your face,' he said.

'I'm Ok.'

'You say this other guy, Pierre, was in a bad way.'

'When I saw him, but I didn't stop to enquire after his health,' said Jacques.

'Course not. But I'm thinking, if he is hurt badly, perhaps I should send the paramedics to check on him. And maybe a couple of gendarmes to accompany them.'

'I think that might be wise, although, lord knows what kind of story they'll cook up at the house. They'll accuse us of trespassing and assault.'

'You've just admitted you assaulted him.'

'He had a bloody rope around my neck, hands tied with tape, and a shotgun sticking in my back. Assaulted him! I let him off very lightly. They'd have killed me, Paul, make no mistake. Not him maybe, but his psychopathic boss. And now he's after Celestine. So, send your paramedics, but let's go. She'll emerge on this road, and we have to find her first.'

It was hard to start walking again, but she felt a little easier now. She didn't know how far the cliff stretched or if there was a way around it, but she now had real distance between her and Jean-Michel. Before standing up, she pulled off the rucksack and put her hands inside; she felt the cold, rather greasy surface of the package, and she gripped it for a moment or two. Then she hitched the rucksack onto her shoulders and started walking away from the cliff edge. It was not easy; the trees grew thickly, and at the base of the broad oaks were colonies of thin saplings and smaller trees. She had to force her way through these thickets, which whipped against her face and arms. She stumbled a few times, grabbing hold of rough branches to break her fall, with hands so shredded that she winced at every touch. Then she saw a light flickering through the branches ahead of her, and she heard the sound of a vehicle. The headlights swept over and away from her, then the roar and the rumbling tyre noise and the car passed on the road, no more than ten metres in front of her.

After the car passed, the dark was absolute, and for a moment she was disorientated. She stepped forward cautiously, feeling with her feet, her hands out in front of her. She came to a bank covered in brambles and hawthorn. She couldn't find a way through, her hands flinching every time she touched the thorns. She reached into the rucksack and took out her mobile phone. She knew she was about to expose her position, but she had no choice, and she hoped her pursuer was now a long way off, searching fruitlessly in the woods below. She switched on the torch light and swung it quickly from right to left. She saw to the right of the thicket there was a thin chute of bare soil, the end of a culvert taking rainwater off the road.

She stepped towards it and switched off her phone. The soil was friable, but she clambered up quickly and took hold of the metal barrier at the top. She climbed over it and stood, breathing deeply, and letting the relief sink down through her whole body. She had reached the road.

It came to her mind Jacques' joking advice to call an Uber, and she had a stab of concern for him. If he was still in hiding, his phone would be switched off and the call would go straight to the answerphone. She tried to call him, but there was no response. He had said to phone Desmarais, but she did not have his number. She decided to start walking, she had learned only to trust herself. Then she saw headlights flickering in the tree branches above her. She crouched down, ready to dive back into the forest. The vehicle was coming closer, she could hear the motor, it was travelling quite slowly. She peered down the road. She saw the leaves in the trees at the side of the road turn purple as the car passed. She realised that she was in a state of intense alertness, it was animal-like, she could pick out details that would ordinarily go unnoticed. She stared, there was a faint blue light behind the white. It was a police car. She stood up, switched on the light on her phone, and started waving it above her head. The car slowed immediately and was almost stopped when it came alongside her. The passenger door opened and Jacques burst out with a yell. He rushed up and wrapped his arms around her, crushing her gently to his chest. She folded then, collapsing against him, all strength now gone from her body. He carried her and lay her down gently on the back seat of the police car, and tucked the rucksack into the well beside her. He closed the door and stood staring into the woods. Then he roared - a great gust of a roar of anger, pain, relief and defiance, an animal howl, savage and wild. At that moment he could have torn flesh from bone.

Desmarais approached him cautiously and touched his arm. He flinched. 'Jacques, we need to think and we need to talk,' he said. 'Then I need to take you to the police poste. This is a shit show and my career is hanging by a thread. I have to take you to see Grimard.' Jacques turned, he could see just a faint outline of Desmarais's face, but he could hear the unease in his voice. He relaxed his clenched fists and let the tension sink out of his limbs.

'You're right,' he said. 'I'll go. But not yet. First, we have to go back to the boat. We need to clean up. Tend to Celestine's wounds. Did you see her hands? Like she'd been savaged by a dog or a wolf. We need to fix them.' He faced Desmarais in the gloom and put his hands on his arms. 'Take us to the boat, let us change and clean up, then I'll come with you. But, Paul, only I will come with you. You haven't seen Celestine, and you don't know where she is. And that will be true, you won't know.' He gripped Desmarais' arms tightly. 'And you know nothing about a package. You found me at the Palomer's place in a state of distress. You brought me to the boat to clean up, I insisted, then straight to the police station. Do you understand? No one must know where Celestine is.'

'You're not going to leave her on the boat?'

'No. But she'll be safe. No one will know where she is. Now let's go quickly. And thank you, my friend.'

Desmarais got back into the car, deeply uncertain, feeling that the last few days had seen him completely cast from his moorings. He felt like he was floating down a channel, without any means of steering, knowing that the waterfall was not too far ahead.

Chapter Forty-Six

Monsieur Lefebvre was still sitting in the same chair, in the bow of the boat, which was now in complete darkness. When he saw them arrive he stood up smartly and took one of Celestine's arms as she stepped onto the deck. She looked up at him and smiled. She said simply; 'Monsieur Lefebvre.'
Jacques took her down into the cabin and then came back to speak to the old man.
'Henri, I have to ask you to help us a little longer, if you will. We can't stay here tonight, but I have another place for you, please be patient. Have you eaten?'
'Sufficiently.'
'Ok, then. I'll be with you in a few minutes after we've cleaned up.' As an afterthought, he asked. 'Have there been any visitors?'
'Visitors, yes,' said Monsieur Lefebvre in his quiet, matter-of-fact way. 'The police, several times, in addition to Agent Desmarais, who came twice. A man from the canal board. A lady who said she was a friend of Celestine and Monsieur Ducrozet, who I met the other day.'
'Ducrozet. Did he say what he wanted?' asked Jacques.
'Only that he was looking for you, to talk to. He looked a little lost.'
Jacques nodded. He went down the steps into the cabin. Celestine was standing in the small shower, with her back to him, letting the warm water run through her hair and over her shoulders. Jacques undressed, and taking a cloth, he gently stroked it over her arms and back. He rubbed carefully at the dirt and scratches on her legs and then turned her around. He wiped her face and kissed it. There were bruises on her shoulders and below her elbows, and her hands were fleshy and raw, weeping blood. He held the back of

each hand and very carefully rubbed the soil and grit from the wounds, while she clenched her teeth and rested her forehead on his chest. He ran the cloth across her belly and gently over the dark weal at the top of her right thigh. Her knees and shins were scraped and scratched, and he knelt down and soaped and cleaned each wound. Celestine took the cloth and wiped around his eyes, the deep scratches on his cheeks, and dabbed softly at the raw cuts on his lips.

'That needs stitches,' she said.

'That needs kisses, nothing more.'

She brushed her lips lightly across his. She wiped his neck where a red weal formed a ring of deeply bruised skin all the way round. Then his shoulders, where the marks were so deep and the bruises would be slow to appear but would be dark and last for weeks. Then his arms, like hers, scratched and bleeding, the legs scraped and battered. She stood up and pressed herself against him. They stood like that for some minutes, saying nothing.

Afterwards, they dried and dressed quickly and sat on the narrow bed. The rucksack was lying there, where Jacques had dropped it.

'We should,' he said.

'I know we should. I want to, but in some ways I don't. What if this is nothing, just a small prize from an old game.' Her eyes were dull with fatigue.

'You need some food. But first, let's open the package. We really need to know and we don't have much time,' said Jacques. He took the package from the rucksack, and with a knife, carefully slit the wrapping along the sealed edge. 'It's waterproof canvas, thick and tough. We'd use plastic now.'

He eased open the canvas wrapper; inside there was a small sheaf of papers. He lay them on the bed. The papers were yellowing in the margins but were a good quality bond. The corners were punctured, and the whole tied together with a burgundy-coloured ribbon. Jacques scanned the first page quickly, then flicked through the next few.

'This is a legal document or documents. It looks like a purchase contract. He untied the ribbon and looked further into the leaves of paper. There were plans, outlines of fields and buildings.'

Celestine looked at him. 'A document of what?' she demanded.

'It looks like a conveyancing document, but I could be wrong. There are names here…. Look we don't have time now.' He folded the papers back into the package and replaced it in the rucksack. 'Whatever it is, it's important enough for people to be killed for, and it won't stop there unless we're very careful. Listen. You must take this. You mention it to no one. They'll be desperate now, and will literally stop at nothing.'

'Where do I take it, not here?'

'No, not here. I have an idea.' He moved his mouth closer to her ear and quietly outlined his plan. He sat back. 'Tomorrow, you must make a copy, at least one. There are a lot of pages, but you must hide the original, you know where now, and bring a copy to the nearest notary. I'll ask Desmarais about that.'

'Where will you be?'

'I think they'll keep me in the police station for questions, don't you? That's fine. The Palomers will think they have me cornered.'

'What exactly did you do to that other guy, the scrawny one?' asked Celestine.

'Enough to remember me by.'

'What about Henri? He can't stay here now. If Jean-Michel comes.'

'Which he will. Don't worry. I have a comfortable place for Henri to spend the night.' He stood up. 'Grab some food to go, then head off. No one can go with you. Only you and I will know where.'

Celestine slipped over the side at the stern end, and keeping in the shadows, hurried away along the towpath. Jacques asked Desmarais to wait in the car while he locked up the boat. Then he took Monsieur Lefebvre by the arm.

'Come with me, my friend. You have food and water in this bag.' He helped him off the boat and they walked quietly along the towpath away, from the town and Desmarais' car. A few boats had moved on, and others had replaced them in the last few days, but not the *Just Left*, the old white cruiser with the for-sale notice. Jacques looked quickly around and then stepped quietly onto the deck. The lock resisted only feebly and he eased open the cabin door. He grasped Monsieur Lefebvre's arm, pulled him on board, and guided him into the interior of the boat.

'You opened that door very easily, Jacques,' said Monsieur Lefebvre, disapprovingly.

'Years of fitting locks and freeing rusty old locks from furniture. They're rarely complex, and I have a few tools of the trade. But listen, Henri. Stay here tonight. I don't think there are any lights, but in any case, you need to stay very quiet and remain unseen. There's a camp bed here. Food and water in the bag. And, Henri, don't open the door for anyone, don't let anyone see you, and as long as you can, keep an eye on the *Incognito*. I imagine there may be more visitors tonight. Whatever you see, just watch, stay here. I'll come for you in the morning.' Monsieur Lefebvre listened in silence, his head slightly bowed. Then he raised it and nodded.

'But, Jacques, is Celestine safe?' he asked.

'As safe as I can make her,' replied Jacques, and quietly closed the door.

Chapter Forty-Seven

Palomer left the meeting with the Maire and Commandant Grimard in a curious state of disengagement. A deeply practical man, hard-nosed, not fanciful, but with sufficient imagination to realise that the control he had had was gone. The certainties of his life were now floating around above him. Although he could tug on one string, he could not pull down all the strings at the same time. Even with dice, there was a large but ultimately limited number of scores, but this was different. His moves now were restricted, but the consequences were more complex than ever before. His best weapons, he had always known, were brutal force, strength of will, the withdrawal from all emotion; fight, deny, fight again. And behind it, cold, methodical calculation and sharp, clear decision-making.

Pierre had been taken away in an ambulance, his breathing uneven, his hand broken and with severe pains in his stomach. Palomer had stood briefly by his head and tapped him on the shoulder until he opened his eyes. He had put a single finger across his lips and looked at him hard. Just then, Jean-Michel had burst into the yard, riding one horse and leading another. He had rushed over to where the paramedics were closing the ambulance door and the gendarmes were standing by their car, watching. His face and arms were scratched and he looked savage and unhinged. His father had put a hand on his chest.

'Pierre?' demanded Jean-Michel.

'Yes. Assaulted by that Lecoubarry. Margot saw him from the doorway.'

'Lecoubarry. Is he here?'

'No, left with a policeman.'

'Pierre?'

'He'll live.'

The gendarmes had approached the two men warily.

'Attacked, my man, attacked by that animal, Lecoubarry,' Palomer had said, angrily.

'Do you know that it was Lecoubarry, monsieur?' one of the gendarmes had asked.

'It was,' said Jean-Michel. He'd paused and taken a deep breath. 'We found him, Lecoubarry, trespassing. Him and a woman, on our land, up in the woods. Asked him to leave. The woman, ran off. I went after her and told Pierre to take Lecoubarry to the house. I didn't think for a minute he'd be attacked. He's fucking dangerous, you must get hold of him.'

'And the woman?'

'No. I lost her in the woods. It was very dark there. Didn't have a torch. I fell, look.' He had shown them his scratches.

'Do you know why they were in your woods?' the younger of the gendarmes had enquired.

'No, how could I? They're troublemakers.'

'How could he know?' said Palomer. 'Who knows with these people? Some wild story, or perhaps looking to rob the place. He was here the other day, Lecoubarry. Just turned up, cock and bull story. Had a good look at my antiques. He's with one of yours. Keep him. He's not safe to be let out.'

'Ok. Monsieur Palomer. Would you come down to the Municipal Poste at some point and make a statement?'

'That's grievous bodily harm. Might have killed our Pierre.' Palomer had screeched at the gendarmes.

But standing now, out in the street in front of the Mairie, he really didn't know if it would hold.

Celestine had waited several minutes in the dark street that she had walked up only a few nights before. It was starting to feel dreamlike; the ancient walls, the great oak door, and the thin breeze blowing down the lane from Calvary. There was no one in sight. She shivered, almost faint with exhaustion. She peered up at the first paring of the moon, lightly curled, just above the treetops, bright as a silver bangle. A rough scraping noise made her look down; the door had opened and a small, weathered face, encircled by a stiff white cowl, leaned out towards her.

'Sister,' she mumbled. 'I need respite.'

Now, lying on this firm, narrow bed in a tiny cell-like room, she looked up at the ceiling. She seemed to sense the presence of the moon, even here, behind these walls, beneath these roofs. She placed the rucksack beside her pillow and draped her arm across it. Then she slept. She woke again several times, her bandaged hands startling her once as she brought them to her face.

The nuns immediately seen the distress she was in. They had taken her to a small medical room and washed and disinfected her hands, covered them with salve and bandaged them tightly. At one point the Mother Superior had come to look carefully at her, but they had asked her no questions, only enquired if she was hungry, to which she had shaken her head. They had taken her up some stairs and along a window-lit corridor, where Celestine had stared at the moon pasted in every pane as she passed. To this small bedroom, where they had told her to rest, and that someone would call on her in the morning. She had wanted to look at the green package again, to look more closely at the papers, but she had no energy for that, only sleep.

Chapter Forty-Eight

Jacques waited more than an hour in a small, airless room. His shoulders ached and the cut on his lip kept weeping blood into his mouth. Desmarais had wanted to take him to the Emergency Department at the hospital, but Jacques had said that he'd rather not, as he wanted to make a good first impression. When Grimard walked in he was ready to blow. He stood up, fists clenched by his side. Grimard came up to the other side of the table and locked eyes with him.

'Sit down, Monsieur Lecoubarry,' he said finally. 'Lecoubarry, is that Basque?' Jacques nodded. 'Your face is a mess. We need to have it seen to. We have an emergency medical person here in the building.'

'Later,' said Jacques.

'As you wish. Then let's start with the reason why you have blood dripping out of your mouth.'

Jacques' version of the events of the afternoon was accurate but incomplete. Grimard listened, making few comments, recording and making notes. He asked for clarification of the kind of tape used to bind him: what exactly had triggered the blow to his face that had cut his lip: the rope around his neck, polypropylene, sisal, what diameter, colour. How many times had he struck Pierre? How, with what part of his body? These last questions were more complicated to answer. Head in the face, bearing in mind that hands were tied behind the back; knees into the middle to prevent him from rising; foot on hand reaching for the shotgun. Did he think Pierre was badly hurt? No, just enough to give him time to get away. Did he see him after the escape? Yes, in the yard. Walking? Walking then doubled up, resting. Did you try to help him? He had a shotgun.

Desmarais called for a paramedic. Desmarais, why was he there? Ask him. I'm asking you. He was looking for me, your orders.

Grimard paused. 'Do you want anything? Coffee, treatment for your mouth?'

'Coffee.'

Grimard waved his hand in the air with two fingers aloft. 'The woman is Celestine Courbet?'

'Yes.'

'Formerly a capitaine in the Police Judiciaire in Bordeaux?'

'Formerly.'

'Where is she now, Monsieur Lecoubarry?' Jacques lifted his head and looked Grimard in the eye, but said nothing.

'You don't know, or you won't say?'

Jacques shrugged. 'Have you arrested Jean-Michel Palomer?'

'On what grounds?'

'Assault, false imprisonment, kidnap,' said Jacques, his voice rising.

'No, we have asked him to come in to make a statement. I would like to hear his take on this afternoon's events.'

'His take, his take. Do you even know where he is? The last time I saw him, when I could see him after my eyes had cleared, he was pursuing my partner through the darkening woods, carrying a shotgun. And I heard two shotgun blasts.'

Grimard looked concerned. 'Shotgun blasts, you're sure. This is the first time I've heard of this.'

'Sure? Oh yes, I'm sure. You can't mistake those sounds, in the country, in the woods where there are few other noises. Two shots.'

'Then, let me ask you again. Do you know where Madame Courbet is now? For Christ's sake, did she get out of the woods?' Jacques didn't speak but only nodded. 'Then she is safe enough?' pressed Grimard. Jacques wiped the blood from his lower lip.

'You have a murderer on the loose, Commandant Grimard. That murderer, I suspect, is the same person who was firing shotgun blasts in the woods this afternoon. The same person who attacked me, and had me bound and dragged through the countryside. "Take him to the grey shed," that's what he instructed his oaf to do. I'm pleased I didn't see the inside of that shed. Perhaps you ought to,' he added.

'Alors. I'm going to assume that Madame Courbet is not in immediate danger or you would be reacting very differently. And I won't ask where she is, for now. But we will have to speak to her. She knows that. She was a flic, for Christ's sake.'

The coffee arrived and they sat back for a moment, Jacques drinking carefully from one side of his mouth. Grimard looked puzzled.

'You and Madame Courbet are partners, a couple?'

'Yes.'

'Do you know why she is no longer a police capitaine?'

'Yes.'

'NO LONGER a police capitaine, I emphasize,' said Grimard, putting his hand flat on the table and levering his body forwards. 'But here she is, and you, in the middle of a murder investigation; a rare, a fortunately rare event in these parts, and you are both here. Can you explain that to me?'

'No,' replied Jacques and dabbed carefully at his mouth.

'You must see it is highly suspicious, highly coincidental, no?' said Grimard.

'Agreed,' said Jacques. 'It is coincidental.'

Grimard pushed his coffee cup aside and tapped his fingers on the table top. The tapping started to form a tune which Jacques recognised. It was an old Basque folk song, made popular throughout France some years earlier, by a band which afterwards disappeared without trace. Grimard was attempting to empathise with him and lower his guard. Jacques looked down at Grimard's hand.

'Crude,' he said.

Grimard sighed deeply, then pressed on. 'You are here on holiday, on a boat, on the canal.'

'Yes.'

'You arrived when?'

'Last Tuesday, late afternoon.'

'Last Tuesday, hmm. Last Tuesday night a man was murdered. Last Thursday night a woman was murdered. Not last week, when you weren't here. Hopefully, not next week, when you will be....' He sat back and shrugged. 'You saw a man running, on the night of the murder.'

'I reported that,' said Jacques.

'Yes, you did, but please, tell me about it again.'

Jacques described the collision with the man running along the towpath. He emphasized the look on his face. He explained about the mooring of the boat in the trees, locating the boat, and confirming the times with Monsieur Lefebvre.

'Oh yes. Monsieur Lefebvre. A vagrant, sleeping rough near the river.' He looked sceptical.

'He's a retired engineer. He's no vagrant.'

'And where is he now? At your boat?' Jacques shrugged. 'Ok. And you found out that this boat belonged to Monsieur Palomer.'

'Yes.'

'How did you find out?'

'We saw it in the boathouse at Palomer's place.'

'And for this, this boat incident, you have concluded that Jean-Michel Palomer is the killer of those two victims.' Grimard shook his head vigorously and wagged his middle finger at Jacques. 'There is more, there must be more. You must tell me all you know, if you want me to take you seriously. And,' he left his middle finger in the air, 'I have to take you seriously. Your partner is....'

'I know, a former police capitaine,' said Jacques.

'Yes. And you are, whatever you are, I do not believe you are a man who enjoys wasting police time. Or even engaging with the police in any form. Am I right?'

'Only former police,' said Jacques.

Grimard smiled. 'Only former police. That, you two, this is a mystery for another day. Come on, what else?'

Carefully, Jacques talked about the link between Malraux, Sister Agnieszka and Ducrozet, who Jacques was adamant was only alive by pure chance.

'I have spoken at length to Monsieur Ducrozet. But, the link,' said Grimard thoughtfully. 'You say the link is this search for a package. Malraux shared some information with the nun and Ducrozet. And that was enough to get two of them killed?'

'Yes.' Grimard commenced tapping out the old Basque melody again, staring down at his fingers, as though they had deserted him and gone over to the side, to this mad, but compelling man opposite.

'But why?' He burst out in exasperation. 'Why would Palomer need to kill them? What on earth does it have to do with the Palomers? Do you know who they are?' he demanded of Jacques.

'Better than you it appears.'

'No. I've just had an earful from Monsieur Palomer Senior and the Maire, accusing me of dereliction of duty, demanding that I arrest you and the woman, who they say, quite accurately as it turns out, were trespassing on their land. And you, you even visited Palomer a few days ago. Just turned up. Casing the joint, that's what Palomer claims. An antique dealer looking for items to steal. He's convinced. Do you deny it?'

Jacques dabbed at his mouth again and sighed. The ache in his shoulders was becoming unbearable, and his patience was now only skin deep. 'Casing the joint, yes, I deny it,' he said. 'I did beat him at Trictrac. He was upset by that. Perhaps that's why he's being so hysterical.'

Grimard ignored that. 'If you weren't casing the place, what were you doing there?'

'Casing him and his ghoulish household,' answered Jacques.

'Casing him?'

'Yes. I wanted to know what kind of man he was. Whether he was capable of murder, or at least of instigating it.'

'Monsieur Lecoubarry.'

'But no, I wasn't looking for antiques to steal. At least half of what he has on display are fakes in any case. And he is, by the way, capable of murder.'

'Oh! So why do you think the Palomers would be interested, concerned enough, threatened by the findings of a…. professor? Threatened enough to kill people, like the nun, why?' Even to himself, Grimard was starting to sound unhinged. Jacques replied slowly.

'That is what we were trying to find out when we were attacked by Jean-Michel Palomer, when I received this lip and the red bruises around my neck. Hauled along the track like a steer.' He pulled down the neck of his shirt to show the angry marks.

'You were trying to find out what?'

'The answer to the puzzle. The one that Malraux dug up.'

'The answer to the puzzle. Which you believed was in Palomer's woods.'

'Celestine thought so, she solved the puzzle. That's what she does. She's brilliant. Although, this was actually much less complicated than you might think. A puzzle left by a father for his young son.'

Exasperated, Grimard sat back and stretched out his arms. 'Monsieur Lecoubarry,' he said. 'Are you going to give me any more information to give substance to these claims? You do understand that they seem very far-fetched at this stage. Tomorrow, the examining magistrate will return and he will want to interview you. He will be very vigorous in his questioning. He may think that if your partner had not been a 'former police capitaine, that he was dealing with a fantasist, a mental delusional.'

'Thank heavens for former police capitaines then,' said Jacques. 'But look Grimard. There is nothing more I can or will say at this time. Therefore, I heartily recommend that you keep me here, in a spartan, but relatively comfortable little room, until the sun rises tomorrow and we can see the world in a new light. Tomorrow is another day and you must give us that time. We are close to finding a link. Or not.'

'You're not going back into those woods again?' asked Grimard.

'Nothing like that.'

'Then you did find something.' Jacques remained silent. 'Did you, or didn't you? Palomer claims you may have stolen something from them, something you found.' Jacques snorted and shook his head,

'Commandant Grimard. I am sure you are going to do this, although it is probably already too late. Search Palomer's place for rope and pieces of duct tape, you'll find my DNA on them, and some of my skin. Find out where Jean-Michel is now, and where he was on the two nights in question. Have you done that? Have you extended your search beyond a Bulgarian patriarch and a Dutch pilgrim?'

Grimard stood up. 'Very well, you can enjoy our hospitality tonight. I am not detaining you, you understand. If you find you want to say more, just call the duty cop. And now, can we get someone to look at your face? It's making me ill just to look at it.'

Jacques grimaced. 'About time. And Grimard, on your way home, you might call on Ducrozet to reassure him that he is safe, and ask him, while you're there, to corroborate what I have been saying.'

'Ducrozet,' mused Grimard. 'You are very keen to offer me instruction on how to pursue my investigation.'

'Ah well,' replied Jacques. 'Perhaps that's down to being the lover of a former capitaine of police. You know what they are like.' Shaking his head, Grimard left the room. Jacques was dead on his feet. He just needed a place to lie down. A cell would do.

Chapter Forty-Nine

Celestine awoke early. A thin wedge of light floated on the wall opposite, early sunlight squeezing in through a narrow slot of a window in the wall behind her. She sat, then stood up. Her hands were still smarting, and her bruised limbs complained when she moved, her shoulders and back were incredibly stiff. Her head, she discovered though, was as clear as a fountain. She sat back down again, opened the rucksack and placed the papers on the bed. She untied the ribbon which held the sheets together and started reading

It was clear that they were, as Jacques had suggested, legal documents. The first pages appeared to be descriptions of the persons involved in the transaction; full names, dates and places of birth. She immediately recognised the name of Samuel Joseph Steinbach, born in 1904, in Bucharest. The following pages included details of a property, the subject of the sale transaction. The pages were yellowing but the text was clear. The contract was dated 1939. Celestine raised her head and stood up to ease the stiffness in her neck and shoulders. Why would someone go to so much trouble to hide a document like this? What did they have to fear? She sat down and started reading again.

At first light, on Grimard's instructions, two police agents and a van of four technical and scientific operatives drove into the yard behind Palomer's house. They fanned out in the zone between the gate and the buildings. One agent went inside the implement shed and started scanning all the surfaces methodically. The first item found was a fragment of grey tape, attached to the tines of a plough. A strip of tape, with blood on it, was also located beside the wheel of a tractor. The search continued for two hours; no rope was discovered, but in the grey shed, a coil of grey polypropylene rope was found, and a small length cut off it and bagged.

Nobody appeared from the house until Palomer came shuffling out of one of the side doors after about an hour. One of the police agents explained that they were merely investigating the attack on Pierre and that it was standard procedure to gather any material pertinent to this. When Palomer demanded to know if Lecoubarry had been arrested, he was told that the officer was not aware of the state of arrest, but that Monsieur Lecoubarry had certainly spent the night in the police station.

After two hours, they all gathered by the vehicles, except one, who was still in the grey shed. They called him out. The senior officer stated that strictly speaking, that was not within the parameters of the search area, as the incident had allegedly happened out in the open, in the yard, by the gate and on the track. That was a pity. They collated the material they had and drove back to Lissac.

Jacques walked out of the police station at seven in the morning and headed straight towards the canal. A wind had blown up, and long, puffy, pink-edged clouds were scudding across the lightening sky. The air was cooler at this time, the weather and the season were changing. He rapped on the door of the white cruiser. Monsieur Lefebvre's face appeared in a side window. He unlocked the door.

'Bonjour, Henri. Do you still have that phone Celestine gave you?' Monsieur Lefebvre rummaged in his pockets and handed the phone to Jacques.

'Did you see anything last night?' asked Jacques.

'Yes indeed. As you suggested. I waited up until quite late. The bed here is quite comfortable, but I resisted, for I could have fallen asleep very easily. I normally do when the sun goes down at this time of the year.'

'And.'

'And yes. I saw a figure, it was quite dark, difficult of course. Shadows, some light from the streetlamps, a little moon. A man, quite tall, tried the door, walked around the deck to the back, pressing on windows.'

'Didn't break in?'

'Oh no. Stayed a little while, looked all around. I thought at one point he had seen me, but no, I was in a dark interior.'

'Did you recognise him?' asked Jacques, hopefully.

'Recognise him. I didn't see his face well enough,' said Monsieur Lefebvre slowly. 'So, I cannot be certain. In build, in movement, I think perhaps the man from the black boat. But of course, that may be because you suggested, or that I was expecting it to be him. Although no, I think it was him. Yes.'

'Right. Well done, Henri. But we'd better leave here now before the boating community start stirring.' Monsieur Lefebvre was looking pensive.

'It is such a shame,' he said. 'So many good places to lay one's head, unused. So many people needing a place to lie down. There is no connection is there? Haves too much and have nots.' Jacques looked at him warmly.

'Come on,' he said, and looking around quickly, he helped the old man onto the towpath and locked the door again. On the *Incognito* he dialled Celestine's number and waited anxiously for her to answer the phone.

'I think you were right. They look like the conveyancing documents for the land and farmhouse at Rama. In 1939. The vendors were a Monsieur and Madame Gattini, and the purchaser, a Samuel Joseph Steinbach. There is an additional note, which I think suggests that it was being purchased on behalf of the 'Eclaireurs Israelites de France. The Jewish Scout Movement. But the purchase was definitely in Steinbach's name. There's a lot of legalise, which I can't quite get my head around, but that's what it appears to be.'

Jacques could hear the tension and excitement in her voice. She was speaking quietly and there was a slight echo. 'Where are you?' he asked.

'In my cell. I can hear singing or chanting. I'm being discreet. I'm ok.' Relieved, Jacques thought about what she had said.

'So, Steinbach or the Jewish Scout Movement owned the land. Are you sure it's Rama?' asked Jacques.

'Pretty sure. It lists fields and has plans of buildings, a few maps of the plot, or plots. It certainly looks like Rama. The land stretching along the river, woods, you know. It looks like it.'

'Ok, so we need to go to the notary. You need to make two copies. Leave the original in the Convent, specifically in their archives. Ironic really. They should have a copier there, it might run on candle wax, but offer to pay.'

'They've been really sweet and kind. I felt safe last night, cocooned. I think the Mother Superior will want to speak to me this morning, and I'm not sure mobile phones are encouraged'

'It's important you speak to her. It's vital that she realises the importance of the document, then they'll keep it safe. I imagine they're still traumatised by the murder of one of their own. Not easy for them.'

'No. But I assume they'll want the matter cleared up.'

'I'm sure. Celestine, stay there until I call you. I'm going to try and get an appointment at the notaries as early as I can, but they do tend to move more slowly than a drunken snail.'

In the case of Maitre Michael Braun-Pivet, the sole notary in Lissac-sur-Tarn, Jacques was mistaken. Intrigued by the brief summary, and the sense of urgency conveyed by Jacques in his telephone call, the notary agreed to meet them at eleven thirty that same morning.

'Most interesting, yes most. Although I cannot offer you a lot of time, and the police are involved in this, yes?'

'Yes. They may wish to send an officer to join the meeting,' said Jacques.

'Well, well. Good. Agreed then. Eleven thirty. Good day.'

He is bored out of his skull, thought Jacques. He immediately telephoned Desmarais. 'Paul, I need you to meet us at the notary's office at half past eleven. Full dress uniform. We have an appointment.'

'I only have one type of uniform, Jacques. But that is remarkable, to get an appointment within hours. It's days or weeks normally'

'I may have stressed the official nature of the matter a little more than is strictly the case at this point. Needs must,' said Jacques.

'I'll meet you outside.'

'Make it quarter past. Is there a café there?'

'A few doors away, yes.'

'Meet there.'

'Celestine?'

'She's ok. She'll be there.'

Celestine had been invited into the refectory and offered breakfast. The Mother Superior joined her, sitting opposite at the table. She reached for Celestine's hands and turned them over to look at the blood-stained bandages.

'We will change these bandages,' she said quietly. 'How did you hurt your hands so badly, and receive your other marks and bruises?'

Celestine sipped the thin, milky coffee. 'I fell, climbing, and then I was being chased through some woods and I had to climb again.' The nun looked at her curiously, searching for any sign of duplicity, but there was a frankness and an intensity in the young woman's quite arresting eyes, which encouraged her to believe the story.

'And your pursuer?' she asked. Celestine shrugged. 'And are you still in danger from him, I presume a him?' asked the nun.

'Yes, him, and yes I believe I am. I believe he is a very dangerous man and I am a threat to him.'

'The police?'

'They know something of it. But they can't or won't act yet,' said Celestine. 'I know how the police work Reverend Mother. Until quite recently I was a member of that force in Bordeaux.' The Mother Superior raised her eyes in surprise.

'Then do you not have friends, ex-colleagues, you could stay with?'

'I have only one friend here, and he thought it safer for me to be…out of the way.' The Mother Superior smiled.

'That's a little old-fashioned I think, but I accept your point.' Celestine leaned forwards a little and spoke quietly and urgently.

'Reverend Mother, could we speak in your office, please? I need to ask you another favour; but first, I would like to give you something of an explanation of why I came here last night.'

'Very well, but in half an hour. Sister Madelaine will redress your bandages.'

The Mother Superior stood up and Celestine felt a wave of guilt wash over her. She looked around the refectory hall, it was not uncomfortable, but it was plain and austere. The women here led restricted lives, built to run on the tracks of a faith, a deep belief in something that Celestine now found frankly inconceivable. Yet here she was, a lapsed catholic girl, pleading for the help of the good and kind-hearted members of this restricted sect, and feeling guilty about it. Which showed, she thought, that quite a lot of her upbringing had lodged deep within her.

She sat on the other side of the desk in the Mother Superior's simple, tidy office; the plainness relieved by a few touches of warmth, a photograph of a woman with two small children, a Chinese vase of flowers, and on the desk, a beautiful, leather-bound volume with fine gilt lettering and marbled edges.

In the end, Celestine told her everything. There was something about the quiet, non-judgemental intensity of her listening, the strength and sincerity of her eyes. Celestine soon realised that this was a confession, an opportunity to divulge, to empty the mind and the emotions of so much material that was clogging the arteries of her thoughts. And to hear it come tumbling out was to clarify her ideas, to validate her reasoning, and to release some of the terror she had felt in the woods the night before.

The Mother Superior was silent for several minutes after Celestine had finished speaking, her head slightly bowed and her hands steepled on the desk in front of her; she almost looked as though she was praying. But it wasn't passive, Celestine could see that she was running over the material in her mind and looking for the next course of action. Finally, she said.

'I knew of course of the visits of Monsieur Malraux. I knew that Sister Agnieszka had been assisting him in his searches. I admit that when I heard of the two deaths, I wondered, I suspected, but I didn't know how there could be a connection. Sister Agnieszka's death has, as you might imagine, shaken this little community to its very roots. For some it is a vindication; Sister Agnieszka was too much "in the world", and look at the dangers of that; for others, they may think that we are too much out of the world, not relevant enough, not engaging vigorously enough in the fight against evil. But however we react, this was a terrible act, two terrible acts, and if you believe you may be on the path to bringing some justice for both of these poor people, then I will offer what little help we can.' Celestine thanked her.

'But it seems to me,' she continued, 'that you are assuming a lot, and that you are taking on a lot of the burden and the risk on your own shoulders. This man Jacques, I don't pry you understand, is he the sort to be steadfast? Goodness, old-fashioned word. I mean, will he be there for you, when he can, is he reliable?' She paused. 'You may think I have little experience to call on in discussing the ways of men, but many of our congregation join us after their relationships with men have been fractured, oppressive, unstable, often violent.'

Celestine nodded and then surprisingly smiled. 'I was married, Reverend Mother,' she said. 'And I could use all of those adjectives to describe that relationship, except violent, I would never have tolerated that. But Jacques, I think he would stand not beside me, but in front of me in any situation where there was danger or extreme difficulty. Yes, definitely steadfast.'

Just at that moment, Celestine's mobile phone rang. Apologetically, she answered it. 'I'm sorry,' she said, after the call. 'That was Jacques, we have an appointment at the Notary's at eleven thirty this morning. So....'

'Copies of the document, yes. Then bring it back to us, and I will place it in the safe in this office. If you need to leave it for another eighty years, then I will have to find a place in the archives for it.'

'No, no. I think a few days will be sufficient,' said Celestine.

'You mentioned the notary. Let me tell you something of what I know of notaries in this town. Maitre Braun-Pivet Senior, the current notary's father, I had dealings with some years ago. Surprising how often matters of legality, of legal advice, arise in an institution such as this. Yes, now. Maitre Braun-Pivet Senior was, I would say, as sound a man of business as you could hope for; meticulous, scrupulously honest, unbending I would say. The current, Braun-Pivet, Michael, the son, took over from his father a few years back. I have heard nothing ill of him, other than that perhaps he is a little less serious than his father. But I don't say that as a criticism you understand, generations are different. What I will tell you is that the office has not always been held by characters of such morality. Of particular relevance, let me say, during the days of which you speak, the black days of the occupation, the notary of that time was a Maitre Vautour. You may ask how I know this, given that although I may look it, I wasn't actually born until fifteen years after the war ended. But this Maitre Vautour was a notorious collaborator, a man also involved in the identification and the rounding up of Jews in this area. He was in fact stripped of his practice when retribution started, and he was not seen in this parish again. I don't know what happened to him, but he was notorious at that time. I'm not sure who took over the practice, but Maitre Braun-Pivet may have worked for him and assumed the business about twenty years later. This may not be relevant at all of course but….'

When Celestine stood up to take her leave she felt somehow lighter, cleaner, yet more focused. The Mother Superior took hold of her hands gently and smiled. Thank you, didn't seem a sufficient response to what Celestine had received, so she merely returned the smile and then followed the nun who had appeared to help her make the copies of the document. The document, that she believed was now at the core of everything that had occurred so far, and everything that would occur in the next few days.

Chapter Fifty

Maitre Braun-Pivet's offices were just off the old market square. They were housed in a fine old nineteenth-century building, solid, but embellished with such small architectural adornments around the windows and eaves, which softened the lines and added touches of quality, enough to lift it above some of the other, rather plain houses in the street.

Desmarais arrived early, but Jacques and Celestine were already sitting in the café, heads together, talking animatedly. Jacques had a copy of the document on the table in front of him. Desmarais sat down and Jacques immediately addressed him.

'This, we think, is the document that confirms the purchase of the house and land at Rama, by Samuel Steinbach, Malraux's great-grandfather, before the war.' Jacques held it so that Desmarais could see the names of the purchasers. 'There is a note that suggests that it was bought for the benefit of the Jewish Scout Movement. The notary will have to clarify that point. Celestine believes it was probably run as a collective farm and a teaching facility for young Jewish adolescents.'

'Until the dispersal of the Jews,' said Celestine.

'What we need to find out from Maitre Braun-Pivet is; A - is the document genuine? He should be able to confirm that from a copy. We're keeping the original back until we know…'

'Who we can trust,' added Celestine.

'Yes, who we can trust and; B - if it has been superseded. There should be a record, a similar document showing the sale from Steinbach to another party, then, or perhaps later, to Monsieur Palomer or his family. Now what is really important, Paul, is that we put and keep the pressure on the notary to get the information to confirm both A and B, as soon as possible, today ideally.' Jacques took hold of the sleeve of Desmarais's uniform to emphasise the point. 'You need to help put that pressure on. This is an official investigation. This matter is extremely pertinent to a murder investigation, and time is of the essence. It is the essence. Got it?' Desmarais nodded. Between the authority of this wild-looking and charismatic man and the weakness he felt every time he looked at Celestine, Desmarais knew he was totally ensnared, and would do whatever he could to help them.

Celestine told him what the Mother Superior had said about the notary who was in practice at that time.

'Notorious. I knew that,' said Desmarais. 'Some names from that time, a few, they are remembered. Well, I hope this comes to something.' Looking at Jacques, he said: 'They did a search of Palomer's yard and sheds this morning, at first light.'

'No kidding,' said Jacques and looked pleased.

'It's too early to know what they found, or the relevance,' he added. 'But April, my mate in the station, said they seemed a little excited. Mind you, in my experience, those technical guys wouldn't get excited if they found the remains of Joan of Arc.'

'They'd certainly be surprised,' said Jacques.

'Ok, let's go in. This could be make or break,' said Celestine, who stood up, clutching the file of copies tightly in her bandaged hands.

Maitre Michael Braun-Pivet was dressed remarkably casually, in a lemon-coloured polo shirt from which his round, fleshy head protruded like a golf ball on a tee. His hair was a dull brown, messy, as though stuck on top of his head carelessly. He wore black-framed glasses; but behind them, his eyes belied any suggestion of a lack of intellect, they were sharp, intelligent and penetrating. He waved them into seats around his large L-shaped desk as if inviting friends to join him at the bar. Jacques made the introductions and the notary looked closely at each of them in turn.

'Agent Desmarais, I have seen before, although I do not think we have met in an official capacity.' His voice was a little high, and his words came out evenly, as though controlled by some filter that released them at pre-set intervals. 'You, madame,' he said turning his gaze on Celestine, 'I would remember, as I would you Monsieur Lecoubarry. I do not believe I have met either of you before today.'

'It's unlikely,' said Jacques. 'We have lived much of our time in Bordeaux, where Madame Courbet was a senior investigating officer in the Judicial Police Force.' Braun-Pivet looked again at Celestine and smiled faintly, rubbing his lips against each other.

'Then this is in the nature of an official visit, I can assume?'

'You can,' replied Jacques, quickly. Celestine placed her bandaged hands on the desk top.

'There is much I am not able to tell you at this stage, Maitre,' said Celestine. 'It is in the nature of such investigations. But I can tell you that there is an urgency in this matter, and your assistance could be vital in bringing a complex investigation to a successful conclusion.'

Braun-Pivet glanced down at her bandaged hands and tutted with concern. 'Well, let us see,' he said, moving his own hands together on the desk and holding them as if shielding his cards from the other players.

Celestine placed the document on the table. 'Firstly, could you look through this and confirm to us, what it is, and whether in your opinion it is genuine.' She pushed the document across the desk in front of the notary.

'But this is a photocopy, madame.'

'Yes. It is an accurate copy. We do have the original and, if necessary, we will produce it. But just now, please accept that this is a true and exact copy of the original.'

Braun-Pivet pulled his spectacles lower onto his fleshy nose and with one hand held up, fingers apart, he began to read. At first, he seemed to read each line, but then he began to scan pages more quickly. He stopped occasionally to focus on certain details, and the final pages he read slowly and carefully, tracing a finger across the paper. Then he sat back and removed his spectacles, leaving them in his left hand to gesticulate.

He addressed himself to Celestine. 'Quite simply, this is a record of a transaction -the sale of a parcel of land, a farm at,' he looked again at the front page, 'at Rama. In the year 1939. A purchase by Samuel Joseph Steinbach from a Monsieur Gilbert Gattini. It is a standard document for this time. It outlines the parcels of land included in the sale, along with the house and buildings, and includes information about any wayleaves, rights and restrictions. Very normal, very standard, I should say.'

'So, for me to be absolutely clear; this document, at that time, would furnish proof of the ownership of that farm,' said Celestine slowly and carefully.

'Yes, precisely. But at that time only. This of course would be superseded on the completion of another transaction, a further sale and purchase.'

'A sale by Monsieur Steinbach to another party?' said Celestine.

'Quite so,' said Braun-Pivet, laying his hands flat on the desk and looking distinctly disappointed. 'No great mystery, an old legal document, nothing more.'

'There is a note. I thought it suggested that Monsieur Steinbach acquired the property on behalf of the Jewish Scout Movement.'

'There is a note there to that effect, but there is no evidence in this documentation that such a transfer took place. Of course, there may well be further documentation to that effect.'

'Of course,' said Celestine. 'But if there were not in existence a document, a sale and purchase document that superseded this one, this document would still be current and relevant.'

'Absolutely. But there could be several documents that reflect the changes of ownership in the intervening years. Good heavens, this is eighty years old. There are sales of land happening all the time, I am pleased to say, or we notaries would be a very thin bunch.' He chuckled to himself and the others smiled, although Jacques thought it unlikely that this notary had experienced thin since the day he arrived on earth.

'These documents. Where would they be held?' he asked.

Braun-Pivet sat back and smiled expansively. 'Why, here of course,' his voice rising as he waved his arms to embrace his office, the building, the whole legal edifice. 'Here we have documents. The Rama Estate belongs to Monsieur Marcel Palomer. It has been in his family for years. Before I, or possibly even my father, assumed responsibility for the legal affairs of that estate.'

'So, you could have the documentation that superseded this document, on file?' enquired Celestine, quietly.

'Certainly.'

'And how quickly could you locate those documents?'

'Ah well. I could dispatch a member of staff into the relevant storage place, and I would be disappointed if they didn't return with the relevant documents in say, eight minutes, or less. Easy.' With an air of triumph, he looked at his three visitors. 'But. I should not be in the right if I were then to show them to you,' he said.

'You mean, you could look at them, but we couldn't?' said Celestine.

'Precisely. They are private. They are retained here for safekeeping, but they are, in essence, the property of Monsieur Marcel Palomer.'

Jacques finally broke the silence that followed this pronouncement. 'Maitre Braun-Pivet. For the sake of argument. If you were to look for those documents, and if you then found that in fact, there were no contracts that superseded this one, or if there were contracts, more particularly, the first contract, a sale by Monsieur Steinbach, and if you found this contract to be in some way, let's say inconclusive.' Jacques raised his hand. 'Please hear me out. If there was a problem with the sale contract, would you, with your extensive knowledge of such matters, be able to establish that it was inconclusive, and in so doing, could you share this information in detail, with us?' He paused briefly, still with his hand up. 'Or will it be necessary for us to obtain a court order to gain access to the files, and to bring in a specialist in this field to provide us with the information we require, and insist on having, one way or the other.'

Braun-Pivet sat up and his whole body seemed to stiffen. 'You would think it necessary to do that?'

'Without hesitation,' said Jacques. 'This is a major criminal investigation. Nothing, no one, can be allowed to obstruct or hinder its progress. So yes, we would do that if necessary. Our preference, not least because of the time involved, would be for you to do this work, today, and for us to all to meet here again at say four p.m.'

'Four p.m. Impossible. I have many other matters to deal with today.'

'I understand. Then let's say five p.m. But we will prepare the paperwork for the court order, ready to be instructed if necessary.'

'All right. Five p.m. But I am sure....' He hesitated, 'but who knows?'

'Exactly, who knows? We have more than a suspicion. Can you not feel the excitement, Maitre Braun-Pivet? The excitement as we move one major step closer to completing this investigation. Your role is crucial, please don't let us down.'

Celestine stood up, her hand on Jacques' arm. 'Thank you, Maitre. We'll take up no more of your time. Until five p.m....' They shook the hands of a slightly bemused notary and left. Once outside Celestine turned to Jacques. 'A bit thick there, Jacques. You laid it on a bit thick.'

Desmarais, who had said nothing except hello and goodbye, looked at them both.

'I didn't realise,' he said, 'that you thought there might be a problem with the ownership of the Rama Estate. It never occurred to me. What made you think of this?'

'Why else would the Palomers be threatened by what Malraux might find? They must know. They know that there is something crooked about their ownership of that land. Do you agree Celestine?'

'I have considered it, but I'd like to wait and see what Braun-Pivet comes up with. It still feels a little nebulous right now. Like it couldn't just be this.'

It's enough,' said Jacques.

'Perhaps, let's wait and see.'

Desmarais took his leave. Jacques called out to him. 'Let me know if Jean-Michel comes into the station, and what he says, please.' Desmarais nodded and walked pensively back to his car. He felt that he was now operating in a very grey area between his official duties and his activities with the unrestricted half-truths of Jacques and Celestine, and he was far from comfortable.

'What now, Raven?' said Jacques. 'Lunch, back to the boat?'

'Henri?'

'He's on the boat. He spent last night in that empty cruiser along the way, the *Just Left*. He saw Jean-Michel come on to the *Incognito* and try the doors and windows.'

'Hang on. The cruiser that's for sale. He stayed there. Was it...? No, of course it wasn't open,' said Celestine.

'It was when he got there.'

'You opened it.'

'And closed it. It's in perfect repair and probably benefitted from the airing.'

Celestine shook her head. 'Buy me lunch,' she said sternly.

A tall figure, dressed in dark chinos and sweatshirt, emerged from behind an advertising board and watched them cross the square towards the cafés on the other side. He turned into the Rue des Mazels and stood at the bottom of the steps leading up to the offices of Maitre Braun-Pivet, Public Notary.

Chapter Fifty-One

'The blood on the tape matches Monsieur Lecoubarry's. Hair on the shreds found on the plough tine is Monsieur Lecoubarry's. The rope; we cut a small length from a coil in one of the sheds, the grey shed, is inconclusive. It's the right colour, it could have made the marks on Lecoubarry's neck, but he had washed and showered before we had him here, so any fragments left in the wound would have been lost. Pity.'

Grimard replaced the phone, then pressed the intercom. 'Jerome, has Jean-Michel Palomer come in to make his statement yet?'

'Not yet, chief.'

'Then call him, and tell him we'd like to see him sooner rather than later. In fact, now.'

'Will do.'

'The guy in the hospital, Pierre. Any news?'

'I'll ask.'

'Do that, and I will want to talk to him, too.'

'Chief. It's not exactly a job for your level, is it? I could send Rabault.'

'How far is the hospital?'

'Just along the road. Two hundred metres.'

'I'm going there now. Text me the ward details.' Bedeau knew better than to query his boss.

Ten minutes later, Grimard stood looking down on the saddest piece of humanity he had seen in a long time. Pierre's face was almost completely covered with the large plaster and bandages over his broken nose. His poky eyes peered out above the bandages with a look of fear and affront. His upper lip was split and held together with steri-strips, and his right hand lay by his side in a plaster cast, his fingers strapped together with splints. He looked at Grimard suspiciously, as though he expected him to start the process of breaking ribs and limbs again. Grimard pulled a chair very close to the bed and laid his hand firmly on Pierre's right arm.

'I am Commandant Jean-Philippe Grimard, Pierre. Commandant, do you understand? Of the Judicial Police. And I want you to tell me exactly, without prevarication, lying to you, what happened yesterday evening in the woods and in the yard at your employer's house.' Pierre looked sideways at Grimard.

'I can't speak well. My nose, my mouth, broken. It's very painful.'

'I appreciate that, Pierre. So, the sooner you start, the sooner you can stop the pain. And, Pierre. Don't you fucking lie to me, or you will find a whole new kind of pain, police business pain, coming down the road to hurt you.'

Fifteen minutes later, Grimard closed his notebook. 'Where is the rope?' Pierre shook his head. 'Did you hear shots, two shots?' Pierre nodded his head. Grimard stood up. 'What the hell possessed you to tie a man up, to put a rope around his neck?' Pierre murmured. 'Oh, I know. Jean-Michel told you to. That is not enough, Pierre. If Monsieur Lecoubarry decides to press charges, you are in a lot of trouble, and what has happened to you, these damages will seem entirely justified to a magistrate. Let's see what happens. Au revoir.'

'I feel that I have not eaten a proper meal for days,' said Jacques, between mouthfuls of duck confit. 'This is not exactly how I envisaged our slow drift through the charming countryside, re-fuelling at small but choice restaurants along the way, lounging together in the dreamy afternoons.'

'No. I didn't expect this either. I think you are trouble, Jacques Lecoubarry.'

'Me, trouble! You're the detective here. You chose to thrust us into these murky waters. But what about dreamy afternoons, are you missing them?'

'I am, and I'll appreciate them when they start up again. But we have to finish this.' She watched Jacques placing food delicately into his torn mouth, and winced for him. 'How is this going to finish? Suppose Maitre Braun-Pivet tells us this afternoon that A: there is something wrong with the conveyancing, the legal train of ownership. Or conversely B: that all is in order, there's nothing to see here. What then?'

Jacques spent some time eating quietly. He took a sip of his beer and flinched as it stung his lips. He frowned.

'A: Palomer is scared. So, we scare the shit out of him some more, to see how he reacts. B: We scare the shit out of him anyway, because he's an unpleasant little bastard.' He went back to eating his lunch.

'Strategy is not necessarily your strong point, is it Jacques? Action, thinking on your feet, putting pressure on. But where and when to press; you're a bit broad brush, a bit agricultural.'

'Thanks very much. What do you think? We show the evidence to the police. The contracts could take months to be verified by an expert acceptable to the courts. Palomers would oppose, counterclaim, for months and months. I just want to pin those murders on Jean-Michel.'

'If he did them.'

'If he did them. But if not, then who?'

'If not he, then we leave it in the hands of the police and drift on down the canal. You can teach me to play Trictrac.'

'For money?'

'For something.'

'Now you're pressing the right buttons. What about the buttons in this case?' Jacques wiped his mouth and leaned across the table to kiss Celestine tentatively on the lips.

'My kissing facility is much reduced at this time,' he said, 'but it will come back stronger than ever.'

'I can't wait,' said Celestine. 'Amazing what a good meal can do for you.'

They sat quietly, thinking. Celestine took a pen and notebook from her bag. Jacques raised his eyebrows.

'Capitaine.'

'Hush.' She began to sketch out a diagram, linking boxes, names and events. She covered the sheet and then turned to a second page and in block letters wrote down a list. 'Evidence,' she said finally. 'There has to be evidence, or if not, it will be impossible to tie Jean-Michel to these murders. The problem, the initial problem, was always to find a motive. But presuming we have that with these contracts, what evidence is there? What evidence do the police have?

If any. Will its relevance only be considered when they can see a motive?'

'What are the alternatives?' asked Jacques.

'If there's no evidence, or nothing conclusive, then you need witnesses, a confession, caught in the act,' suggested Celestine.

Jacques pushed away his empty plate and looked quizzically at her. 'Caught in the act of what? Committing another murder. You mean you need a tethered goat.'

'Something like that, but I don't think that's what we are looking at.'

'Let's go back to the *Incognito*. I think better on the high seas, and Henri will need feeding again.'

'Yes, bless him,' said Celestine. 'He's been really sweet and helpful, hasn't he?'

'He has. I shall miss his gentle smile and the slight aroma of old sweat and leaf mould.'

Grimard sat in the small conference room with his team of four officers, three men and a woman. There was a knock on the door and a tentative Paul Desmarais half-entered.

'Come in, Agent Desmarais. I want you to sit in. I will have some questions for you.' Desmarais took the seat nearest to the door and stared at the table top. Grimard looked around.

'Mathieu, physical evidence from the murder scenes, what do we have?'

'Chief. We have some small fibres, most likely from a glove, found on the surface of the body of Monsieur Malraux, and also in his hair.'

'Gloves, type?'

'Nitrile, nothing unusual, not uncommon.'

'Sometimes used by people allergic to latex,' added Bedeau. 'Something.' He shrugged.

'Same fibres on the clothes of Sister Agnieszka, dress and cape thing,' continued Mathieu.

'Same gloves?'

'Same type.'

'Anything else?'

'Some dark fibres on Sister Agnieszka, possibly a sweatshirt or similar. More on the nun as the body had been…. searched.'

'The note?'

'Nothing much else, chief. Careful or lucky.'

Grimard turned to the youngest member, who had a yellow file in front of him. 'Jean-Paul.'

'Pathology says, same knife, or very similar, used in both killings. Medium-sized blade, smooth, very sharp, possibly agricultural use.'

'Ok, Anna, you look desperate to speak, or something. What've you got?'

'Just come in, chief. CCTV. A residential camera. A Monsieur and Madame Briseau. They live on the Route de Calvaire. They were away on holiday for a few days, seems their camera caught a car driving along that road, the only road that goes to Calvary.'

'Go on.'

'This couple live on a bend and the camera points out of their gate and slightly up the road.'

'And.'

'And we have a registration number, and we've traced it.'

'Go on,' said Grimard, a little excitement now stirring.

'The picture is not very clear and you can't make out the identity of the driver, but the registration number is clear. The car belongs to Jean-Michel Palomer of the Rama Estate.' Agent Anna Froissart beamed, her face glowing as she became the centre of attention in the room. Grimard sat back, whistling through his teeth.

'Does it indeed? And where is Monsieur Jean-Michel Palomer? He was supposed to come in to make a statement. Where is he, Jerome?'

'Chief, we've tried calling him several times. No answer.'

'At home?'

'Home and mobile.'

'No answer from the house?'

'No, sir.'

'Get a car over there now. If he's there, bring him in. The number of questions I have for Jean-Michel Palomer is growing.' Several of the team left, only Bedeau and Desmarais remained.

'Jerome, give me a few minutes with Agent Desmarais, will you.' Bedeau smirked and looked across at Desmarais.

'Go on. And find where that big, Basque bastard, Lecoubarry is. I want to speak to him again.'

Grimard turned towards Desmarais, who, much as he tried, was unable to look him in the eye. Grimard spun out the silence a few more moments before speaking. 'Now, Agent Desmarais. "Get a fucking grip". Appropriate language with which to address a superior officer in the police force?'

'No, sir. I apologise of course. It was unacceptable.'

'Unacceptable, yes.' Grimard paused, picked up his pen and opened his notebook.

'Then let's see if you can redeem any of your rapidly diminishing prospects by squaring with me, and telling me everything you know about what Lecoubarry and that former policewoman are doing. Because I know he has kept a lot from me. A lot.'

Chapter Fifty-Two

At five p.m. Jacques and Celestine sat down opposite Maitre Braun-Pivet, who nevertheless, remained standing. Jacques studied him carefully; there was an increased wariness in his eyes, his round fleshy face seemed to be arguing with itself as he rehearsed what he was going to say, and his hand moved restlessly. He started to speak, then stopped and leant forward with both hands on the desk.

'I had a visitor today. An unexpected visitor. Yes, not scheduled, not expected at all. A quite unpleasant visit. A rather abrupt and indeed rude man, Monsieur Marcel Palomer.' He paused to see the effect of this on his current visitors. 'An unpleasant, rude man. One shouldn't, you know, talk of one's clients in such terms, but....'

'I have met Monsieur Palomer,' said Jacques. 'I completely understand your sentiments. But why was he here?'

'A coincidence you think? Hardly. Our discussion this morning, the questions you raised, and suddenly, poof, Monsieur Palomer arrives. Angry, oh so angry. Wanting to know why you and Agent Desmarais had visited here this morning.' Jacques and Celestine looked at each other. So, they were being watched, followed. 'I told him,' continued Braun-Pivet. 'I told him it was no concern of his, and that I could not discuss another client's matters with him. Oh, he was most insistent, called me several names. But I did not disclose any details of our meeting this morning. None.' Braun-Pivet sat down, pleased with this display of bravado.

'That was well done, Maitre,' said Celestine.

He continued, 'But, and here I had to give way a little, but, well you'll hear. He then demanded, there and then, all the details we held on file in relation to the Rama Estate. Now, immediately. Said he was going to engage a different firm of notaries and legal representatives. Well, as I explained to you this morning, these documents are, by rights, the property of Monsieur Palomer. No question.'

'You didn't give them to him, did you?' asked Celestine anxiously.

'I did not. Although, I will have to in due course. No, I told him that it would take some time to extract them from the secure archives and that he would have to wait until tomorrow. By then, I assumed, you would be able to obtain a court order to seize them. No?'

'I presume so,' said Jacques.

'Thank you for that. But why? Wouldn't it have been easier just to give him the contracts? Easier for you, I mean,' said Celestine.

'It would, it would, but you see,' and he leaned towards them in a confidential way.

'I have unearthed, yes unearthed, anomalies. More than one, most surprising, most....' He paused, searching for the word. 'Incomplete.' Jacques and Celestine looked at each other again.

'Please explain, Maitre Braun-Pivet,' said Celestine, and smiled at him. Jacques settled back in his seat.

'Very well, and you appreciate this was a quick, almost superficial review of the paperwork.' Braun-Pivet, who did not give the impression of being a man who had ever done anything superficial in relation to legal documents, opened the file in front of him. 'A number of things.' He ran his fingers down the pages. 'For instance, the vendor; described differently on two different pages - a Samuel Joseph Steinbach acting on behalf of the Jewish Scout Movement, and a Monsieur Steinbach - no mention of an organisation. Now instructions from a client must be very clear, and must be agreed with the vendor; very clear, who is the vendor, in what name, and indeed details like date of birth, place of birth. Missing you see, missing. Now, normally this information is extrapolated in large part from the previous documents, the preceding sale and purchase documents.' Braun-Pivet scratched his head. 'Yes, more of those details that should be transcribed, not included, or included in a very limited, vague way. The descriptions of the fields, unclear, dimensions, too well-rounded. Wayleaves, rights of way, sketchy details.' He looked up. 'Perhaps I am not explaining myself very well. The relevance. Let me put this document alongside the copy that you gave me this morning. If this copy was indeed the contract that succeeded, and only one by the way, there is no evidence that the property has been sold since 1943, when it was acquired by Monsieur Palomer's grandfather, also a Marcel Palomer. Sorry. If this copy followed this copy, the information, the details of the property should have been transposed, in detail, to this contract, give or take any changes that may have taken place in the meantime. But the estate was held by, according to your contract, Samuel Joseph Steinbach, for only a few years, so it is unlikely that there were many changes made in this time.' He stopped and dramatically drew in a deep breath, whistling through his nostrils. 'So, if I were to summarise, I would surmise, although there could be other explanations, perhaps. I would suggest that the current contract was prepared with little or no access to the previous contract - your copy. And with only limited information provided, if at all, by the vendor.'

'What you are saying,' said Jacques, but Braun-Pivet held up his hand.

'Please let me finish. This is unusual enough, and very inconsistent with good practice. But then I found a clue, you might say, as to why that might be the case. I expected to find, you see, in the files, our, the notaries copy of the contract that you left with me this morning. A copy of the previous contract, and even contracts going further back still; why we have contracts going back even into the nineteenth century. Where was I? Yes. In the file there was indeed a large envelope, the kind of envelope used, now and then, to hold these contracts. Sealed, oh yes. Undoubtedly the envelope where one would expect to find a contract, but what did I find inside?' He pulled a thick, sturdy-looking envelope from below the other papers and placed it dramatically on the desktop. 'Paper, yes, but blank, look. Just blank pieces of paper. Except on the final page, the last page of perhaps forty leaves. A number, just that. A number, 37. Remarkable, 37. Just that.'

He sat back and looked at them one by one. Celestine's face was actually shimmering, he thought. Behind the even features and the depth of the dark pools of her eyes, he could almost see the brain working, calculating, evaluating the information he had given out. It was most alluring and disconcerting at the same time. Encouraged he continued.

'One more thing, or one more thing of note; and bear in mind here that I am not a handwriting expert, but one gets used to different signatures, the squiggles, the flamboyant, the reticent. Yes, but look here, at the signature pages where the vendor must sign, and compare that signature with the signature of Monsieur Steinbach on the contract you gave me. No comparison, not even similar. Different, yet purporting to be the signature of the same person. I do not think so.' He shook his head. He was addressing everything to Celestine now. 'There are other details you know, only a cursory look really, but well, they are the main anomalies that I have found in reviewing these two contracts.'

They lapsed into silence as Jacques and Celestine considered the import of this information. Finally, Celestine broke the silence.

'So, in your opinion, this current contract was prepared without any access to the preceding contract, and the fact that the envelope where the preceding contract should have been, included only blank paper would rather confirm that.'

'I think it most likely, and don't forget, none of the details that would have been provided by a vendor during the signing of the *compromis de vente,* the initial meeting to instigate the sale process, the confirmation of dates of birth etc. etc.'

'Yes, yes,' said Celestine. 'And the signatures on the two contracts are totally different, which would suggest strongly that the person who signed as the vendor was a different person to the one who signed to purchase the property a few years earlier, and who was called in both cases, Samuel Joseph Steinbach.'

'Precisely.'

'So, would you go so far as to say that this current contract, proving ownership of Rama Farm by Monsieur Palomer, is quite possibly a fake, a contract prepared without the knowledge of, or agreement with, the owners of the property, Monsieur Steinbach, possibly and Associates.'

'Fake, strong terminology. Not enough evidence to hang that hat on the peg. But suspicious, suspicious, oh yes, most certainly. There are questions to be answered.'

'And if it should prove to be a fake,' said Jacques, 'then Palomer is not the actual owner of the property, it still belongs to Monsieur Steinbach or his heirs, as I am sure poor Monsieur Steinbach is dead by now, and probably not long after, or even before this contract was drawn up.'

'Well yes, I feel that must have been the case, for there has been no query raised on this matter afore now. It would be in the file you see. And yes, two other things, not conclusive in themselves, but in the context of all the other anomalies. Invoices; there are no copies of invoices for the work done by the notary at the time, for the sale and purchase. One would normally find a record of these, although this could certainly be an administrative issue. It's possible. And correspondence; again, nothing on the file. It is almost, yes, as you said, as though the whole process were conducted without recourse to the vendor at any stage. Most remarkable, most suspicious. There, I've said it,' and he looked across at Celestine for her admiration. She was, however, at that point, looking through some other papers in her shoulder bag. She drew out several sheets and scanned them quickly.

'37. 37 is the pillar with the carving of Judas' betrayal in the Garden of Gethsemane.'

Braun-Pivet looked at Celestine questioningly.

'It's a theme, running through all of this,' she explained. 'Monsieur Steinbach used a simple code to be deciphered by his son. The code was a set of numbers relating to the pillars in the cloisters of Saint Pierre. Unfortunately, his son never came back to receive the letter which included the code. Monsieur Malraux, who was murdered, he came. He came to look for a message, something left by his great-grandfather, and he died because of it.'

Braun-Pivet went pale. 'You suspect?'

Celestine nodded slowly. 'I beg of you, do not say a word of this to anyone, you mustn't. And you must not give that file to Palomer. You must delay him, do whatever is necessary. We will aim to get a court order, but it may take some time. Please hold on to it, it's crucial evidence.'

'In fact, Maitre Braun-Pivet,' said Jacques. 'I would advise that you make a copy, probably several copies of that fake contract, and keep them all under wraps.' The Notary looked quite shaken, excited by the work he had done, and a little proud of his insight, but the implication of these discoveries left him drained and not a little fearful. 'Make the copies now, while we are here, then lock them away. And take a copy home with you, you may find a few more anomalies.'

'Quite so, yes.' He pressed a button on his intercom system and a stern, middle-aged woman came in, looking disapprovingly at Jacques and Celestine.

'Paulette, I want two copies of this made, right now. Thank you.' Jacques and Celestine waited until the copies had been brought, and Braun-Pivet had tucked one into his briefcase and taken the other, with the original, to a safe storage place. They shook hands, the notary now with a little more colour in his cheeks. 'Most remarkable. Never in all my experience, no, remarkable,' he said as he showed them out of the door.

Desmarais was waiting on the *Incognito* when they returned. He was sitting quietly next to Monsieur Lefebvre, and he scanned their faces as they stepped over the side. Celestine smiled at him.

'We were right,' she said. 'There's a…what would you call it?'

'Fraud,' said Jacques.

'Yes, it looks like. It looks as though the Palomers never actually bought the land they are living on.'

'And thriving on,' said Jacques.

'The sale contract was something cobbled up by the notary at the time, the notorious Maitre Vautour, and Palomer's grandfather, in 1943. The real owner, Samuel Steinbach, disappeared, taken to the concentration camps, and presumably died there,' said Celestine. 'But he must have been suspicious of Vautour, so he took the deeds from the notary and hid them where we found them. God, was it just yesterday? And he left a message for his son to be able to find the contract if he didn't return.'

'And then left an envelope of blank papers, sealed in an envelope for Maitre Vautour to keep,' added Jacques.

'I wonder how long before Vautour opened the envelope? Probably not until Steinbach was well out of the way and he could draw up a new contract for Palomer.'

'And be well paid for it, I've no doubt,' said Jacques.

'But not as much as actually buying the land.'

'Vautour must have known he'd been rumbled as soon as he opened that envelope. But he went ahead anyway. Palomer was in it for the long haul. Who would look at the contract? No one until the property was sold again, and it hasn't been in eighty years.'

'No, the only concern would have been if the true contract turned up somehow, and someone contested their ownership. I guess it must always have been a fear.'

'I hope so,' said Jacques fiercely. 'I hope it shortened their lives and ruined their livers.'

Transfixed, Desmarais moved his gaze from one to the other as they batted these insights back and forth. He ventured to ask.

'Aren't all properties registered? Somewhere.'

'I don't know if they were in those days, but in any case, it's down to the notary to register it,' said Jacques impatiently.

'Then Malraux turns up, asking questions,' continued Celestine. 'A little loose-tongued, given to taking drugs, finding a letter relating to these matters from all that time ago, and suddenly the Palomer family nightmare is real. The land was stolen and all that family wealth was under threat.'

'They must have thought Malraux had made more progress than he actually had.'

'Perhaps he gave that impression. In effect, they didn't know how much Malraux had learned, how close he was to exposing the fraud, nor how much he had told Sister Agnieszka and Ducrozet. But they couldn't take any chances.'

'And then we entered left,' said Jacques. 'Unknown quantities. They must have wondered what the hell we were doing. Had we in fact talked to Malraux before they killed him?'

'In some ways, they were lucky though. Two murders, two plausible suspects. Nothing to link the Palomers to any of it.'

'No motive,' said Desmarais, 'until now.'

'But now a big fat motive - the preservation of the family fortune, the prestige, the social position, the political power.' Jacques paused. 'But hell, I wouldn't kill for that, no way.'

'I'm glad to hear it,' said Celestine. 'The question, as always, is what now?'

Desmarais looked down into the canal waters and then back at the space between Jacques and Celestine. 'I have to take this information to Grimard. I had a bollocking this afternoon, but he was really quite fair. He wants to see you both, right away. That's why I came, well that and….'

'That and Henri's Tales of the Riverbank. Irresistible,' laughed Jacques and patted Monsieur Lefebvre gently on the back.

'But first, Agent Desmarais, you must do your duty as a municipal officer, dedicated to serving the needs of the community, and give us a lift to where we left our bicycles yesterday afternoon. And if they're not there, you must arrest the whole Palomer family for larceny. Do you think you'll be able to cycle with your hands like that, Celestine?'

'That's not possible,' spoke up Monsieur Lefebvre quickly. 'I will go. I'll ride the bicycle back.' Jacques looked doubtful.

'I don't really like leaving you.'

'I'll be fine, don't worry,' said Celestine. 'And thank you, Henri. I keep saying that, don't I? But don't go racing down those hills. I want the bike and you in one piece.'

Jacques looked at her. 'Or two pieces,' he said.

'I'm tired, you know. So, sod off, Jacques, I'm going for a lie-down and a think.'

'Lock the door.'

The bicycles were where they had left them. Jacques lifted them over the chain and Monsieur Lefebvre marvelled at the instruments on the handlebars.

'You'll be ok on that, Henri?'

'Certainly. I will have to get used to all the gears and gizmos, but I think I can handle it.'

Jacques stared down the track, through the trees in the gloom. Desmarais put a hand on his shoulder.

'Jacques, you really must come into the poste again, with Celestine, as soon as you've taken the bicycles back. It's honestly my job on the line.'

Jacques turned to him. 'Don't worry. I need to talk to Grimard. I have an idea, and I'll need his help with it.'

Desmarais looked askance at him. 'Don't hold your breath. I believe he's expecting you to help him, not the other way round.'

'It will be mutual,' Jacques assured him. Desmarais' face suddenly lit up.

'Damn, I forgot to say. Jean-Michel's car was caught on a CCTV camera, going to and leaving the hill at Calvary, at around ten o'clock on the night the nun was killed. Definitely his car. Grimard sent men to encourage him to come in for some questions.'

'That is interesting,' said Jacques thoughtfully. 'Look, tell Grimard we'll be in before dinner, so he mustn't expect to keep us very long. Seriously, we'll be there. Go back and tell him how much we've cooperated with you. Go on, get yourself away. And thank you, Paul. You have been exceptional.'

Desmarais climbed into his car, uncertain of whether he was going to come out of this as a hero, a villain, or just a fool. But there was something about that pair, Celestine and Jacques, something like a force of nature, pointless to resist, he thought. For him in any case.

Cycling along the peaceful country lanes, as the light gradually seeped away and the colours faded, Jacques felt calm for the first time in days. He felt the breeze gently washing over his face, blowing back his hair, and it was as though he was moving slowly away from the agitated, angry world he had lived in since his arrival in Lissac-sur-Tarn. Monsieur Lefebvre was tootling along behind him, looking clumsy on Celestine's bicycle, muttering unintelligible engineering babbles about gearing, bearings and links. There were good things, the neat gardens of the small country houses, the rows of fruit trees in their net cages, the sweetness of the country air. He felt as though they had passed through the thunderstorm, a maelstrom of death and destruction, but now the dark cloud was passing away and the new sky would be rinsed blue, clearer than ever. Then the storm might seem, somehow, a good thing. He knew he was thinking of Celestine. How would this affect her? How would it affect them? He steeled himself. Time to think of those things when the work was over. There was more to do yet. There was, of course still, the tethering of the goat.

Chapter Fifty-Three

Commandant Grimard was professional and courteous. He expressed concern for the injuries that Celestine had suffered and was at pains to point out that he had no intention of prying into the reasons why she had left the police force. He wanted merely to ensure that there was no additional information, held by them, that was relevant to the investigation. An investigation that he assured her was making progress.

'Have you arrested Jean-Michel Palomer?' demanded Jacques.

'No. He appears to be un-locatable at this time. We have tried to contact him.'

'And his father?'

'His father says his son is away on business, and will of course be happy to clear this up when he returns. He is still insisting, incidentally, that we arrest you for your unprovoked attack on his employee.'

'Unprovoked!' said Jacques.

Grimard held up his hand, desperate to stop another tirade. 'We know what took place between you and Pierre Mignot last night. I have interviewed him myself. We have some evidence also. We could possibly put both Jean-Michel and Mignot formally under investigation for this. Whether we do so rather depends on you, Monsieur Lecoubarry.'

'What I want, Commandant Grimard, is to see Jean-Michel and his father formally investigated for the murders of Malraux and Sister Agnieszka. And I have a plan. But first, let us help you with the issue of motive.'

Celestine briefly explained the findings of that afternoon at the offices of Maitre Braun-Pivet. Grimard listened attentively, scribbling notes and puffing out his cheeks at regular intervals. When she had finished, he said quietly.

'That does put a different perspective on it.'

'Yes, it does,' said Jacques. 'But is it enough to prove murder?'

'It helps, let's say,' said Grimard. 'We have the CCTV evidence, which shows that Jean-Michel was in the vicinity at the time of the second murder. We have a little bit of physical evidence, which perhaps we could find a match for if we searched the Palomer's property. Although I am afraid I'm not hopeful.'

'No,' said Jacques. 'But I think you should do it anyway. Might strike lucky.'

'And it would be the normal procedure after receiving the CCTV evidence,' stated Celestine. 'Especially as he doesn't seem to be cooperating.'

Grimard was pleased that none of his subordinates were in the room; they would be amazed at how he was letting these two civilians dictate the progress of his investigation. He determined to assert his authority, when Jacques continued.

'Can you leave off that search until tomorrow afternoon?'

Grimard looked astounded. 'Why?'

'Why? Because I intend to visit the Palomers tomorrow morning. I have a matter I wish to discuss with them.'

Grimard looked at him doubtfully. 'What are you thinking of, Lecoubarry? I am grateful for your assistance, I really am. But I think you can step back and let the current forces of the law follow this to its conclusion.'

'Well, perhaps,' said Jacques. 'But he does have a Trictrac table I am rather keen to acquire, and I think he may be willing to sell it to me, in the current circumstances.'

Grimard shook his head. 'I don't begin to understand what you're talking about, or even believe you, if I'm honest.' He stood up. 'Madame, it has been a pleasure to meet you, and I am sure you are a great loss to the force.' He shook her hand. 'And Jacques Lecoubarry, well….'

'One more thing, Commandant,' said Jacques. 'Can you secure the fake contract held by Maitre Braun-Pivet, but again, not until tomorrow afternoon? Very important, the timing.'

'It's probably material evidence, I think I can arrange that,' said Grimard, and sighed deeply as they left and closed the door behind them.

As they walked down the street from the police poste, Jacques stopped and held Celestine's arm. 'I have to make a phone call. Henri is waiting in the market square, by the fountain. I said we'd go for dinner at Le Margoton. He, we, need a good dinner.'

'Who are you calling?' asked Celestine.

'Just go on. I'll tell you later.' Celestine walked around the corner towards the square, and Jacques took out the mobile phone that Monsieur Lefebvre had used. He stepped into the doorway of a shop, now closed, and dialled. He recognised the clipped, unemotional tones of the housekeeper, Margot. 'Madame Margot, it is Jacques Lecoubarry. It is imperative that I speak to Monsieur Palomer Senior, immediately. Please tell him that I have something to his advantage. Just that.' Jacques waited several minutes before Palomer grunted into the phone.

'The fuck,' he said. 'Disrupting my family, attacking my worker, coming into my home with some cock and bull story. You will pay, I will make you pay.'

'Well, what you say may be correct, Palomer, but let's not dwell on past disagreements. The fact is, you're in the shit. And I have something that, I would suggest, holds great value for you, something that could sink you, or let you swim.' There was silence on the other end of the line, except for a low grumbling sound which assured Jacques that someone was still there. 'Ownership. Ownership of the Rama Estate. Now that would give you peace of mind, certainty in your old age, security. The lack of it, the presence of it on the open market, as it were, would cause you deep, such deep distress and anguish, loss beyond imagining.' Celestine's words about laying it on too thick came back to him, but he felt in this case it was necessary, and quite pleasurable.

'What the fuck are you talking about?'

'The deeds, Monsieur Palomer. The deeds; the original, the authentic, as opposed to the fraudulent, deeds to Rama. I have them.' He paused. 'And you can have them, but for a very substantial sum of money. In fact, let's not be coy - 100,000 euros. That's the price.'

'You're mad.'

'I don't think so. You see when you look at these original documents, you will see what shifting sands you are standing on. I'll bring you a copy of the document, a copy mind you, to your house tomorrow morning at ten. Then you can decide whether I am crazy or not. Or whether you'd be crazy to let this get into the wrong hands.' Jacques could picture the sphinx-like face of Palomer, staring ahead of him, his mind quickly calculating all the different permutations.

'Money, you just want money,' growled Palomer.

'Just money. Frankly, I don't give a damn about anything else. Ten o'clock then.'

'I want to see the original. Copies are no good.'

'You will, but only once we've made our deal. The original is safe, very safe. No one knows about it except me and Madame Courbet.'

'The Notary? You visited him this morning.'

'Following me, Palomer? We did visit Maitre Braun-Pivet. We had some technical questions to ask him, which he answered very well actually. Put our minds at rest. But he doesn't know the context. He hasn't seen the document. Nor will he, if you come up with the money. Well?'

'Bring that woman with you,' said Palomer.

'No chance. She'd tear your fucking head off after what happened to her in the woods.'

'I want to know she won't talk.'

'It's just money, Palomer. We get the money, you get the contract. Talking isn't going to mean anything after that. And you get to save the family and lift the cloud you've been living under all these years. Legitimate at last, like Michael Corleone. Huh.'

There was a long silence.

'Ten.'

'Ten. Bonne soirée, Monsieur Palomer.'

Celestine raised her eyebrows as Jacques sat down at the restaurant table. Monsieur Lefebvre was reading each line of the menu, enthusiastically.

'Can I borrow your phone, C.? You have Ducrozet's number on it.' She passed it to him, saying nothing. 'Ducrozet, Jacques Lecoubarry. Thank you, and you. I still have the key for your boat.

I wonder if I might borrow it once more, for a short trip tomorrow morning. Not far. Excellent, thank you. Progress, yes. I'll let you know. Meanwhile, keep safe with your family. I don't believe you are now a target, but it pays to be careful. Good man. Au revoir.'

'Food,' said Jacques, beaming at Celestine and Monsieur Lefebvre. 'The hearty man ate a condemned meal, or some such.'

'Jacques, what is going on?' demanded Celestine. She looked at the glassy, slightly disconnected look in his eyes. 'You need to tell me, now.'

Jacques raised his eyebrows and opened his eyes wide, then extended his arms and bowed slightly. 'Act One of that famous play, *The Tethering of the Goat*, has been performed,' he said. 'All the players acted their part, some more enthusiastically than others. But I think, as the audience, you should sit tight as the scenery is changed.'

'Jacques!' said Celestine loudly.

'Let's order some food and I will tell you all. Henri, we don't eat the menu, we just order food from it.'

Monsieur Lefebvre looked up with a serious and concerned expression. He was uncomfortable with the slight madness in the air. 'I'll have the Boeuf Bourguignon with Dauphinoise potatoes,' he said.

'Splendid choice. We'll have you fattened up in no time. You'll have to strengthen the frame of your bicycle. And wine. We will have wine.'

The food was good, but the meal was not a success for Celestine. Jacques' fantastical behaviour continued, only slightly less frenzied, for ten minutes or more and then he lapsed into an uncharacteristic silence. She spoke to Monsieur Lefebvre, who answered her quietly. She tried to uncover a little more about his past, but very politely but firmly, he seemed not inclined to elaborate. Eventually, she lapsed into silence herself and watched the small groups of people, mainly young, wandering carelessly around the square. It seemed a long time since she was so young, so carefree. I have assumed so many burdens, she thought, because I believed it was the right thing to do. For a short time, I thought, or I imagined, that I was on a new path, lighter, footloose, carrying no baggage. But it's always there. We might outrun it for a while, but it catches up when we ease off. We can't outrun our natures. Moths to a light. A crime is committed, and there I am flapping around the candle flame, singeing my wings. She looked ruefully at her bandaged hands. And Jacques, always the question. She sensed the darkness in his mind, his lively, humorous eyes now seemed shaded and withdrawn. It was as though he had experienced a short phase of madness and was now exhausted, pulled back into his own space. He called for the bill and paid it without speaking. Monsieur Lefebvre, now embarrassed, pulled a number of creased notes from the depths of his trouser pockets and tried to pay for his part. But Jacques dismissed the idea with a wave of his hand. They stood up and walked back to the *Incognito* in silence, like three strangers thrown together carelessly by some random chance.

At the boat, Monsieur Lefebvre suggested that he wouldn't mind spending another night in the cruiser. It was quite comfortable, he said, and he would not be intruding on them. This roused Jacques a little, and he placed an arm around the old man's shoulders.

'Henri, you are a legend. You deserve so much better. Grab your things and let me open the door to your floating palace.'

Celestine started to say something then thought better of it. There were bigger battles to be had, and it would be helpful if they could have them uninhibited by social niceties. When Jacques returned, Celestine was sitting in the salon, her notebook on her lap, and her eyes and lips compressed. Her glance at him was as hard as acacia wood. He sat down opposite but didn't touch her.

'Perhaps I should explain my plan,' he said. She nodded and pursed her lips forward even further, which made him suddenly conscious of the continuing pain in his own lips, and his anger started smouldering again. He spent the next five minutes outlining the actions he had taken so far, and the actions he intended to take to, as he put it, bring down the final curtain. Celestine listened with increasing alarm, and when he had clearly finished she almost shouted.

'Absolutely not. You're out of your mind. No, no, Jacques. No.'

Jacques placed his hands on her arms and looked up at her. 'Yes. You said it yourself. It's the only alternative. If there are no witnesses, little evidence, you said it yourself, a confession, never going to happen, or catch him in the act. Tether a goat.'

'And you're the goat,' said Celestine, incredulously.

'Not totally out of character, I would say,' replied Jacques.

'Be serious man. This guy has killed two people, with a fucking knife. I'm not letting you be the third.' She was shaking her head violently and threw off his hands. Jacques held his palms out to suggest calming down.

'That's actually not exactly what I had in mind, martyr though I am to justice. It's more in the nature of a flushing out, I would say, a showing of the animal in its true colours.'

'It's incredibly risky.

'Not if we're well prepared. This will do it, this will bring the curtain down at the end of Act Three. Meanwhile, this is what I want you to do during Act Two, tomorrow morning.

Chapter Fifty-Four

The next morning, Celestine eased Ducrozet's boat alongside the jetty by Monsieur Palomer's boathouse. Jacques leaned over, took hold of a post and swung himself out. He squatted on the wooden boards and whispered to Celestine.

'Half an hour. Tuck in upriver there, around the bend. In half an hour come past, and go back and forwards on the other side until you see me.'

'You just be bloody careful,' said Celestine.

Jacques nodded and stood up. He pushed the boat off and watched as she reversed into the current and then turned her head upstream. In the distance, he heard a church clock strike ten. He had never thought of the sound as ominous before; not so much a tolling as a calling out to the people in the vicinity. Ten o'clock, halfway through the morning. If you're working in the fields, lift your head a moment, acknowledge that the morning is passing and it won't be long before the lunchtime bells ring. This morning Jacques felt the sound was most definitely a tolling - life is short, and here's another marker passed.

Gathering himself, he strode across the lawns where a peacock raised its fine tail fan in vanity and bravado, but it moved quickly out of the way as Jacques approached. This time he skirted around the house and came to it at the front door. Stone steps led up from the curved gravel driveway. He pulled on the brass chain and could hear the bell ringing inside. As he waited, he looked out at the land on that side of the house - the formal lawns, the ornate benches beneath the fig and mulberry trees, the fence and then the vines, shorn now of their grapes. He looked up to where the drive came down the gentle slope, and at the woods behind where so much had happened just two days before. It really was a beautiful spot, an awful lot to lose. Worth killing for? Perhaps for some.

He heard the door open behind him, but he didn't turn around.

'Well.' Palomer had come to the door himself. Jacques waited. Impatiently, Palomer pushed the door wider and stepped out just behind Jacques. 'Well,' he said again.

'I was just thinking,' said Jacques, calmly, 'and looking at this scene. You really have made a wonderful place here, haven't you? I mean, the location itself is special, the woods, the river, and in between, all these vines, all this golden money literally growing on trees. And this house, not quite a chateau, but your family has spent a lot of money on it, nevertheless. And the antiques.' Jacques paused and turned to face Palomer. 'What I mean to say, Palomer is, it's a shame, because it's not really yours. It doesn't belong to you. It belongs to the heirs of a Jewish gentleman or men, and I think, yes, I do think, they'll want it back. And you, Monsieur Palomer, will be turfed out, along with your chattels. You'll lose everything. Shame. It wasn't you who stole the property, was it? It was your grandfather. And you have looked after it very well in your time here. They'll probably take that into consideration. Yes, definitely you'd have a good case for some compensation for the work you've done. Good case. But then again, it depends on what else you've done to keep your hands on it. What have you done, Monsieur Palomer? Murder. Is that what you've done?'

Palomer's face was blank, it might have been a death mask if not for the slight twitch in the corner of one eye. 'Have you finished your rambling? I thought you had a proposition for me, so let's hear it. Inside.' He turned about and swaggered across the hallway and into the study. Jacques followed and closed the door behind him. Palomer was standing beside his desk. He had picked up a large, glass paperweight.

'Baccarat, circa 1850,' said Jacques. 'Or more likely, made by the Czechs in 1986 by the thousands and filtered into auction houses throughout Europe, particularly France.'

'You're a smart arse, Lecoubarry, but your smartness isn't nearly a match for mine. You are so far out of your depth you can't see the next wave coming towards you. Coming to drown you.'

Jacques sighed. 'Ok. You can posture as much as you like, but let's just cut to the chase.' Jacques took the copy of the original sale contract and slapped it on the desk. He sat down and crossed his legs. 'Read it, then we'll talk,' he said.

Palomer snatched it up and walked over to the window, he sat down heavily on an embroidered stool and started to read. Jacques watched him closely, but there was no indication on his face, or in his body, to suggest that any emotions were passing there. Finally, Palomer laid down the contract on a small, marble-topped side table, and looked flatly at Jacques.

'So, let me get this straight. You're trying to extort money out of me, on the basis of this old contract. Is that your line, extortion, blackmail?'

'Yes, to the first point,' replied Jacques smoothly. 'But extortion is a bit strong. A trade is what I suggested. You buy this contract from me, then you're the owner of it, and you can do what you like with it after that. It never has to see the light of day. It didn't see the light of day for eighty years. But here's the crux. If it does see the light of day, you are fucked. You'll lose everything, the house, the farm, everything, including your liberty.' For the first time, Palomer's eyes opened wider than a slot. 'Oh yes,' continued Jacques. 'The police already suspect you, or more likely your son, of murdering two people. Disappeared, your son, I understand. They have some evidence, fibres, CCTV that places Jean-Michel's car on the road to Calvary at the time the nun was murdered. A nun for Christ's sake, what were you thinking? But you see, the puzzle for them is why. Motive. Why would people like you kill these people? Beggar's belief. Unless, unless there was a motive, a big fat smouldering motive. Malraux was the heir, the phantom that finally came out of the woods to claim his inheritance. And he was getting closer. The nun, Sister Agnieszka was helping him, she knew what he was looking for. A few more steps and Malraux would have come up with the answers. The puzzle wasn't complicated, it was designed by a father for his son to figure out. It was the puzzle that led us to the ruins in your woods. That helped us to find this.' He pointed at the contract. 'So now there is a motive. And the police love those, trust me.' He paused. 'So here is the choice. Either you pay us one hundred thousand euros in exchange for the original of this contract or you lose all of this, and your son and you go to jail for murder and incitement to murder. Come on,

Palomer, decision time. That's what Trictrac is all about, isn't it? Make a decision, you have two minutes.'

Palomer looked down at his hands for several minutes in silence, and when he looked up again there was at last some emotion in his eyes – hatred. He spoke slowly, in a scratchy monotone, choosing each word carefully before releasing them.

'I admit none of this, of course. You are raving. You're a conman, a gypsy. We had nothing to do with the murder of those people. And I won't be extorted by you. But I am interested in artefacts, ancient documents related to this estate of mine. I am interested in history, and that old, but clearly superseded document, is part of the history of the place. And on that basis, I'll give you fifty thousand euros for it. And I want every copy you've made.'

'Seventy-five,' said Jacques.

'Sixty. I won't pay a cent more. You can go to hell.'

'Sixty, cash,' said Jacques. Palomer looked at him with anger and distaste.

'You may get some money out of me this time. A lot of money for a shiftless scavenger like you. But I'll be on your tail. You will never raise your head around here again, or by God, I'll cut it off.'

'Yes, whatever,' mocked Jacques. 'Arrangements.'

'Bring the original here this evening. I'll have the money,' said Palomer.

'Oh, no. I don't intend to come back here. No, we'll exchange somewhere neutral, somewhere well-lit but private. You'll want to check over the document, you can keep that copy by the way, and where I can count every bill of the cash. Calvary. Symbolic no? I went there the other day. A bit ghoulish, but that's where they found the body of poor Sister Agnieszka. Cut down, throat slashed by person or persons unknown. There's a Dutch woman, or Polish perhaps, they think she may have something to do with it, got a motive apparently, but no evidence you see. You need both to square the circle. Calvary at nine o'clock. And I'm a big man, Palomer. Don't try anything stupid.'

'This policewoman.'

'What about her? She's an ex-policewoman, read into that what you wish. She knows nothing about this… arrangement, and she'll know nothing about the money. That's my gratuity.' Jacques stood up. 'One more thing, Palomer. If this doesn't happen today, I'm off to find some relatives of Monsieur Malraux, who I've no doubt, will be happy to part with a few shekels to get their hands on this valuable document. It would be life-changing, wouldn't it? Especially for you,' he sneered.

Jacques strode out of the room and across the hallway, hands clenched. He reached the front door before he heard a sound behind him. Palomer had come to the door of the study. The sound wasn't words, it was a deep, guttural grunting, the angry moaning of a wounded animal. Jacques turned and for a moment they locked eyes. Palomer's face was blank, but his eyes were terrible, boiling with fury and hatred. For the first time, Jacques felt afraid, and began to doubt the wisdom of his plan. He opened the door, stumbled down the steps, and walked quickly across the lawns to the river.

Celestine was passing on the other side, and she changed direction and headed across stream to where Jacques was pacing on the jetty. He stepped onto the boat and waved her to move off quickly.

'You've been more than half an hour. I was really concerned, Jacques.'

'I know, but it's ok.'

'You don't look ok. You look… shaken,' said Celestine.

'Mm. Let's get back to Lissac. I have to talk to Grimard.'

Chapter Fifty-Five

Commandant Grimard was at lunch, so Jacques and Celestine went to the café opposite the abbey. Celestine disappeared into the cloisters and emerged a few minutes later with the deputy curator. Celestine was holding her upper arm gently and propelling her towards the café.

'Jacques, this is Catherine. Catherine, Jacques.'

Jacques leaned forwards and kissed her on both cheeks. 'Enchanté, Catherine. Please join us.'

Suddenly, life was normal again. A group of friends having lunch together in a café; chatting, laughing about trivial, everyday things. Just like the bike ride yesterday, an interval, or the other version of the parallel universe Jacques felt he was living in. Jekyll and Hyde. Now Dr Jekyll, charming, engaging; now Monsieur Hyde, hanging out with his friends, blood and gore. It was too much, it was disorientating, unbalancing, even for a man as well ballasted as Jacques. Much of the conversation wandered around him. He heard snippets, occasionally he realised a remark had been directed at him, and he blustered to answer it. Eventually, Catherine left, and Jacques watched Celestine walk over to the abbey with her. He needed space to think. He knew there were flaws in his plan, and he was trying to think methodically through each possible situation. He wanted to see the scene play out in his head and to look for grey areas, for leakage or for weaknesses.

Suddenly, Celestine was standing over him. 'Catherine thinks I should leave you and come and live with her. Until I sort my life out.'

Jacques looked up at her and seemed to ponder the remark. 'She's probably right. Life would be simpler for you. No climbing through woods being chased by a maniac with a shotgun.' He shrugged. 'Sexually, I would suggest, less than interstellar, but hey, no maniacs.'

'I told her that you were not always so unresponsive. That you were preoccupied with this case, and that normally you were a man of infinite good humour, charm and raconteurship. Can you say that?'

'And?'

'And a couple of other minor plus points, which on balance, left me leaning ever so slightly towards you.'

Jacques clapped his hands lightly. 'A victory I would say. But I do believe that you have come down on the right side of the scales.'

Celestine smiled and stroked her arm across his shoulders. 'We need to finish this thing, Jacques. I need you back.'

'Believe me, I need me back. Let's go and see Grimard.'

In the small, windowless and featureless conference room, Jacques and Celestine sat opposite a Commandant Grimard who looked weary and dispirited, his eyes were bloodshot from lack of sleep, and his shirt was crumpled and sweat-stained. He appeared to listen carefully as Jacques outlined his plan, but kept shaking his head.

'Out of the question,' he said several times, until Jacques, exasperated, demanded.

'Ok. What is in the question? What are you willing to do to bring these people to justice? What? You haven't got enough evidence. If you go down the legal route of proving that the contract is a fraud, it could take years in the courts. And at the end, Palomer will say he knew nothing about it. You'd have to trace relatives of Malraux, convince them of the value of committing thousands of euros in a court case to prove ownership of some land in Tarn and Garonne. Years. We have to demonstrate that Palomer did know about the presence of the original contract, that he recognised the threat it was to his position, and that he was willing to act to secure it. Act violently, extremely, to stop that contract coming out into the open.' Jacques leaned forwards on his fists and stared into the face of the Commandant.

Grimard was not a man easily swayed, or willing to be browbeaten by anyone, especially not a civilian. He kept his seat and held the gaze for as long as he could, but there was something unnaturally powerful in that great shaggy head leering up at him, and the eyes so dark and penetrating, that eventually he looked away. And he was so tired of this case and this town.

'Palomer must know it would take a long time to prove the validity of the original contract, he's no fool,' he said, trying to gain a foothold again.

'No. But he can't take that risk,' said Jacques, aware now that he had control. 'If he loses, he loses everything. What's more, it's motive. He doesn't know how much evidence you have.'

'Very little.'

'But he doesn't know that. He's scared. Angry as hell. But underneath, he knows that only one thing can make this go away - getting his hands on the contract and destroying it. Come on Grimard. We can finish it tonight.'

Grimard sat back and closed his eyes to get the sight of that Basque and his disturbingly attractive partner out of his head, while he thought. He knew he would have to keep this to himself. He couldn't involve Drouillard at this stage. There were so many risks. Civilians running loose in a police operation. Perhaps if he had not been so tired. Maybe if he could see some other clear threads to follow. If he didn't have to argue with these two again. Perhaps. He opened his eyes.

'On your own head be it,' he said finally.

'One thing, Commandant,' said Celestine, who had remained silent through most of the meeting to this point. 'I'd like Jacques to be wearing a stab vest. Ok.'

Grimard eyed Jacques up, doubtfully. 'I'm not sure they make them in that size,' he said. 'You might have to stick two together.'

Sitting quietly in the salon of the *Incognito*, Monsieur Lefebvre listened carefully to Jacques' instructions. He sat with his head bowed, and his hands on the worn, shiny knees of his old flannel trousers.

'Above all. You must keep out of sight. He mustn't see you if he comes that way. And call as soon as you safely can. If we don't hear, we'll assume he's come a different route. If he does come by boat, stay hidden until well after nine o'clock, and until we call you. Is that clear?'

Monsieur Lefebvre nodded slowly. Jacques couldn't see, but the old man's lips were moving, repeating the instructions to himself. He looked up, Jacques was smiling at him.

'After tonight, we will stop enlisting you in our murky dealings. By God, you could never have expected to end up in this production. Look what happens when you stop to speak to beautiful women on the towpath. Bear that in mind, Henri. Dangerous animals.'

Monsieur Lefebvre chuckled.

'You are both dangerous animals, Jacques. But it has been good to be involved. It has been… spicy,' he said, clearly delighted with the description.

'Spicy?'

'Yes. And you and Celestine have been so very kind.' He paused. 'Kind and rather alarming. I'm not sure the towpath is going to be quite the same for me after this.'

'No. But kind and alarming and a bit spicy, that's us. In any order you wish,' said Jacques, and squeezed the old man's wrists tightly.

Chapter Fifty-Six

At eight p.m. Celestine slipped into the door of the Convent, while Jacques waited outside in the shadows. She was taken by the same sister to see the Mother Superior who was waiting for her in her small office. She immediately handed Celestine the envelope containing the original contract for the Rama Estate.

'That was not a very long safe-keeping, Celestine. Have you found a more suitable location for that purpose?' she asked, running her eyes over Celestine's face and down to her hands.

'No, not at all,' replied Celestine. 'But I think, after tonight, it will be in the hands of the police, and my responsibility for it will be ended.'

The Mother Superior waved Celestine into a chair and sat down herself. 'I am relieved to hear it. You take on too much responsibility, I think.' Celestine sat down uneasily on the edge of the chair. 'Then, perhaps it is time to let that past go, and to move forward taking responsibility only for yourself.'

Celestine was struck again by how this elderly woman, whose life was so different from hers, could combine sternness and kindness, be firm yet also soft, so that her words didn't jar, but seeped in slowly, unresisting. She felt herself close to tears, which was a useless and dangerous weakness to show at this time. She stood up, gripping the envelope tightly in her still bandaged hands. The Mother Superior stood also.

'Take good care, my dear. I can see that you are strong, but also a little brittle, I think. Make your next moves carefully. And come back and visit us again, sometimes.' They kissed on both cheeks.

'Thank you so much,' said Celestine.' It's funny, but this Convent has played a critical role in this whole odyssey, from beginning to the end.' The Mother Superior smiled and nodded sagely.

'Perhaps, that is because we are a place apart, where things can be lodged and left unchanged while the world outside rages around itself, fighting its wars and all its other horrors.'

Celestine left the office and walked along the quiet musty corridor. She was full of trepidation for the night's action to come. But the ageless, timeless serenity of the Convent calmed her a little and brought her some focus. She spoke to the sister who had opened the gate.

'Would it be ok if I waited here for an hour or so, just here by the gate? I won't trouble anyone.' The sister pointed to a small stone bench in an arbour set into the outer stone wall.

'There, you can sit there.'

'Thank you, I just need to speak to someone, briefly, he is just outside the gate.'

'I'll wait,' said the sister, her hands folded in front of her, and her face framed by the stiff cowl of pure white.

Celestine opened the gate and Jacques was immediately by her side. She handed him the envelope. He gripped it tightly and shoved it with difficulty inside his jacket.

'I can hardly breathe in this armadillo shell I'm wearing,' he said.

Celestine smiled and suddenly felt tears welling in the corner of her eyes. 'Just… just.'

'I know, be careful. Don't worry, everything is well prepared. Now go and stay with your sisters. But don't get hooked on that celibacy lark. Go on.' He ushered her through the door and it closed behind her. He suddenly felt very alone and exposed, and not for the first time, wondered if his bravado had landed him straight into the lion's den.

He walked slowly up the lane, climbing gradually, then more steeply. It was still quite light although the sun had set, and the few clouds, with their salmon pink bellies and dark blue backs, seemed to be swimming very slowly, like fish, across the sky. Each tree had its surround of shadow and uncertainty, and Jacques kept firmly to the centre of the lane. Until he reached a bend in the path, he could hear traffic sounds from the town below, but after the bend, the silence was complete. He could hear his own footfall, a slight dragging of his right foot, the muscles not completely in harmony anymore. He emerged from the path at the top, into the drama of the tall white statue, lit by the wide halogen lamps around the base. It was a stark contrast and it took him a few minutes to adjust to the brightness. So that would work in reverse he thought; anyone leaving this well-lit area quickly, would need time for their eyes to adjust to the darkness. He walked all around the statue and the flat area behind it, the empty car park, the railings guarding against the steep drop below the viewpoint. He looked down; the town lay out before him like a model. He looked everywhere, anywhere someone could hide or watch, and then he sat down on the small wall at the front of the statue of the Virgin, and waited. It was twenty minutes to nine.

Grimard sat uneasily in an unmarked police car in a parking space beside the railway line. From there, he had a view of the small road that led up from the town to the Convent and to Calvary. Bedeau sat alongside him in the driver's seat. They didn't speak. Across the road was a terrace of tall but shabby-looking houses, mostly unpainted, with shutters hanging carelessly and tiny gardens behind block walls.

A small group was gathered by one of the gates; the men smoking; short stocky men, dressed, in the main, in T-shirts and tracksuit bottoms. One of the men flicked a finished cigarette into the middle of the road, and following its trajectory his eyes met Grimard's. He tapped another man on the arm and gestured with his head towards the car. A third and fourth man looked around. Bedeau hadn't noticed and was focusing on the Convent road end. The Bulgarians waited for a truck to pass, then crossed the road and came up to the car. One of them slapped his hand on the bonnet making Bedeau jump.

Grimard wound down the window. The youngest of the men leaned his head towards him. 'You watching us again? You want search our houses again? Maybe you want arrest all?' Two others came on either side of him and leaned heavily on the car.

'This has nothing to do with you, so move away from the car. We are not interested in you, just back away.'

Bedeau leaned over. 'You're obstructing a police operation, go back to your houses,' he shouted.

'Police operation, what operation? Fuck the Bulgarians, your operation?' said the young one and slapped his hand on the top of the car. Bedeau made to get out but Grimard restrained him.

'It's all right. We are not interested in you tonight. This has got nothing to do with you. Go home.'

The men stepped a little away from the car, then with several parting oaths in Bulgarian, they crossed the road again and went inside their houses. Grimard breathed deeply. Bedeau went back to looking at the road end, but for several important minutes his attention had been elsewhere, and both men's unease grew accordingly.

Jacques sensed, rather than heard, the presence of another person on the hilltop. He looked around quickly, thought he caught a shadow moving behind one of the cypress trees, then the rustle of leaves. He stood up quickly and stepped onto the low wall.

'Palomer,' he called out. There was no answer for a moment and then, from the other side of the statue, came the voice of Jean-Michel.

'Put the document on the wall beside you, by the light. Then move clockwise around the statue, slowly. Your money is in a sack here, on this side. You count your money here, I check the document there. If we are both satisfied, you walk away in that direction, I walk away in this direction. You fuck off to your next swamp. You never come back.' The voice was flat without emotion, the words spat out like lumps of gristle, and slightly muffled, as though he was speaking through a screen.

'No.' said Jacques. 'You come around here, to this side. It's good and light. Then I can see that you really have got my money. We stay two metres apart. You check, I check, No tricks.'

There was silence for a minute, and then suddenly Jean-Michel was standing in front of Jacques. For a tall man, he moved so silently. He was dressed all in black; black trousers, black leather jacket and he was also wearing a black motorcycle helmet and black gloves. He had a plastic bin liner in his hand. Jacques placed his hand inside his jacket and pulled out the large brown envelope.

'Open it, let me see the papers,' demanded Jean-Michel.

Jacques slipped his fingers into the envelope and pulled out the pages. He held them so that Jean-Michel could see the first page, and then he rifled through them, picking out the final, signature page, and showing it to him.

'Now open the bag, take out some of the money, let me see it,' said Jacques. Jean-Michel rested the sack on the wall, took off his gloves and put his right hand inside the bag. He took out two bundles of notes and flicked through them for Jacques to see. He replaced the notes and then tossed the sack onto the wall nearer to Jacques.

'Put the papers on the wall there,' Jean-Michel pointed. 'Then move back and count your money.'

Jacques looked at the document in his hand. This was the moment when you step onto the wire, impossible to turn back, set on a course which could lead to the other side of the chasm or a plunge into the abyss. He carefully put the document back into the envelope, and tossed it onto the wall towards Jean-Michel who immediately reached for it, and tore it open. He pulled out the papers and scanned them, counting the pages as he did so. He didn't notice for a moment that Jacques had not moved towards the sack of money. He was standing, legs apart, arms by his sides, and staring. Jean-Michel suddenly looked up.

'What's the matter? Count your fucking money.' Then a realisation came into his eyes. 'You bastard.'

He rolled the document up quickly and stuffed it inside his leather jacket, at the same time he drew a knife from one of the pockets. Jacques stepped back and Jean-Michel lunged at him. Jacques felt a sharp pain in his left arm. Jean-Michel slashed at him again, and then lunged hard for his body, aiming for the heart. Jacques fell backwards, his head bouncing off the low wall. Just then, torchlights came on as two police agents emerged from the track on the other side. Jean-Michel turned quickly and sprinted onto the path down to the Convent. He plunged into darkness and stumbled as his eyes adjusted to the change in the light. He could hear a voice calling behind him, and he ran more quickly again. He knew the path, every metre of it, he knew where the steps gave way to concrete - by the dogleg in the wall, and then to tarmac, and the little dark yard where his motorcycle was waiting.

He hurtled around the bend at the bottom of the steps. Too late, he saw the tall, lean figure of a woman standing there. He felt the agony as the hard, oak beam crashed into his knees, and again as he toppled forwards, skidding across the rough concrete on his bare hands. Agony, his breath knocked out of him, agony as the beam crashed down across his back, twice, three times. He tried to turn on his side, away from the beating and managed to look up. He realised then who was assailing him; he could see the fury and the joy in her eyes as she crashed the oak beam down again on his hip and then his ankle, and then it stopped, and he was pushed roughly onto his front, his arms pulled back and handcuffs snapped onto his wrists. The police agent looked up at Celestine who was breathing heavily, her eyes glazed, holding the beam above her head. She laid it down carefully by the side of the path and rested on her haunches. Another police agent arrived from the hill, he was speaking into his radio. Celestine heard him demand an ambulance. She snapped out of her daze and grabbed the agent by the arm.

'Jacques,' she screeched. The young man looked at her in some awe.

'Cut, but ok. Yes, madame, I think he's ok.'

For a second, she was Capitaine Celestine Courbet of the Bordeaux Judicial Police. She set off running up the hill, it seemed forever, but she reached the top, and in the bright lights she saw Desmarais helping Jacques to strip off his outsize stab vest. Jacques' arm flopped by his side. She rushed up to him, but then stopped and looked. There was blood dripping from his hand onto the stone parapet of the wall. Jacques raised his eyes and grinned, then grimaced.

'That hurts.'

Desmarais looked around. 'Madame, help me please. Hold his hand and lift his arm, keep it still.' Celestine gripped the hand, she could feel the blood, soft and slippery between her fingers. She looked at Jacques' eyes, almost turquoise in the spectrum of the halogen lights. Desmarais was wrapping a bandage around the cut. Jacques flinched but kept looking at Celestine.

'Let me drown in your eyes,' he wheezed, 'let me die in your… Fuck that hurts, Desmarais,' he growled and tears bubbled up in her eyes. Some capitaine of police, she thought. She gripped his hand more tightly as Jacques flinched again. 'That hurts. What are you? A prop forward playing at doctors?' Desmarais ignored him and pulled the bandage tighter. 'The contract?' murmured Jacques.

Celestine nodded. 'I felled the bastard with a piece of wood.'

'No. He got that far. I'm sorry,' he whispered hoarsely. 'I tried to detain him but he was impatient to be off. You stopped him with a piece of wood. Hear that, Paul, poetic justice. Ouch, you butcher, you need to go back on the training course.'

Chapter Fifty-Seven

Jacques had twelve stitches in the arm, and four in the back of his skull where he had tried to dismantle the wall with his head. There was a risk of concussion, so he was kept in the hospital overnight. Celestine stayed with him until a police agent arrived and told her she was needed to make a statement at the police poste. Jacques was sleeping when she left and when she returned three hours later.

Less sympathy was shown to Jean-Michel Palomer, whose own injuries were not minor, and included: three broken vertebrae, a dislocated knee, a fractured ankle and masses of bruises. His hands, Celestine was told, were cut and scraped to the bone, with flaps of skin hanging off them, and fingers scorched by the friction of his fall.

Celestine gave an accurate and factual account of her actions. She did not mention where the oak beam had come from, with the suggestion left there that it had been fortuitously lying by the side of the path where she had found it. Grimard came into the room and read her statement. He nodded appreciatively.

'That is how a statement should read. You're a loss to the force. Perhaps you might reconsider?'

Celestine looked down at her hands; the bandages dirty and scuffed, splinters of wood caught in the creases. She looked up at Grimard. 'Thank you, Commandant, but I don't think I am ready for that. Not at this time.'

The morning was stormy, a blustery wind had risen, and dark clouds raced across a greening sky. Jacques and Celestine left the hospital and walked through streets drained of their summer colour, past planters and hanging baskets full of tired, fading blooms and crisp dry leaves.

'Old Lefebvre was right, the season is changing, shifting gear,' said Jacques.

'Feels like spring to me after the last few days,' said Celestine. 'Coming out of the shadows again. Like I don't have to look over my shoulder anymore or think about death and killing. And I can stop worrying about you. That would be a blessing.' Jacques stepped to her other side so he could link his good arm in hers.

'It'll take a little while to clear it out of our heads, for you in particular,' said Jacques.

'Why me?'

'That time in the woods. The terror you must have felt. I won't forgive myself for that.'

'If I remember rightly,' interrupted Celestine. 'I fell on top of you, then you were knocked down, trussed up, and dragged through the brush like a steer.'

'Or a goat.'

'A goat. Jesus. The tethering of the goat in three acts. It's not funny, Jacques, it's really not funny.' They walked silently until Celestine felt the pressure on her side, guiding her towards the café across the street from the Abbey.

In the Poste of the Municipal Police, Commandant Grimard was waiting for them. He enquired after Jacques, then sat in, as an agent took down his statement. The agent read it back to him.

'Anything you'd like to add to that, Monsieur Lecoubarry?' asked Grimard.

'Not a thing,' replied Jacques. 'What's your verdict now, Commandant? Do you have enough to charge Palomer with murder?'

'We're getting there. We're searching the house and the boat as we speak. A little more scientific evidence would be helpful. Early suggestions are that he used the same knife for each attack, including the one on you.'

'Arrogant prick,' said Jacques.

'Yes, untouchables. Palomer Senior is kicking up a hullabaloo, as you might imagine, but it's all bluster. Seems the Maire never really liked him in any case, and is only interested in seeing justice done.' Grimard raised his eyebrows. 'This case with the contracts, that's complicated, and better minds than mine will be working on it.'

'It's safe?' asked Jacques.

'Oh yes, very safe,' he said.

Monsieur Lefebvre's bicycle was leaning against the side of the boat. The panniers were bulging as usual, and in the front basket was an assortment of waterproof clothing. He came out of the cabin when he saw them, his battered old straw hat jammed down tightly on one side of his head against the wind. He looked at Jacques' bandaged arm and the shaved patch on the back of his head. He pressed his lips together tightly and shook his head a little.

'I'm going now,' he said. 'I know of a comfortable little hut about twenty kilometres along the canal, where I can shelter when this storm breaks. It could last a couple of days, end-of-season storms do.'

'We have some food, Henri, take some please,' said Celestine.

'No, thank you. I have sufficient. I bought a few things this morning. I can't carry too much, and besides, there is a lot of free food out there at this time. The telephone I have left on the table.'

Celestine put her arms around him and hugged him tightly.

'Thank you for all your help and your company. Take good care of yourself. And if you're ever in trouble or need help....'

The old man chuckled. 'I think from my experience of the last few days, if anyone is going to get into trouble it's not me, Celestine, it's you two.'

Jacques helped him over the side and hugged him with one arm. Monsieur Lefebvre pushed off slowly and with a dangerous wobble until he gained a little speed. He cycled off along the towpath, flapping from his various parts. He did not look back, and they lost sight of him as he passed the lock and as the canal gently curved and the trees hid him from view.

Twenty-four hours later Jacques fired up the engine. It shivered a little at first, then settled into a steady pulse. Celestine untied the ropes at both ends and stepped lightly onto the moving bow deck. Jacques edged the *Incognito* into the middle of the canal to pass the various boats moored along the quay. They passed under the footbridge and came quickly to the first lock. As the great wooden doors closed behind them, and the rushing waters poured in, lifting the boat slowly higher, Celestine tried to imagine herself being lifted in a similar manner, to a new level.

As the waters reached the top and the exit gates opened they chugged forwards into the open channel. Around the gentle curve, and the canal stretched straight and true for as far as the eye could see. The plane trees, their speckled trunks lining the sides like sentinels, cast shade across the water as their branches swayed in the wind. White caps were ruffling the khaki-coloured waters of the canal. There was nothing to do but settle into the gentle rhythm, and let life slowly come to them. Jacques steered, nonchalantly, one-handed at the stern. Celestine sat on the bow deck, watching the countryside passing, thinking of the winter ahead.

They exchanged an occasional word.

Authors Note

The title of the story was taken from the ancient French game of Trictrac, a game played on a similar board to backgammon but with many differences and more variables. *The Devil's Point* is the second most difficult position to achieve but does not mean that the game is won. I wanted this to represent the position of the Palomers before the intrusion into their affairs by Celestine and Jacques.

The story itself was inspired by the drama of the ancient and more recent history of the town situated near the confluence of the great rivers Tarn and Garonne. A town which is also connected through South West France by the Canal des Deux Mers. There, the wonderful 12th-century Abbaye de Saint Pierre and its cloisters seem to emanate mystery and permanence, and to me suggested a continuity of stories told through the generations. Equally important was the uplifting chronicle of the actions of the people of the town and surrounds, who saved the lives of nearly five hundred Jewish children by concealing them from the Nazis. In many cases taking them into their own families.

The book is of course, a work of fiction, and I have taken certain liberties with geography and locations to meet the needs of the narrative. Lissac-sur-Tarn does not exist, but it would not be difficult to discover the real name of the town portrayed in the novel. It would be well worth a visit. It is a town that rewards digging under the skin of its more modern exterior.

This is the second book in the series which finds Celestine Courbet and Jacques Lecoubarry slowly travelling along the great canal that runs from the Atlantic Ocean to the Mediterranean Sea on their barge, the *Incognito*. Far from enjoying a tranquil time, these two are drawn repeatedly into mystery, murder and complex investigations, putting their lives in peril and straining their already complicated relationship. It is great to write about them. I hope you will return to enjoy the future books in this series.

If you would like to be kept up to date with any new releases, just send me an email or log onto my website.

Website: tombecketauthor.com

Email   mailto:tom@tombecketauthor.com

Best Wishes

Author Page

Tom Becket is the author of the Celestine Courbet crime thriller mystery series. Living in the South of France with his wife and an energetic spaniel, Tom draws his stories out of the rich history and colourful landscapes of this beautiful region. He writes about authentic characters in conflict who inspire affection and concern in the reader. His research for the novels takes him outdoors, walking the long-distance footpaths and cycling along the towpaths of the French Canals.

Tom taught English and ran his own company for many years before committing to writing fiction full-time. He invites you to join him in discovering the mysterious and fascinating France described in his novels.

By the same author

WEEP FOR THE DEAD

BEAUTIFUL DECEPTION

The Celestine Courbet Murder Mysteries based in South West France

www.ingramcontent.com/pod-product-compliance
Lightning Source LLC
LaVergne TN
LVHW011759060526
838200LV00053B/3634